POLICY, PRACTICE AND PROVISION FOR CHILDREN WITH SPECIFIC LEARNING DIFFICULTIES

Policy, Practice and Provision for Children with Specific Learning Difficulties

JILL DUFFIELD
SHEILA RIDDELL
SALLY BROWN
Department of Education
University of Stirling

Avebury

Aldershot • Brookfield USA • Hong Kong • Singapore • Sydney

Published by
Avebury
Ashgate Publishing Limited
Gower House
Croft Road
Aldershot
Hants GU11 3HR
England

Ashgate Publishing Company
Old Post Road
Brookfield
Vermont 05036
USA

British Library Cataloguing in Publication Data

Duffield, Jill
    Policy, Practice and Provision for
    Children with Specific Learning
    Difficulties
    I. Title
    371.90941

    ISBN 1 85628 928 1

Library of Congress Catalog Card Number: 95-77822

Typeset by
Department of Education
University of Stirling
Stirling FK9 4LA
Scotland

Printed and bound by Athenaeum Press, Ltd., Gateshead, Tyne & Wear.

Contents

List of figures and tables		vii
Acknowledgements		xi
Chapter 1	The context for research on provision for children with specific learning difficulties	1
Chapter 2	Regional provision: recognition, identification and meeting needs	16
Chapter 3	Specific learning difficulties and the public examination system	35
Chapter 4	The contribution from teacher education	47
Chapter 5	The perceptions of learning support teachers	67
Chapter 6	Parents of children with specific learning difficulties	92
Chapter 7	The voluntary organisations and specific learning difficulties	121
Chapter 8	Illustrations of provision and practice	141
Chapter 9	Provision for specific learning difficulties within the health service	176

Chapter 10	Specific learning difficulties: a focus for debate	190
References		210
Appendices		
A:	Definitions of specific learning difficulties	216
B:	Definition of social class	225
C:	Summary of education authority policy documents	226
Index		236

List of figures and tables

Table 2.1   Definition of specific learning difficulties: 20
             local authority views

Table 4.1   Distrtibution of pre-service teachers by   53
             course and college

Table 4.2   Primary and secondary student teachers who   54
             said they would discuss a child's learning
             difficulties with colleagues

Table 4.3   Student teachers' understanding of the   55
             learning support teacher's role

Table 4.4   Student teachers' identifying direct tuition/   55
             withdrawal as part of learning support teacher's
             role

Table 4.5   Primary student teachers' accounts of aspects   56
             of the teaching of reading covered in their
             course

Figure 5.1   People with whom learning support teachers   71
             would use term 'dyslexia'

Table 5.1   Confidence in identifying specific learning   74
             difficulties reported by learning support
             teachers using term 'dyslexia'

Figure 5.2	Estimate of percentage of children with specific learning difficulties	74
Figure 5.3	Person responsible for identifying specific learning difficulties	75
Table 5.2	Learning support teachers reporting school has systematic procedures for identifying children by sector	76
Figure 5.4	Stage at which children most likely to be identified	76
Figure 5.5	Where children receive education	78
Table 5.3	Learning support teachers reporting child likely to receive education in mainstream class only by sector	79
Table 5.4	Learning support teachers reporting child likely to receive education in mainstream class plus withdrawal for individual tuition by sector	79
Table 5.5	Learning support teachers reporting awareness of regional policy on specific learning difficulties by sector	81
Figure 5.6	Learning support teachers' views by sector of the effectiveness of regional policy for children with specific learning difficulties.	82
Table 5.6	Learning support teachers' views of the importance of individual tuition outwith the class by sector	83
Figure 5.7	Learning support teachers' view of the most important aspect of their role	84
Table 5.7	Learning support teachers' contacts with voluntary organisation by sector	86

Figure 5.8	Learning support teachers collaborating with other professionals on specific learning difficulties	87
Table 6.1	Social class of family by means of contact	97
Table 6.2	Method of contact by type of school attended	98
Figure 6.1	Age when learning difficulties first identified	98
Figure 6.2	Parents reporting child experiences particular difficulty	99
Table 6.3	Parents' account of whether child experiences numeracy difficulties by sector	100
Table 6.4	Parents reporting use of term 'dyslexia' by method of contact	101
Table 6.5	Person who first suggested child had learning difficulties by method of contact	103
Figure 6.3	Person who first carried out test to identify learning difficulties by method of contact	105
Table 6.6	Type of support received after identification of learning difficulties by method of contact	107
Table 6.7	Parents reporting that child has Record of Needs by means of contact	108
Table 6.8	Parents reporting that child has Record of Needs by social class	109
Table 6.9	Parents reporting satisfaction with school support by means of contact	109
Table 6.10	Parents reporting satisfaction with school support by class of family	110
Table 6.11	Parents reporting school tuition inadequate by class of family	111

Table 7.1   Types of support provided by voluntary   132
             organisations which parents found useful

Table 9.1   Learning support teachers reporting   187
             collaboration on specific learning difficulties
             with speech therapist by sector

Acknowledgements

This book is based upon research funded by the Scottish Office Education Department into policy, practice and provision for children with specific learning difficulties, briefly updated to 1994. The project was carried out by a team from the University of Stirling and reported to SOED in 1992. The authors acknowledge the help and support of all the teachers, parents, voluntary organisations, and educational advisers and managers who gave time to the research. We also thank colleagues in the Department of Education, University of Stirling, especially Carole Ogilvy, who carried out early stages of research, and Louise McKinsley, Lisa Davies and Carla Shepherd who have given secretarial support.

1 The context for research on provision for children with specific learning difficulties

When we embarked on the research embodied in this book, it was not our intention to settle any of the debates on the nature or aetiology of specific learning difficulties. We did not ask, 'What should be done about dyslexia?'; still less, 'How do we make schools do the right thing?' Rather, the task which we set ourselves was to draw out the various perspectives of a range of concerned groups and individuals and to clarify the implications of the different positions in terms of appropriate identification procedures and educational provision. We are aware that the text refers frequently to 'children with specific learning difficulties' and that this might be interpreted as reifying a phenomenon whose definition and boundaries are strongly contested. However, the phrase 'children who are believed by some to experience specific learning difficulties' seemed unnecessarily pedantic. Whilst the terms 'specific learning difficulties' and 'dyslexia' are sometimes used synonymously, each conveys particular understandings of the nature and origin of the problem. The use of terminology by different interest groups emerged as a focus of the research, while we ourselves endeavoured to retain an agnostic stance. Our aims over and above the fulfilment of the contracted objectives of the research project were to shed light on the implications of policy options for all children with special educational needs, contributing to educational debates rather than simply reflecting the agenda of government or pressure groups.

The project *Policy, Practice and Provision for Children with Specific Learning Difficulties*, carried out by a team at the University of Stirling Department of Education between 1990 and 1992 was commissioned by the Scottish Office Education Department with the following four aims:

1   To describe current policies and practices for the recognition, identification, assessment and provision to meet the needs of children with specific learning difficulties.

2　　To identify the criteria used, by providers and 'customers', to judge the effectiveness of different approaches.

3　　To report on how current policies and practices perform in relation to those criteria.

4　　To present this information in a way which informs and advises those who make decisions (particularly policy makers, teachers and teacher educators) on how to deal with the problems of these children.

Our study clearly focuses on aspects of specific learning difficulties associated with literacy and, more particularly for some of those involved in the research, dyslexia. Some readers may be concerned that there are other aspects, particularly connected with numeracy, to which we have paid relatively little attention. Our decision to focus on literacy was based on an initial trawl of the views of principal educational psychologists, who clearly indicated that in their view this was the most salient aspect. Many felt, however, that numeracy was also important and this aspect was addressed by a teacher researcher who worked in conjunction with us throughout the course of the research. His report (Weedon, 1992) was presented to SOED alongside our own.

In order to understand the nature of the debates surrounding specific learning difficulties, it is important to have a sense of the various frameworks which may be used in conceptualising learning difficulties and the historical relationship between them. Research and writing in the area of specific learning difficulties is characterised by heated debate. A report published by the Division of Educational and Child Psychologists of the British Psychological Society noted:

> The conceptual complexity of this area, the problems of carrying out both basic and applied research that will resolve controversial issues, the ambiguities in the terminology used by those involved in the work, all testify to our limited knowledge (DECP, 1983, p.8).

Tomlinson (1982) provides an overview of the development of special education which she claims is characterised by

> power struggles between medical, psychological and educational personnel, who all have an interest in dominating definitions of special education (p.27).

The medical classification of disabled children for educational purposes began in the mid-nineteenth century, and initially produced an increasingly complex medical taxonomy of disability and associated forms of educational provision.

More recently, there has been a shift from a medical to an educational paradigm. Classification of children according to the nature of their disability is no longer seen as an adequate means of establishing their intellectual potential. Recent policy reflected in official documents and legislation has made it clear that the focus should be on understanding the way in which a child's educational environment needs to be designed in order that his or her disability may be overcome.

Specific learning difficulties, however, represent an area where the supremacy of the educational over the medical paradigm may not have gained full acceptance. Among professionals, parents and other advocates, a significant group (but by no means all) insists that children with specific learning difficulties or dyslexia comprise a discrete category whose problems are physiological in origin and may be circumvented, but will not disappear simply by modifying the curriculum. This position is likely to be at variance with at least some aspects of the official conceptualisation of learning difficulties which currently holds sway. This policy context has had a profound influence on the nature of provision for children with specific learning difficulties and in the following section we review its key features. Subsequently, we explore the contribution of different conceptual frameworks to an understanding of specific learning difficulties and the on-going debates within each area.

The policy and legislative framework

Over the past decade and a half, two key documents have had a major impact on policy and provision for children with learning difficulties in Scotland. These are the Warnock Report (Department of Education and Science, 1978) and an HMI report entitled *The Education of Pupils with Learning Difficulties in Primary and Secondary Schools in Scotland* (Scottish Education Department, 1978). We outline the key points emerging from both documents and go on to consider their implications for children with specific learning difficulties.

Major findings of the Warnock Report

A key theme of the Warnock Report was that a continuum of special education needs should be recognised and the rigid distinction between handicapped and non-handicapped children should be abolished. This entailed taking account of the fact that as many as one in six children might experience some form of learning difficulty during their school career. Arguing against the use of statutory categories of handicap, Warnock suggested that they stigmatised children unnecessarily and led to the mistaken assumption that all children

3

experiencing a particular form of handicap would require similar forms of educational provision. For the future, Warnock advised that the term 'children with learning difficulties' be used and that the emphasis be on identifying their needs and modifying their educational environment accordingly. The Report also stressed the need for the 'closest possible involvement of parents in the assessment of the child's educational needs and in the provision made'.

The report of Scottish HMI on children with learning difficulties

The influential report of Scottish HMI on children with learning difficulties focused on those in mainstream rather than special schools and on the role of remedial teachers. As in the Warnock Report, the conceptualisation of learning difficulties was a major theme. Rather than attributing learning difficulties to problems residing within the child, HMI shifted the focus to a curriculum and teacher deficit model:

> Many learning problems arise because the demands being made by schools are still too great for the linguistic competence of some of their pupils. They may then modify the language element to match individual capabilities, or they may provide pupils with individual help. (Scottish Education Department, 1978, para 4.9, p.24)

Echoing doubts which had been raised for some time on the efficacy of remedial teaching (Yule 1976; Tobin and Pumfrey 1976; Carroll 1972), HMI pointed to some of the dangers of the withdrawal of pupils for individual tuition, the traditional work of remedial teachers. Such practice was likely to create difficulties for pupils when they were reintegrated into their mainstream class since they might well have lost touch with the general work of the group. In addition, decontextualised drilling in particular skills was unlikely to be of long term assistance since pupils might well be unable to apply what they had learnt without ongoing support. Practice in deficient skills should be context-specific and should generally occur in the mainstream class. One of the most significant points made by HMI was that the ultimate responsibility for dealing with children's learning difficulties lay with subject or class teachers:

> Pupils with learning difficulties should be taught, as far as possible, by class and subject teachers. If they are unable to give the proper kind of help, then the pupils involved should be given the additional support of a remedial teacher. That fact, however, does not reduce the class or subject teacher's responsibility for the pupils, or absolve him from continuing his own endeavours. (para 4.11, p.25)

This emphasis on the paramount responsibility of the class or subject teacher had implications not only for the individual remedial teacher, but also for the remedial department. HMI commented:

> There has been a steady trend towards the establishment of separate 'remedial departments' in which they (remedial teachers) offer separate courses. Such a trend appears to be at odds with the indicators of our survey which suggest that remedial education is a whole-school responsibility and an inherent element of the work of subject departments. (para 4.17, p.27)

As Allan, Brown and Munn (1991) have noted, there is a certain ambivalence in the HMI report with regard to the status of the remedial teacher. On the one hand, it is suggested that the new tasks and responsibilities, particularly consultancy and co-operative teaching, are 'considerably more exacting' than the traditional concerns of the remedial teacher. On the other hand, the report implies that remedial teachers no longer require a departmental base from which to operate but does not consider the extent to which the loss of such a base might undermine their status and capacity to act effectively.

The Scottish Committee for Staff Development Education document *Guidelines for Diplomas in Special Educational Needs* (SCOSDE, 1990) went some way to clarify and modify the recommendations of the HMI Report. Summarising the roles of learning support teachers, they suggested that such teachers are concerned:

(a)   through consultation and collaboration, in helping class and subject teachers to plan and develop responses to the range of learning difficulties;
(b)   through consultation and collaboration, in the development of a differentiated curriculum at whole school and department levels to meet the range of learning difficulties found in mainstream classes;
(c)   in supporting individual learners, either through direct teaching or through co-ordinating support from visiting teachers, parents, or specialist services;
(d)   in working with management on the formulation and implementation of whole school or college policy;
(e)   in initiating and contributing to staff development related to their other roles.

The Guidelines emphasise that learning support teachers should be able to offer specialised individual help to children 'with specific learning difficulties, including those of a dyslexic kind' (para 4.1, p.22).

The Education (Scotland) Act 1980 (as amended)

The Education (Scotland) Act 1980 (as amended) incorporated key aspects of the Warnock Report and the HMI Report, in particular the anti-categorisation perspective, the recognition of the continuum of needs and the importance of parental partnership. (The Act was amended in 1981, and is generally referred to as the 1981 Act; we shall follow this usage from now on). Although a key theme of Warnock, parental partnership did not feature prominently in the Inspectorate report. Parents were not mentioned until the final paragraph, and then in the context of the responsibility of the school to maintain their interest in their child's progress, which might otherwise be likely to flag.

Under the terms of the Act, following a multi-disciplinary assessment, a Record of Needs may be opened for a child whose needs are regarded as pronounced, specific or complex relative to those of his or her peers, are of a continuing nature and cannot be met by the classroom teacher unaided. The Record contains a statement of the child's special educational needs and their curricular implications. An education authority is legally obliged to meet these needs, subject to the availability of resources. Provision is made for parental involvement throughout the recording process and parents are allowed a number of rights of appeal.

There were, therefore, a number of themes emerging from these various documents which were relevant to all children with learning difficulties in mainstream schools:

1   The abolition of categories of handicap and a shift from a child-deficit model to a focus on educational needs.
2   A recognition of a continuum of learning difficulties, ranging from children with severe and profound difficulties to those experiencing short-term difficulties in particular areas.
3   A new emphasis on the consultancy and co-operative teaching roles for the learning support teacher, as well as that of individual tutor.

The implications of policy for children with specific learning difficulties

The anti-categorisation theme which permeates the documents reviewed above is certainly one of the most significant for children with specific learning difficulties. As we have noted, some professionals and parents have argued strongly for the use of categories such as specific learning difficulties or dyslexia as a means of drawing attention to the qualities which distinguish this group from the generality of children with global learning difficulties. The anti-categorisation perspective of the Warnock and HMI Reports might be interpreted as having negative consequences for this group in terms of obscuring their particular needs and causing them to merge into the continuum of learning difficulties. Warnock, however, did suggest that 'distinctive arrangements' should be provided for 'children whose disabilities are marked but whose general ability is at least average' (DES, 1978, para 11.48). The HMI Report, on the other hand, made no reference to specific learning difficulties as such, although it noted that

> a good number of pupils with particular learning difficulties go into the 'certificate' courses which begin in stage S3 (SED, 1978, para 2.22, p.13).

No further discussion of the characteristics of these pupils occurred in the HMI Report, although the SCOSDE guidelines did recommend that learning support teachers should be able to offer specialised individual help to children with specific learning difficulties including those of a dyslexic kind. In the 1981 Act, although specific, profound and complex difficulties were mentioned with regard to children for whom a Record of Needs should be opened, there was no definition of what these terms might mean in practice. Riddell, Thomson and Dyer (1992) have drawn attention to variations in the interpretation of the Act in different authorities and it was apparent that in a number, children with specific learning difficulties would not be recorded because of fears that the authority did not have the resources to meet their needs. In terms of singling out children with specific learning difficulties as a group for whom special provision should be made, therefore, there was a degree of ambivalence in the official policy documents.

The redefinition of the role of the learning support teacher might be seen to have had both positive and negative implications for children with specific learning difficulties. A potentially positive implication was the awareness of the need to address the learning difficulties of a wider group of children and not simply those whose difficulties were most marked and who were generally of low ability. Balanced against this, however, was the notion that withdrawal for individual tuition would no longer be seen as the only role of the learning support teacher, but rather as one of a number of functions including consultancy and co-operative teaching. Although a learning support teacher working co-operatively or as a consultant might well be helpful to children with specific learning difficulties, many parents and other advocates of such children have emphasised the need for intensive **individual** tuition to help with the acquisition of literacy skills. They might be wary, therefore, of the broader concept of responsibilities of learning support teachers recommended in the HMI report and the SCOSDE guidelines.

Finally, the emphasis on the importance of parents as active partners in educational decision-making (a strong theme of the Warnock Report, the 1981 Act, the Parents' Charter in Scotland (Scottish Office, 1992) and the document *A Parents' Guide To Special Educational Needs* (SOED, 1993a) but less marked in the HMI Report) might be regarded as extremely helpful to parents of children with specific learning difficulties. The principle that the parent should be seen as the consumer of educational services whose wishes must be taken into account would be likely to raise expectations of the delivery of quality services. However, since the 1981 Act was not accompanied by additional financial resources, potential problems were likely to arise concerning the ability of education authorities to meet those expectations.

This discussion of the overall policy context has suggested that, despite the general anti-categorisation theme of the Warnock Report, children with specific learning difficulties were to some extent recognised as a distinct group for whom special provision should be made. There was no such clear statement in the HMI Report, although the SCOSDE guidelines did recognise dyslexic children as a discrete category requiring special provision. The 1981 Act, whilst recognising that children with specific, profound or complex learning difficulties should have their special needs met by additional resourcing, failed to define these categories. Given this degree of ambiguity in official documents, combined with the encouragement of consciousness among parents of their rights as consumers, the potential for conflict over the interpretation and implementation of policy is apparent.

The effect of devolved school management - looking towards the future

Other features of more recent government policy are likely to have an impact on provision for all children with learning difficulties. Particularly significant has been the shift of responsibility for educational finance from the education authorities to the schools. Local management of schools is already in place in England and Wales and devolved school management (DSM) will be in place in all mainstream schools in Scotland by 1996 and in special schools by 1997. The change is likely to have particular significance for children with learning difficulties, especially if they do not have a Record of Needs. Under DSM, education authorities will continue to fund centralised services such as peripatetic learning support, but it is unclear as to whether there will be sufficient funds retained centrally to safeguard existing provision. Schools may buy in additional services (publicly centralised or private) as required and, where finances are tightly stretched, additional learning support for individual children may be reduced. In the future, debates on priority for learning support are likely to take place at the school rather than the regional level and are likely to be influenced by a range of factors outwith the school's control, such as Government's determination to curb the spending of local authorities through the process of local tax capping and the reorganisation of local government in Scotland into 32 unitary authorities in 1996. Bowe and Ball (1992) have noted the strains placed on provision for children with learning difficulties by LMS in England. Where resources are scarce, some form of rationing is inevitably imposed and within the population of children with special educational needs, those with specific learning difficulties will be part of the competition for dwindling resources. It remains unclear how these children will be affected by the further progress of national testing, (albeit with the degree of flexibility which Scottish teachers have won), and by assessment of children's progress against the levels of the 5-14 curriculum programmes.

Changes to the public examination system for the upper secondary school in Scotland, set out in *Higher Still* (SOED 1994) could enhance or further diminish opportunities for educational achievement of pupils with specific learning difficulties. *Higher Still* (para 10.4) expresses a commitment to 'ensuring that the arrangements for the new awards do not place any artificial barriers in the way' of students with 'dyslexia' among a number of special educational needs.

Specific learning difficulties and competing explanatory frameworks

Within this general policy context, let us now look more closely at recent research and development in the area of specific learning difficulties.

The summary of definitions which we provide in Appendix A illustrates the complexity of terminology and the continuing influence of a range of paradigms. The DECP report, reviewing the field in 1983, optimistically predicted the end of terminological confusion in the wake of the 1981 Act:

> The new Act goes much of the way to make the debate on terminology irrelevant. Because of its emphasis on presenting problems, it will encourage all of us working with children with specific learning difficulties to pay more attention to assessment and educational provision than to spend time debating matters of nomenclature (p.6).

9

In the light of developments since the implementation of the legislation, such optimism appears somewhat premature. Pumfrey and Reason (1991) have suggested that the persistence of debates over terminology is not simply because of conflict between various interest groups, but also because of:

> the complexities of the issues, the involvement of different professions, the contrasting levels and natures of explanatory theories available, the different interventions advocated and the evidence adduced as to the efficacy of the latter (p.18).

Like Tomlinson, cited earlier, they recognised the involvement of three distinct approaches, the psychological approach (which emphasises learning processes and products) the psycho-educational approach (which focuses on pedagogy) and the psycho-medical approach, which focuses on the treatment of disorder or disease. Not only do conflicts arise among these three explanatory frameworks, but also between different theories within the same paradigm. The nature of these debates is summarised briefly in the next section.

Debates within the psychological approach

Among those who have investigated literacy problems from a psychological perspective, the fundamental disagreement has concerned the way in which children acquire literacy skills and hence the action which should be taken when problems arise. Pumfrey and Reason (1991) summarised the two views as the top-down and the bottom-up approaches. The top-down approach, based on psycho-linguistics, emphasises the social, political and cultural influences which impinge on the acquisition of reading skills (Smith 1990) and the importance of encouraging the child to move quickly from text to meaning. Proponents of this approach suggest that it is counter-productive to break down the immensely complex business of learning to read into sets of sub-skills. By analogy, you learn to swim by swimming, not by doing exercises on dry land. The 'real books' method of teaching reading is based on this theory. The bottom-up approach, on the other hand, stresses the importance of helping the child to master the skills of decoding written language and stress is placed on the acquisition of pre-reading skills. The significance of phonemic awareness has been explored recently by a number of psychologists (Bryant, 1990; Bradley, 1990; Snowling, 1990). For instance, Bradley (1990) has demonstrated that the achievement of nursery children on rhyming and alliteration tasks is related to their progress in reading and spelling ten years later. (An association between two variables does not, of course, necessarily imply a causal relationship. Children may develop reading skills by responding to the social and cultural

10

meanings of nursery rhymes, as well as developing understanding of the relationship between sound and symbol.)

Pumfrey and Reason argued that an eclectic approach is called for and there is danger in the rigid adherence to either a psycho-linguistic (top-down) or grapho-phonic (bottom-up) approach. Children use a range of strategies in learning to read and the insights gleaned from both approaches may be applicable in different contexts. Indeed, a small-scale study conducted by Pumfrey (1990) suggested that teachers' repertoire of teaching methods was influenced by both grapho-phonic and psycholinguistic approaches.

A further area of debate within the psychological approach has concerned the extent to which children with specific learning difficulties experience a range of problems which are **qualitatively** different from those of other children with literacy difficulties. Bryant and Bradley (1985) maintained that reading failure is caused in all children by the lack of common crucial skills connected with phonemic awareness. Developing this perspective, Bryant and Impey (1986) suggested that whilst there are no qualitative differences between children's reading difficulties, these may range from mild to severe and should be regarded as developmental delays rather than permanent defects. Snowling (1985) on the other hand, asserted that some children do exhibit qualitative differences in the nature of their problems. She commented that:

It seems highly likely that some dyslexics will show a delayed pattern of development, whereas others will show one which deviates from normal. The appropriate research has yet to be done to tell us 'who is who'.

Debates within the psycho-educational approach

Important implications for teaching have spilled over from the debate on the nature of children's literacy problems. Those who deny qualitative differences between children with specific learning difficulties and others would argue that teachers should use the same repertoire of teaching methods with all children. Those who assert that at least some children with specific learning difficulties have qualitatively different problems from 'normal' readers recommend particular remedial approaches. The latter are likely to use highly structured teaching methods, generally based on a multisensory approach and providing practice in phonics. Some educationists maintain the value of a basic starter repertoire which benefits **all** pupils while being of essential importance to those with dyslexic problems.

However, even among those who assert the need for a particular approach, there is a lack of unanimity over what this should be. For instance, Brown (1978) claimed that an emphasis on phonics actually inhibited reading because

11

of its emphasis on verbal processing. His alternative was based on the look and say method. He divided words into morphemes (the smallest meaningful part of the word) and taught children to link the morphemes to a visual signal which he called an icon.

It would appear that the superiority of one method of teaching reading over another has not been demonstrated, although a multi-sensory approach has been generally advocated by the Dyslexia Institute and dyslexia associations. Arguments for one teaching method rather than another have tended to rest on observations of what seems to work rather than on a sound theoretical basis. This has been inevitable, given that many key aspects of the acquisition of literacy have remained unresolved. Nonetheless, the hope is widespread that future developments in fundamental research will lead to greater theoretical rigour and so more effective practice.

Debates within the psycho-medical approach

As the summary of definitions provided in Appendix A indicates, there is a continuing debate concerning the role of the medical profession in the identification, assessment and possible remediation of children with specific learning difficulties. In 1980, following meetings with the Schools Council and examination boards to formulate a working definition of dyslexia, the British Medical Association advised its members that dyslexia was not a medical problem but a learning disability and as such responsibility for diagnosis lay with educational psychologists. The following year, Education Acts in both England and Wales and Scotland made provision for the compulsory representation of medical personnel on multi-disciplinary terms concerned with assessment of children whose special educational needs were to be set down in a record or statement. This effectively undermined the compartmentalised areas of responsibility which the BMA had attempted to define.

Despite the BMA's reluctance to involve itself in such matters, a number of researchers, notably Critchley (1981) continued to argue that neurologists had a major role to play.

> I have always insisted that the diagnosis of specific developmental dyslexia is a medical responsibility. This view is not popular among certain educational psychologists, but its truth can scarcely be denied (p.2).

Pumfrey and Reason (1991), reviewing recent work in this field, commented:

to date, the evidence for a neuro-pathological aetiology of specific learning difficulties is not conclusive but is very persuasive (p.158).

They acknowledged the contribution to be made by occupational and speech therapists to identification and remediation, but were more sceptical of causal theories and proposed remedies which had been advanced by those involved in other branches of medicine. Within the psycho-ophthalmological literature, for instance, the finding that there were significant differences in the eye movements of dyslexic and normal children was used to posit a causal connection, with various exercises recommended to normalise eye movement. Pumfrey and Reason pointed out that the original finding of difference in eye movements might well have been an **artefact** of the delayed acquisition of literacy, rather than its **cause**. Further, improvements in literacy skills after treatment might simply be due to the increased time spent practising reading.

A further example of work in the area of psycho-ophthalmology is that of Helen Irlen, who has claimed that impaired reading performance is caused by sensitivity to light which she has termed scotopic sensitivity. It has been claimed that the problem can be cured relatively simply through the use of coloured plastic filters to lay over pages or by wearing tinted glasses (Reid, 1994 p142). The Irlen Institute, which has branches in the United States and the United Kingdom, has published this work, although a convincing theoretical explanation is still lacking. There have also been contradictory findings on the overall effectiveness of the treatment.

Other areas which have been suggested by those approaching the problem from a psycho-medical perspective involve the use of drugs. For instance, it has been claimed that piracetam, a drug originally used in the treatment of memory disorders in the elderly, has led to improvements in reading among dyslexic children. Vitamins and trace elements are also claimed to have a beneficial effect. In reports of such treatments, a central problem lies in establishing a causal link between the medical intervention and the observed improvement.

In the light of the inevitable difficulties in interpreting conflicting findings, Pumfrey and Reason (1991) advocated the cultivation of an open-minded but sceptical attitude.

> The simplistic appeal of snake-oil solutions to children's specific learning difficulties will continue to be exploited. The armour of informed scepticism is an important protection for professionals and parents against exploitation by the unscrupulous (p.181).

It appears, therefore, that disagreements about the best means of identifying, assessing and making educational provision for children with specific learning difficulties persist for a number of reasons. First, educationists, psychologists and the medical profession have all approached the problem from different directions, asking different questions and so, inevitably, coming up with different solutions. Secondly, even within the confines of a particular discipline, many key theoretical issues remain unresolved. Pumfrey and Reason (1991) have argued strongly for an escape from the blinkered view which is offered by reliance on one particular vantage point.

An adequate understanding of aetiology, prognosis and the effects of interventions on children's reading difficulties is unlikely to derive from the efforts of any one group of specialists (p.8).

They have not suggested, however, that the problems are incapable of resolution. On the contrary, they have seen a need for careful and rigorous work in fundamental research so that important questions about the acquisition of literacy may be resolved and the knowledge used to inform practice. We would concur with this recommendation.

Research questions and methods

In addressing the aims of this research, the focus has been on three central questions:

1   To what extent are pupils with specific learning difficulties recognised as a group with distinctive needs and how is the nature of their difficulties perceived?

2   Where specific learning difficulties are recognised, how are they identified?

3   How are the needs of these pupils met and their identified difficulties remedied?

During the course of the project, both qualitative and quantitative methods were used. Detailed semi-structured interviews were conducted with principal educational psychologists, education officers and advisers in all regions. These were carried out either face to face or by telephone. Secretaries of local branches of the Scottish Dyslexia Association, Scottish Examination Board officers, teacher educators and medical personnel were also interviewed using semi-structured schedules. Questionnaire surveys were used with pre-service teachers, parents and learning support teachers. In addition, analysis of a wide range of relevant documents was undertaken. We thus gained the following distinct perspectives:

1   local policy makers (principal educational psychologists, education officers, special educational needs advisers);
2   consumers (parents and voluntary organisations);
3   grass-roots practitioners (learning support teachers);
4   trainers and recent recipients of training (teacher educators and pre-service teachers);
5   other professionals with an interest in the area (Scottish Examination Board officers, medical and para-medical personnel).

A central focus of the research was to contrast these perspectives to see how specific learning difficulties were construed and the contexts within which these constructs arose. The project began with the precise aim of looking at policy and provision for children with specific learning difficulties. As the work progressed, however, we became increasingly aware that the issues which were arising took us to the centre of debates on the conceptualisation of learning difficulties. It was not possible to think about specific learning difficulties without considering

the nature and extent of inter- and intra-individual differences in cognitive abilities, and the modifiability of these (DECP, 1983, p.8).

2 Regional provision: Recognition, identification and meeting needs

The main source of information about policies, practices and provision for specific learning difficulties in the Scottish education authorities was a set of interviews carried out with regional officers. From these interviews a picture was built up from the distinctive perspectives of psychologists, members of the directorate and advisers. In this chapter, their views on the recognition, identification and meeting of the needs of children with specific learning difficulties are analysed. Their perceptions of their relationships with other facets of this study such as the Scottish Examination Board's special arrangements, voluntary organisations and the medical profession are included in chapters 3, 7 and 9 respectively.

The collection of data

The intention was to interview three individuals within each of the 17 regional/divisional authorities: the principal educational psychologist (PEP), the directorate officer with responsibility for special educational needs and the adviser for special needs or learning support. In practice this range of individuals was not always available, and relevant alternative personnel such as primary advisers, have, therefore, also been included. In total, 49 individuals were interviewed: 18 principal psychologists, 11 education officers and 20 advisers or similar.

As a preliminary, a sheet of basic questions was sent out to the 17 principal psychologists in the region or division to ascertain the range of difficulties which, in their view, should be included under the heading of specific learning difficulties and the type they considered to be the most salient for education authorities' decisions about special provision. Twelve responded and while there was some variation in the range of difficulties included under the term, the majority (10/12) described reading, writing and/or spelling as being the most salient for special provision. On this basis, it was decided that the focus of the interviews would be on specific learning difficulties in the area of **literacy**. Special provision for consideration of difficulties with numeracy was made in a parallel project reported by Weedon (1992).

The interview schedules for principal psychologists, education officers and representatives of the advisory service were broadly similar in structure with changes in detail reflecting the different perspective of each group's work. The common structure consisted of questions about definition, identification and assessment, meeting children's needs, evaluation, training and associations with other professionals, parents and voluntary organisations.

Conceptualising specific learning difficulties

All interviewees were asked the same preliminary questions:

1   Whether they thought that children may have such a thing as a specific learning difficulty

2   If so, whether they thought that literacy problems were the most salient type of specific learning difficulty

3   Whether they considered children with specific learning difficulties to be a discretely identifiable group with a special category of needs which is different from that of other children with literacy-type problems.

The responses to these questions reflect **individual** opinions, and the analysis was carried out in the first instance according to individual responses. The consistency among individuals within regions or professional groups will be commented on in later sections. Where more than one member of staff was interviewed in any department, one view only was coded. Such individuals were usually in agreement but, in the case of disagreement, the view of the most senior person was coded. In total forty-four responses were coded, seventeen from principal psychologists, eleven from education officers and sixteen from advisers.

All forty-four interviewees agreed that specific learning difficulties existed and forty-one agreed that literacy problems were the most salient. (One person felt that other areas such as numeracy were as salient and the data are missing for the other two interviewees.) There was, however, less agreement about whether children with specific learning difficulties constitute a discretely identifiable group, which is different from other children with literacy problems. Thirteen people thought that they could be considered as a discrete group.

> Their difficulties are not similar to those of slow learning children; they are different in that they are often more intelligent and often able to conceptualize in a way other children can't. (Adviser)

However, few people made as categorical a statement, and were likely to add qualifications such as: the boundaries of this group are not 'tightly defined'; or there is some overlap with children with more global difficulties; or they are only considered a discrete group to a certain extent, e.g. in terms of their need for special examination arrangements.

The remaining thirty-one interviewees did not agree that such children constituted a discrete group. Of these, twenty-one described specific learning difficulties as part of the spectrum of literacy problems. They referred to a continuum of learning difficulties, ranging from children with global problems to those with specific learning difficulties. They pointed out that there was no absolute dividing line between specific learning difficulties and moderate learning difficulties; it depended on how you defined your criteria. Moreover, they did not see specific learning difficulties as confined to children of average or above average intelligence, it was just easier to detect in a bright child. Specific learning difficulties were not regarded as a distinct category, in the sense of a medical condition.

> [These children] do not exist as a separate group showing identical characteristics, having identical needs or having identical causes of their learning difficulties. (Psychologist)

> There are common elements between these kids but the variability among them is greater than any commonality. (Psychologist)

It was pointed out, furthermore, that specific learning difficulties were also on a continuum, ranging from the normal strengths and weaknesses that everyone has, to severe difficulties which significantly impede a child's learning. The problems of identification, therefore, were not only to do with the **nature** of the child's difficulties but also with the **degree** of difficulty (e.g. a 3 month lag in reading attainment would not constitute a specific learning difficulty).

18

There was a considerable amount of overlap in the two positions described. Almost half of those who considered children with specific learning difficulties to be a discrete group conceded that this group was not tightly defined; a similar proportion of those taking the continuum view felt that at the extreme end of it there were almost qualitative differences between children with specific learning difficulties and other poor readers, although it was difficult to be precise about what those differences were. Basically these children appeared to be 'reasonably intelligent' yet did not make the progress one would expect of someone with a moderate learning difficulty. They might also be getting into 'serious social and emotional difficulties' (Psychologist). Across both positions the term specific learning difficulties appeared to serve the function of highlighting these children's needs. An adviser noted the need

> to label in order to identify special educational needs but we don't want to separate these children... they are not discrete in terms of a population but in terms of practice in schools and the way you respond to them. (Adviser)

There were some individuals, however, who did not find labels such as specific learning difficulties or 'dyslexia' helpful (although they had all agreed initially that some such difficulties could occur). Ten interviewees rejected the notion of a discrete group, either because they were against categorising children according to their disabilities, preferring an approach based on individual needs, or because they felt that it was impossible to separate specific learning difficulties from other factors, such as emotional problems or inadequate teaching. Again there was some degree of overlap, with a small minority of those holding the 'continuum view' also expressing such reservations: 'the learning support system meets a continuum of need without categorising' (Education Officer).

The analysis so far has been across individuals; it is also interesting to look at the pattern of responses within each professional group. The variation was considerable (see Table 2.1); only among the psychologists did there appear to be a trend as indicated by twelve of the seventeen taking the continuum view. For the rest, there appeared to be no correlation between how specific learning difficulties were conceptualised and the area of responsibilities or the seniority of the interviewee.

Table 2.1   Definition of specific learning difficulties: local authority views

	Discrete	Continuum	Anti-categorisation	Total
Psychologists	3	12	2	17
Education Officers	4	5	2	11
Advisers	6	4	6	16
	13	21	10	44

At this stage, we move on to piece together the responses of those interviewed and try to characterise the ways in which the **regions or divisions** recognised specific learning difficulties. In doing that, we will endeavour to note where conflict or tensions between professionals within authorities, or across regions/divisions, were apparent.

Local Authorities' policy and practice

Regional/divisional recognition of specific learning difficulties

The views of individuals within each region on the definition of specific learning difficulties (i.e. the extent to which such children are a discretely identifiable group) were not always in agreement. In only one of the eight regions where three or more people were interviewed were the individuals in complete agreement.

Each region could be characterized , however, by a dominant view: in more than half of the regions the continuum view was dominant (7/12), in two regions (rural) the view that children with specific learning difficulties form a discrete group was dominant, while in two regions (central belt) the notion of any categorization was rejected in favour of a more individualistic approach. In one region we were unable to identify a dominant view; the data were missing for the education officer and the views represented by the PEP and the adviser were not in agreement.

Principal psychologists were asked if there was a regional policy on specific learning difficulties and, if so, whether it was documented. Over half of the authorities (7/12) had some kind of written statement. In three regions, policy statements had been issued by the directorate. Interestingly, in two of these the statements had been written by education officers, but the predominant view (i.e. that expressed by both the PEP and the adviser) was against the notion of categorising children. A fourth region had policy statements on recording and assessment in draft form. In the remaining three regions where documents were available, these had been issued by the psychological service, usually as a statement on practice and provision for schools and/or parents. However, the documents in one of these cases were 'for discussion' only, and the education officers interviewed were not aware of it at the time and considered that the matter was subsumed within the general policy framework on learning difficulties and learning support. Two of the five regions with no explicit statement on specific learning difficulties, also considered that the needs of these children were subsumed under more general policy documents, such as the aim of providing 'appropriate education for the whole range of ability', or within the general special educational needs policy.

> These difficulties are recognised and accepted as special educational needs. We do not 'label' or distinguish between different special needs. (Psychologist)

All of the policy documents available to the research are summarised in Appendix C. However, in three regions (one central belt, two rural) there were no relevant 'umbrella policies' to refer to; specific learning difficulties were considered as part of the continuum of learning difficulties and there were no guidelines on how the needs of these children should be met.

Given this general framework for the recognition of specific learning difficulties what did the data say about how regional authorities identified children with such problems?

Identification of pupils with difficulties

Three-quarters of the regions followed the Warnock stage model as the procedure for identifying and assessing needs. The first two stages were school-based, starting with class and head teachers, then involving advisory or specialist learning support staff. Stage three brought in the educational psychologist and moved on to stages of multi-disciplinary assessment. Progression through the stages was only as required and three regions described schools as mainly identifying the problem themselves with the assistance of learning support staff, only consulting an educational psychologist occasionally. In three other regions, mainly rural, referral of suspected specific learning difficulties to the psychological services was done almost automatically either through the learning support teacher or the parents. The final stages, involving multi-disciplinary assessment with a view to opening a Record of Needs, were

21

recommended by Warnock only for children whose needs could not be met within the ordinary school.

Those interviewed were asked at what stage in their school careers children's specific learning difficulties were most likely to be identified. In the majority of regions (two-thirds) children's difficulties were reportedly usually picked up at the end of the early primary stage, (i.e. P3 to 4). However, it was conceded in all regions that children's difficulties do not always come to light before secondary school.

> If it's picked up at 7 or 8 years you can do more...By secondary school it's too late unless they're picked up straight away. Plus there's the factor of attitude. Adolescents don't want to be singled out. I don't think we identify early enough. (Learning Support Coordinator)

Screening for reading and number difficulties was routinely carried out in one rural region at the P3 stage. Although not asked directly for their views on screening, two PEPs volunteered that they did not think it was an effective way of picking up specific learning difficulties since screening for reading cannot detect bright children who are underfunctioning, a view which was confirmed by the evidence of a 1985-86 psychological service survey in one of the regions.

In two regions, concern was expressed that children with specific learning difficulties were not being identified frequently enough; because their needs were not being defined, appropriate provision was probably not being made. Those interviewed found it difficult to estimate the incidence of specific learning difficulties in the school population in their region because of problems of definition. In three regions no one would hazard a guess. Elsewhere, estimates ranged from 0.5 to 10% depending on the severity of the cases included. In 5 regions it was estimated that between 0.5 and 1% of the school population had severe specific learning difficulties. The figure increased to 4 or 5% when children 'experiencing problems in schools' were included, whereas at 10% 'run of the mill low achievers' would be encompassed.

The identification of specific learning difficulties is likely to be the first stage in the process. The next question to address is whether this leads to an opening of a Record of Needs for the child.

Records of needs for pupils with specific learning difficulties

In the majority of the Scottish authorities (ten out of twelve) assessment procedures had led to the opening of Records of Needs for children with specific learning difficulties. There was, however, considerable variation among regions in the frequency of this: in three authorities, it had occurred only once or twice and was described as a rare event relating to the severity and complexity of the child's difficulties, whereas in another authority such children were recorded 'almost routinely'. The reasons for recording children were, as Warnock recommended, largely to do with securing extra provision for those whose needs could not be met within existing mainstream resources. However, in three authorities recording was not done to secure special provision, which was already available, it was done mainly at parental insistence.

> Why would you need to draw up a Record of Needs if everyone is aware of his needs and provision is made? (Adviser)

This argument was used as the reason for not recording in two other authorities. One PEP added:

> I don't think the record has much to say about specific learning difficulties . . . it's inappropriate to see the child as disabled. I don't think that's what parents want. The supply of resources to schools is part of the general structure and learning support should be part of every school. Recording doesn't make more resources generally available and that is what is needed.

In one island authority there was no philosophical objection to recording children with specific learning difficulties; the decision not to record was purely to do with the limited number of personnel available.

The incidence of recorded pupils with specific learning difficulties in two regions (both rural) was estimated at 3 to 4%. In one region (also rural) strict criteria for such recording were laid down as part of the written policy on recording special educational needs. In another region (central belt) a working group had been set up to establish recording criteria and the education officer who chaired the working group indicated that specific learning difficulties would be set down as one of the categories to be considered for recording. The aim was to improve the consistency of recording across the divisions of this region, where estimates of specific learning difficulties as a percentage of the total recorded population ranged from 0 to 60% depending on who was asked and the division represented.

Principal educational psychologists and advisers were asked about the type of diagnostic techniques they would recommend to identify specific learning difficulties. Advisers in half of the regions relied upon observation and/or a criterion-referenced approach aimed, for example, at detecting a discrepancy between oral and written language or between oral language and reading performance. In the other regions, standardized tests were also used by learning support teachers, although not widely. The battery of tests most frequently mentioned was the Aston Index which was designed for the early screening, diagnosis and categorization of 'dyslexia-type language difficulties' (Newton et al 1979, cited in DECP Report, p 78, 1983). It is interesting to note that Tansley and Panckhurst (1981) are most critical about this 'hotch potch' of tests and question its validity (see p 224-228).

Two-thirds of the sample of PEPs advocated the use of normative tests to detect a discrepancy between general ability and attainment in reading/writing. Such tests might also be combined with other tests to identify particular areas of difficulty, such as perception or memory. Diagnostic teaching and direct observation of how the child goes about the task of reading were other strategies recommended (either in addition to or instead of psychometric tests). Three PEPs were explicitly against the use of 'specific dyslexia tests', such as the Bangor Dyslexia Test, describing such checklists as having low validity, associated with false positives and false negatives and unable to pick up an unusual style of learning. However, one PEP said that he did use this test.

In three regions neither the PEP nor the adviser favoured the use of normative tests.

> It's not useful in going forward to find out what the child needs to improve learning... Viewing the whole child in the whole context is the important thing and how the child extracts learning from the context. (Psychologist)

This approach emphasized the child's interaction with the curriculum as the central focus rather than the child's deficit. Those interviewed were also asked how standard the procedures described were in terms of regional practice. In most regions, PEPs thought practice would vary according to the professional judgement of the psychologist, but there was a general move away from normative psychological assessments:

Psychometric tests are about putting children in categories and if you're not using a categorical frame of reference they don't help. (Psychologist)

Except for two areas, where standard assessment procedures had been established in schools to enable them to carry out the bulk of the assessments, there was reportedly little consistency in the procedures employed within schools. Variation in the ability and level of training of learning support staff to carry out assessments was commented on in several regions. Steps towards achieving greater within-region consistency were being taken in a number of regions by means of guidelines (for educational psychologists and schools) and staff training.

Current provision

Provision for most children with specific learning difficulties was within normal mainstream resources, i.e. help from learning support staff and the class/subject teacher. In two-thirds of the regions this was the only provision available. However, three large regions also had a number of specialist reading centres for primary school children with severe specific learning difficulties. One had extended its learning unit provision over recent years to three units sited within primary schools. The children attended on a full-time basis with some mainstream integration. Those admitted were typically at P4 to P6 stage. The authority also funded the placement of some pupils in independent schools providing specialised provision for such children. In a second region, attendance at the six reading centres was on a part-time basis from P6 to P7.

In the third of these regions, there was considerable variation in the range of provision available. Three divisions of this authority had specialist tutorial centres. One of these divisions had two such centres, both providing part-time places for 30 primary school children, and one part-time one-teacher unit, plus a number of teachers working in child guidance clinics who also went into schools to advise or carry out assessments. While secondary school children were not withdrawn for tuition, they were given a 6-week intensive assessment by reading centre staff who then made recommendations to the school on teaching materials and equipment. In a second division, four centres run by the psychological service provided a limited amount of within-centre tuition for small groups of primary school children, plus a consultancy service to the area schools. The balance had shifted towards more in-class and less in-centre support from the specialist teachers, after monitoring showed that the effects of withdrawing children for intensive tuition were short-term if not maintained by good in-class support. This was also the model followed in the third division, where three reading centres run by the psychological service acted primarily as resource centres. About 90% of the provision was given on an outreach basis, with specialist teachers providing support to both children and teachers in primary and secondary schools. Children were still brought in, however, for individual tuition when necessary. In one other region, specialist advice/support was given in primary schools by five teachers attached to the psychological service.

There was debate about the desirability of withdrawing children for intensive tuition. In two regions, PEPs expressed reservations about this practice, objecting that it distorted the child's curriculum and focused on the deficit rather than the whole child. Elsewhere the PEP thought that some educational psychologists might not refer children to the tutorial centres because they were against separate provision. Specialist unit provision was, however, seen as desirable by the PEPs in one region; in his 1988 report to the region, the PEP in one of the region's divisions recommended part-time attendance at a specialist centre for children with severe specific learning difficulties. Despite this, the general trend appeared to be that increasingly the specialist goes to the child rather than the child to the specialist.

Where relevant, interviewees were asked if the type of provision made for recorded children was any different from that for non-recorded children. In no region was a place at a reading unit or help from specialist staff dependent on the child having a Record of Needs. In two regions, provision for recorded children was the same as provision for non-recorded children i.e. learning support. The only difference was that recorded children would get more learning support time. This was viewed as a matter of concern by the adviser in one of these regions, who was worried about the shift of resources within the mainstream budget away from non-recorded children to recorded children.

In the other two regions where records were regularly opened for specific learning difficulties, extra learning support was available for recorded children out of the special education budget. In one rural region, where the extent of mainstream learning support was poor, support for recorded children was allocated on a one to one basis. Another made available an extended learning support facility for recorded children in a small number of primary schools and over half of the secondary schools. Each facility was staffed by an additional teacher and a supervisory assistant to provide back-up help with preparation of materials.

In the five divisions of the region where recording for children with specific learning difficulties was carried out, there was a range of practice. Two tutors allocated to both primary and secondary recorded children gave a small amount of extra help in schools beyond that given by area learning support staff. These tutors were not, however, specialists in teaching children with specific learning difficulties. In another division special educational needs teachers, managed by the psychological services, saw some children with specific learning difficulties (recorded and non-recorded) but on a limited basis with little direct tuition given. Only one division had no back up facility for recorded children; any extra help requested on the Record of Needs had to come from existing learning support provision within schools.

Provision seen as desirable for children with specific learning difficulties

The discussion so far has concerned the broad categories of provision available in the different regions. We turn now to interviewees' recommendations on the type of support/teaching which **should** be given. Learning support was described by one psychologist as having a dual role: to improve the child's literacy skills and to help the child access the curriculum. In relation to the first of these, most advisers said that some direct tuition was given. Many psychologists felt that this was not enough, however, and that intensive tuition on a one-to-one or small group basis was essential for the progress of children with severe specific learning difficulties.

> Specific learning difficulty requires more individual attention, more direct instruction because the degree of difficulty goes beyond that of the slow learner. (Psychologist)

It was recognised, however, that there was tension between this view and that held by at least some learning support teachers:

> Learning support [teachers] often see themselves in an advisory role and some are actively hostile to the idea of working with children one-to-one. (Psychologist)

In one region both points of view were evident: the PEP recommended once-a-day learning support withdrawal for a small percentage of pupils with extreme specific learning difficulties (there were no reading centres in that region) but the learning support adviser saw too much direct tuition as against the interests of the child (it was, 'not a questions of the more he gets the more likely he is to be cured'). Moreover, the latter suggested, without a special needs budget, one-to-one support was at a cost to the other children and the broad curriculum. Instead, she advocated that the balance should favour support in class, making sure that the learning materials were appropriate and giving the child as many strategies to help him or her cope as possible (be they special schemes, computers or coloured overlays). Another adviser pointed out that it was not

27

practical to allocate learning support help on a one-to-one basis, there were just not enough staff.

Teaching methods and learning materials

In the majority of regions it was considered that there were some differences in the teaching methods or learning materials used with children with specific learning difficulties compared to children with global learning difficulties. A more structured teaching approach with the former was frequently recommended, using techniques such as repetition and over-learning; a more curriculum-oriented approach would be used with the generally slow learners. Multi-sensory methods, using materials such as Hickey or Alpha-Omega, were mentioned in a third of the regions. However, it was more often claimed that the approach was pragmatic, that there was 'no magic formula', you just look at the approaches the child responds to: 'no fancy ideas - good teaching practice and attitude'. (Learning Support Adviser)

In one region, advisers emphasized the use of normal teaching methods in order to 'quell the panic' amongst teachers who feel they 'don't know how to teach a dyslexic child'. The main difference in approach, however, lay in teaching those with specific learning difficulties alternative strategies to enable them to access the curriculum without being hampered by their difficulties.

> With slow developers the work is on concepts and content as well as mode. Children with specific learning difficulties cope with more complex ideas and therefore may need extra help to access the curriculum - more direct help because they have no reading skills. The slow learners may have one foot on the reading ladder and with appropriate books and reading group tuition you can expect progress. (Psychologist)

In two-thirds of the regions, interviewees advocated teaching children with specific learning difficulties to by-pass their problems by using various technological aids (e.g. tape recorders and computers). Teaching such children was described as striking a balance between 'remediation' of their difficulties and 'compensation' through the use of technology. The emphasis placed on one or other aspect varied across the regions and the balance between the two depended on the individual pupil and the stage of schooling. It was suggested that by the secondary school stage, if not before, the balance should have shifted towards compensation.

Evidence about the effectiveness of the provision described above was not plentiful. Opinion varied on the extent to which specific learning difficulties could be remedied. In one region with reading centre provision it was claimed that 'most children who attend the units become functional readers, although residual problems with written work remain' (Psychologist). In three regions psychologists rejected any notion that the difficulty could be overcome. While considerable progress was possible, it was more appropriate to think in terms of teaching children 'to cope with' their difficulties and 'not feel swamped' by them.

> Severe specific learning difficulties are not remediable. Part of their definition is that they are resistant to easy or normal means of remediation. They're still going to have that discrepancy at the age of 55... I think it's dishonest to say that we can fix their difficulties; [rather] we help them address or cope with their difficulties and make sure the child gets as full an education as possible. (Psychologist)

Dissatisfaction with the provision offered to children with specific learning difficulties was expressed in a third of the regions. A psychologist commented that there was a

> definite gap. [Without a specialist centre] the needs of the severest cases are not being met.

Others were more satisfied but felt there was room for improvement. A common response in more than half of the regions (7/12) was that more staff development was needed both to change attitudes and to train teachers how to assess and work with children with specific learning difficulties. Two regions also felt that they were more effective at the primary than the secondary stage.

Three-quarters of the regions provided some guidance on specific learning difficulties for learning support staff either in the form of written guidelines or through in-service training (INSET). INSET ranged from optional one-day sessions or other ad hoc arrangements to college courses on specific learning difficulties. By comparison, little was done to raise the awareness of the ordinary classroom teacher. In a minority of regions, INSET on specific learning difficulties was available (or about to be) on an optional basis; elsewhere it was explained that other claims, such as the 5-14 curriculum programme, were more pressing. Where efforts were made to develop the skills of learning support staff by, for example, training them to diploma level, the intention was that their expertise would filter down to the mainstream teacher. In two regions, programmes had been developed to raise class teachers' awareness of learning difficulties in the primary and secondary sectors respectively. There was, however, some resistance to focusing on raising awareness about specific learning difficulties in particular:

> We don't go out of our way to categorize children, therefore that wouldn't be our aim. (Education Officer)

Although not asked about this directly, a small minority of interviewees volunteered that they had a poor opinion of the standard of teaching of reading in schools and wondered if poor teaching might be a contributory factor to the incidence of specific learning difficulties.

> I wonder if better teaching of reading, the old-fashioned approach [look and say plus phonics] would lower the incidence of specific learning difficulties. Nowadays there's not the same degree of over-learning and repetition. It's OK for children who pick it up easily but not for others. (Psychologist)

There were also criticisms about the standard of initial teacher training:

> The teaching of reading is one of the least well-taught elements of teacher training. (Psychologist)

PEPs were asked if there was any support available for psychologists in the area of specific learning difficulties. This had been addressed in a third of the regions through the organisation of seminars and meetings.

Summary

Recognition of specific learning difficulties

From the start of the collection of the regional data it became clear that although the vast majority of those interviewed agreed that specific learning difficulties had a distinctive reality (and were overwhelmingly affecting **literacy**) there was great variation (even within regions and professional groups) about how this was conceptualised.

Nearly half of the education officers, principal educational psychologists and advisers interviewed saw such difficulties as **part of a general continuum of learning difficulties** stretching from the global to the specific. This conception did not conform to that of others (just under one third) who recognised pupils with specific learning difficulties as a **discrete group** with particular problems in some areas (usually literacy) which did not appear to match their abilities in others. This was not to say that specific learning difficulties occur **only** in children of average or above average ability, but in those cases they are more readily detected. The rest of those interviewed (just under a quarter) were **against any categorisation** of children, did not distinguish specific learning difficulties from other problems in learning and emphasised the importance of identifying and meeting the different needs of each individual child.

Our classification of the views of regional officials into these three categories is, of course, an artefact to make communication easier. Whether these second order concepts (i.e. introduced by researchers) would stand up to the test in a wider area remains to be seen. They have been useful to us, however, and provided it is realised that there is considerable overlap in the details of the three kinds of views expressed, we believe it is helpful to sustain these distinctions for the time being. In the final chapter, we return to this matter and discuss some of the philosophical, ideological and economic factors which impinge on the conceptualisation of specific learning difficulties.

The inferences we were able to draw about the dominant concepts of specific learning difficulties held at the regional level, suggested a similar distribution to that among individuals. There was evidence, however, of differences among officers within regions in their perceptions of the difficulties. Policy documentation varied greatly among regions and was not such that a clear **analysis** of the assumptions made about specific learning difficulties could be accomplished. In Appendix C we **summarise** the documents, but that is not the same thing.

Variation in responses made it difficult for us to summarise the proportion of the population which, it was believed, exhibited specific learning difficulties. Our 'best guess' was that the modal estimate suggested about 1% of children had a severe form of such difficulties; 10% of the school population would include **all** children with specific learning difficulties, but that 10% would also encompass other low achievers who could not easily be distinguished from those on whom this research is focused.

Identification of specific learning difficulties seemed to occur mainly in the middle years of primary school. Diagnosis in the secondary years was seen both as too late and introducing problems of social stigma for adolescents. For the most part, the identification of children followed the pattern of the five stages described in the Warnock Report, but was usually confined to the first two school-based stages with, perhaps, some subsequent consultation with the psychological services. Only a minority proceeded to diagnosis by professionals outside education (see Chapter 9 for a discussion of this).

There was some unease expressed about using routine screening to detect specific learning difficulties - it was seen as unlikely to reveal the inconsistencies across different abilities which are regarded as characteristic. Concern was also evident about whether teachers were sufficiently aware of how to identify these children and, if not, whether children with such problems were being 'missed'.

The great majority of regions accepted that children with specific learning difficulties should be considered for a Record of Needs, though only one did this routinely. For the others, the stimulus for starting the recording process might be the severity of the difficulty, circumstances in which the childs' needs appeared not to be met within mainstream education or pressure from the parents.

Diagnostic procedures used included observation of the child and both criterion-referenced and normative tests to detect discrepancies among the child's various abilities. These and other standardised tests, the Aston Index and the Bangor Dyslexia test were all mentioned and most were adversely criticised. These criticisms were of three kinds: technical (eg low validity, identify false positive or false negative cases), inconsistent with the conceptual view of the difficulty (eg tests do not pick up unusual styles of learning or particular needs of the individual pupil) and practical (eg. great variation among schools' practice and teachers need more training).

For two thirds of the regions, provision was made entirely within mainstream schools. Three regions had specialised reading or tutorial centres, almost all of which catered for the primary sector. Some of these were attended full time by children over an appropriate period, others had part-time attendance with the children based in mainstream schools. These centres, however, served a minority of children with specific learning difficulties. The trend was towards specialist staff supporting schools and pupils in their own classes; this preference was based, to some extent, on evidence about the effectiveness in the long term of withdrawing pupils from mainstream education. It also resulted from beliefs that withdrawal of this kind was likely to distort the curriculum for the individual, focus on a 'deficit in the child' model, hamper social relationships with peers and work against the policies of the previous decade which had tended to discourage ideas of extending separate provision.

Within mainstream schools, withdrawal from class for intensive tuition on literary skills seemed to be favoured by educational psychologists. Learning support advisers, however, were more likely to resist this in the spirit of the SOED sponsored move away from 'remedial education' over the 1980s. Furthermore, limited staffing levels inevitably meant that individual tuition of this kind was at the expense of attention to other children with learning difficulties.

The uncertain future of both psychological and advisory services in the light of devolved school management and local government reorganisation in Scotland makes it difficult to predict how policy and provision for specific learning difficulties will develop. In the meantime, SOED have issued new guidelines (Support for Learning 5-14, SOED 1994a) which accord more recognition to specific learning difficulties than previous official documents.

At the time of our research, more structured approaches to the development of reading and writing (e.g. more repetition, over-learning) were seen by local authority informants as necessary for children with specific learning difficulties in comparison with those with more general literacy problems. While one third of regions recommended multisensory approaches, the common stance was pragmatic and suspicious of any so-called magic formula.

A continuing aspect of the debate concerned the extent to which specific learning difficulties could be overcome, or whether the most sensible course of action was to help the pupils find alternative strategies (such as using technical aids) to by-pass their problems. While slow learners more generally have difficulties in coping with complex ideas, this was not seen as a major factor for those with specific learning difficulties. For them, the issue was access to the curriculum. The general consensus seemed to be that at the primary level the emphasis should be on overcoming the difficulties, but if they persist into secondary the balance should shift towards compensatory measures.

In Chapter 8, we give an account of some specific kinds of provision. These are illustrative but not typical. It is relatively easy to gather more detailed information in centres which draw in identified pupils from a large number of schools; the more common practice of providing for perhaps just one pupil in a classroom is difficult to capture within the resources of a project of this kind.

3 Specific learning difficulties and the public examination system

An important element in the framework of provision in Scotland for children with specific learning difficulties is the Scottish Examination Board's arrangements for special educational needs. Views of these arrangements propounded by regional/divisional officers, learning support teachers and representatives of voluntary organisations are also included.

Scottish Examination Board (SEB) arrangements for special educational needs

It became clear from our policy interviews and from investigation of the views of voluntary associations (see chapter 7) that the opportunity for candidates with specific learning difficulties to enter and obtain examination qualifications was a topic that required further study; past special arrangements were regarded favourably by dyslexia association speakers, but anxieties were expressed about current developments in the system, not only by the voluntary groups but by psychologists and some of the education officers and advisers. Additional information was gathered from two interviews, with the SEB's Examination Officer for Special Educational Needs, and with the secondary head teacher who chaired the Board's sub-committee on these examination arrangements. The Association of Scottish Principal Educational Psychologists (ASPEP) had also set up a working group to monitor the effects of the 1990 revised arrangements; the report of their survey of psychological services was made available to us.

The Examination Board undertook a review of procedures in 1987 which led to the setting up of a sub-committee to consider the whole question of special arrangements. In 1989, revised arrangements were introduced, which were applied in the 1990 examination diet. The booklet, *Guidance on Examination Arrangements for Candidates with Special Educational Needs,* addressed to parents and teachers, was issued in 1990, incorporating comments from consultations the previous year. It was founded on the principles of:

1   assessment for all
2   descriptive certification
3   a common basis of treatment for all candidates with special educational needs
4   reflection of classroom approach on examination arrangements.

An important further undertaking was the development of independent courses for those Standard Grade examinations which required substantial modification to make them accessible to candidates with various special needs. Two such courses, Standard Grade Spoken English, and Standard Grade English, Alternative Communication, have been developed and piloted. The examination diet in 1994 included these special English pathways for the first time.

Rationale for the revised examination arrangements

The system for special examination arrangements up to 1990 distinguished between sensory and/or physical disabilities on the one hand, and 'dyslexia or other related severe communication difficulties' on the other. Thinking about the whole field of special educational needs developed in the light of the argument of the Warnock Report for rights of access to the curriculum in spite of disability. In Scotland, progress towards the principle of assessment for all continued during the years leading to the establishment of the Standard Grade examination in the mid 1980s. Standard Grade required a fresh look at the application of special arrangements for two reasons:

•   Examinations for all meant finding ways of involving the many candidates for whom the old Ordinary Grades were never designed.

•   The increased coursework element called for special conditions outwith the examination itself.

Effects of the 1990 arrangements

The introduction of the revised arrangements led to some misunderstanding. The broader terminology of 'specific learning difficulty' was accepted rather than restricting concessions to those defined as having 'dyslexic or severe communication difficulties'; but this was interpreted variously, and in practice the Board still required to know that the difficulty was either sensory or a specific learning difficulty of a dyslexic or similar nature:

> After one year of the diet of exams it became apparent that we were having great problems with using that terminology . . . there was a feeling that it was for all special educational needs; it was never intended to be that. We were allowing special arrangements to get over a disability but the whole ethos out on the teaching side is enabling the pupil with special needs to get there. Where do you draw the line? Any pupil at the bottom end might be helped by extra time in an exam, by a reader or scribe, but that was never the Board's intention; the Board is working on the presence of an identifiable disability that can be removed by using the arrangements, not to make up for a lack of ability. (SEB Officer)

The tighter interpretation of the new wording required by the Board appeared to be becoming familiar to users. The success of the revised arrangements in spite of these problems was seen by the Board in the increase in numbers of candidates permitted special arrangements:

> It was always envisaged that numbers would increase. Before 1990 special schools and people in the know applied. One of the recommendations of the sub-committee was to circulate all schools and put the onus on schools to ask for what a candidate needs. (SEB Officer)

Approximate numbers of candidates taking advantage of the arrangements in 1991 were:

Candidates with SpLD	-	1400
Blind candidates	-	26
Partially sighted	-	148
Other disabilities	-	578
TOTAL	-	2000

This was a rise of just under 300 from the previous year. Special examination arrangements still accounted for only a small percentage of the total number of candidates, however, and a still smaller percentage of all presentations.

Identification of candidates

Schools had the responsibility for nominating pupils under the revised arrangements. Nominations were referred to local authorities who had to validate them for the Board. Eligibility might vary from subject to subject; where the grade related criteria did not include the skills of reading and writing as such, it was much easier to certify that a reader or scribe would allow the candidate to display his or her knowledge and understanding without distortion:

> In English or Modern Languages, the use of a reader/scribe inevitably confers advantage, particularly for candidates at the lower end. We have had teachers upset because a candidate helped by a reader/scribe has ended up with a better folio of work than another child who is 'better at English'. It is very hard to control the amount of support a reader/scribe gives. (SEB Officer)

> The school is the prime mover; it does happen that a school puts forward a candidate who is not validated, but not very often. If a school puts forward a candidate on the grounds of being a 'poor reader' and it is validated as 'poor reader' then we would not allow it without more details: full evidence from the psychologist that it is specific learning difficulties. (SEB Officer)

Nevertheless, the principle was followed that provision must be made to allow all children access to the curriculum; that implied access to assessment. Some schools were well organised, with documentation prepared from the different subject departments co-ordinated by learning support, and a case conference at the end of S2 with the assistant head teacher responsible for examination presentation and the psychologist.

Validation by the local authority

The educational psychologists' survey cited in the introduction to this section identified variations in existing practice among the 17 local authorities. Applications forms from the schools were returned for validation either to psychological services or to directors of education/education officers. The almost equal split in practice in this respect seemed not to affect the essential elements of the application process. While educational psychologists were consulted on the cases of individual children in all authorities, in only about half of the areas were they always involved in requests for special examination conditions. In 10 of the 17 psychological services, information on applications was automatically received. ASPEP recommended that all authorities should make this information available, and in considering the criteria for validation cited by the authorities, recommended that the validation process include close co-operative working and discussion between school learning support departments and local psychologists. In 3 cases, school forms were said to be accepted without further check; ASPEP indicated dissatisfaction with this practice.

The criteria used by psychological services for decisions on validation showed only five answers based on the notion of a discrepancy between a candidate's knowledge of a subject and his/her ability to display this knowledge; other answers were expressed more vaguely. The ASPEP authors conclude that while national guidelines would be useful:

> it would be a retrograde step to attempt to define more stringent criteria for determining eligibility for support . . . We are of the opinion that special examination conditions should be offered to any pupil who would benefit from them with the proviso that there is no infringement of the Grade Related Criteria. (ASPEP report)

Both ASPEP and other informants agreed that the identification and validation of candidates for special conditions should be part of a process extending over some years: 'There should be no dramatic turn of events that causes the Board to phone an educational psychologist in a panic to certify a child'. Among ASPEP's conclusions was the recommendation that schools should maintain a folio of work for pupils for whom they foresaw a need for concessionary arrangements, and that this folio should be central to the validation process.

Terminology

As with other sections of this research, controversy over terminology was evident. The change in 1990 from the previous separate categories had led to expectations that concessions would be made available for all special educational needs; this was not the case. Three psychological services reported to ASPEP that they had been refused applications for special arrangments on the grounds of the terminology used. The 'specific' learning difficulty cited still had to be specified, and the earlier acceptable wording of 'dyslexic or similar difficulties' remained the clearest route to reaching understanding with the Board. The Examination Board Officer expressed surprise that 'some people used "specific" to mean "particular"':

> we had forms saying specific learning difficulty but ... it might turn out that the child had a physical problem. It was becoming a catch-all phrase ... Downs syndrome may well be a 'specific learning difficulty'. It was being used as a label; we wrote and enquired if this child had been officially identified as having specific learning difficulties. It is not so bad this year because we have stated in our correspondance that learning difficulties must be clearly identified, and must be distinguished from general or moderate learning difficulties. (SEB Officer).

There was substantial confusion among the different interpretations. Where schools or psychologists had an objection to categorising learning difficulties, or to the word 'dyslexia' in particular, it was implied and apparently accepted that they could get round it by using phrases such as 'similar to dyslexic-type problems'. The Board's sub-committee 'certainly gave the question of categories of difficulty a good innings', but its chair claimed that he tried not to let his doubts about the concept of dyslexia permeate the committee's work. The doubts appeared to centre upon a suspicion of what was seen as a middle-class pressure group rather than on the existence of 'such a thing as dyslexia'. The Board meantime reserved its position on the definition of specific learning difficulty. It took the term to mean:

> whatever the authorities have in mind. We are not psychologists here. Schools can give details of a child's difficulties but I am not in a position to say if he is a poor speller or a child with specific learning difficulty. We want the authorities to make the definition for us... It is fraught with problems. (SEB Officer)

Inequalities in access to special arrangements

It was acknowledged that applications for special examination conditions were unevenly spread, between authorities and between schools. The socio-economic status of the catchment area was stated to be the main determinant of unequal demands from schools, although other sources of know-how were mentioned.

> I have to admit that interpretation varies widely ... from presenting centre to presenting centre. We were aware that in some schools there was a good service to candidates; perhaps the LS teacher had been on a committee; whereas there were other schools, not necessarily in the

backwoods, which do not avail themselves of the opportunities. (Head teacher, Chair of SEB Special Educational Needs Committee)

There are discrepancies in take-up at present ... the chances of unfairness creeping in are there. Some schools are more clued in, particularly special schools which have had a lot of special provision; also independent schools clued into the dyslexia aspect or perhaps with more pupils assessed outwith local psychologists. Inconsistencies are bound to occur, but the fact that numbers are increasing means that more people are aware. (SEB Officer)

Discrepancies among the authorities' policy positions on the categorisation of learning difficulties were seen as less important; the expectation was that staff would be willing to use the system, even if it involved modifying their preferred terminology. The ASPEP recommendations, if followed, would enable schools in different authorities to gain more uniform access to the arrangements. The social class aspect of variations in access to special arrangements may be more difficult to eliminate. Hints of resentment at the demands of parents seen as relatively advantaged come through some of the data:

We have had experience of parents who tend to become dogmatic; they are talking prematurely about exam presentation during the first or second year. They don't stop and consider the rate of maturation...[in one instance] the parents arrived on the day of the examination and said the boy was dyslexic and had a certificate to prove it. They had never given us any clue of this. Our view of that boy was that he was what used to be called retarded. (Head teacher, Chair of SEB Special Educational Needs committee)

Certificates obtained under special arrangements

One of the 1990 changes proposed to endorse certificates on the basis of the special arrangement where the grade related criteria were modified, not on the basis of the child's special need. The Scottish Dyslexia Association had been unhappy with the endorsement of certificates in the past, but the Board expressed the hope that the new arrangements were 'more consistent and defensible'. The Scottish Dyslexia Association responded positively to the consultation about the development of the Spoken English examination. The independent courses would preclude any need for endorsement of certificates as they were designed to test candidates rigorously by alternative means of communication. They were intended not to be a soft option; the intention was

41

that the credibility of the award would remain intact. Where scribes and readers continued to be used in subjects where no independent courses existed, endorsement would also continue.

User's views of the examination arrangements

Regional officers

Not unexpectedly, the main concern of the regional officers related to terminology. They reported that they had to return applications to schools because the terminology preferred by the SEB had not been used. Unfortunately, they felt they themselves were not clear about exactly what that preference was. Most of them argued that any application had to include the term 'specific learning difficulties' in order to be accepted, but in several instances there were rejections apparently because the term 'dyslexia' had not been used.

Many of those interviewed welcomed the opportunity for schools to take the responsibility for nominating children. However, the system of validation (through the principal educational psychologist or education officers) had some disadvantages. Two regions expressed dissatisfaction with the arrangement because the children concerned were not known by the validators - a 'blind' process.

Like the Examination Board, the regions were aware that nominations were not evenly distributed across the authority but tended to concentrate in certain schools. This was attributed to parental pressure on the schools:

> Most come from middle class areas and least from areas of priority treatment. One school is 2000% more in terms of its demands. (Education Officer)

The SEB's intention that the request for special arrangements should be a reflection of current classroom practice (i.e. if a child is getting extra time or a reader/scribe in class then these arrangements will be made for the child in the examination) was posing problems in a quarter of the regions. Many schools were uncertain of the type of special support which should be given in class. It appeared, in some areas at least, that satisfactory special examination provision was viewed as something still to be achieved.

In one region advisers were concerned that the arrangements might encourage too much external support which was not necessarily in the child's interest. They emphasised the importance of striking a balance between support and encouraging independence. It was too easy for a child to become dependent on a scribe or reader, whereas good teaching was about encouraging the child to learn to cope with his/her difficulties and making him/her independent.

A number of authorities had responded, or were in the process of responding, to schools' uncertainties over exam-related issues by providing guidelines and/or holding INSET days. In one divisional document schools were told that special arrangements needed to start at the primary/secondary transition.

Psychologists in two authorities criticised the SEB for attempting to focus on too narrow a group as eligible for the revised special arrangements:

> I thought we'd got rid of this dyslexia differentiation and any child who had difficulties in demonstrating knowledge would be eligible for a scribe, word processor or whatever. It should be negotiable regardless of the disability which gave rise to it. They still want a diagnosis. If a school has had to modify the class approach to the child, special provision should be available; it shouldn't depend on classification. (Psychologist)

The development of the new independent courses may help to meet this objection, at least for English, as entry is to be open to any candidate for whom the school and family together decide it is the best pathway. However, once the new courses are in place, the availability of scribes and readers for Standard Grade English will be reduced.

> We would want a decision taken about which path the child is on, regular or independent course, as early as possible in the secondary career, the teaching aligned appropriately and the assessment falling in with it. We would perhaps be harder on the dyslexic child than we have been previously. (Head teacher)

Learning support teachers

In chapter 5 we shall describe a survey of learning support teachers' views on specific learning difficulties. In response to a question about the SEB arrangements, 75 (88%) of secondary learning support teachers said that they had made use of SEB dispensations for pupils with specifial educational needs. Nearly two thirds of those who had experience of the arrangements thought them good to some extent with only 6% describing them as no use.

Most of the additional comments were critical of the system: 'too much red tape'; 'some specific learning difficulties are difficult to prove'; 'ten minutes extra time is not nearly enough'; 'confirmation comes too late to set the pupil's mind at rest, or to give counselling if special arrangements are not permitted'. One respondent raised the problem of social class bias: the Examination Board special dispensations were seen to meet the needs of middle class children from an articulate, educated background very well, but were not at all good for 'poor' children. Two teachers expressed the hope that the new independent courses for Standard Grade English would improve on the present provision for examination candidates with specific learning difficulties.

Voluntary organisations

In chapter 7 we will report on interviews with various voluntary organisations. Although the SEB arrangements for candidates with specific learning difficulties were not an important focus of this part of the research, it became clear that they were well known and approved of in this sector. The degree of satisfaction varied sharply, however, where education authorities or individual schools would not recognise specific learning difficulties. This aroused frustration that the possibility of concessions existed but that children in particular areas were debarred from benefiting from them. There was some dissatisfaction with the year to year changes which the current re-organisation of the system had entailed, and a desire to see a settled, well-publicised system. The paradoxical stance of certain authorities was noted, where specific learning difficulty 'is not supposed to exist then suddenly it does for the purpose of the examinations.' One speaker was critical of the endorsement of certificates currently awarded under the Scottish Examination Board dispensations.

Summary and continued debate

There is no doubt that considerable efforts have been made by the SEB to introduce examination arrangements which give young people with special educational needs the opportunity to acquire qualifications. These arrangements have had to evolve as the assessment procedures for certification have changed and from 1990 onwards references to dyslexia and related severe communication difficulties have been replaced by the broader term 'specific learning difficulty'. This has led to a number of problems.

Some interpretations of the term have equated it with **any** special educational need. The Board's intention, however, was not to facilitate the performance of all children who would benefit from having a reader or scribe. Its concern was with pupils with particular 'disabilities' and not with those with general learning difficulties. Support for this stance was evident in the voluntary organisations. Teachers and regional officers welcomed the arrangements at a general level, but they had reservations about the terminology and its implications for the identification of children who could take advantage of the scheme. Some individuals saw no reason why **all** those children who have difficulties in understanding the task which is set, or in demonstrating the knowledge and skills they have acquired, should not be eligible for support from a reader, scribe or computer.

The tensions arising from these distinctively different sets of assumptions about who should and should not receive support within the arrangements, are unlikely to be easily resolved and may even increase. Standard Grades in Spoken English and English: Alternative Communication were being introduced from 1994 onwards and the Board had decided that concessionary arrangements for the use of a reader and scribe in Standard Grade English would, therefore, be phased out from 1997. Decisions about who is to be provided with a scribe for the examination would become a thing of the past as the choice of the alternative course would have been made earlier. It would be important, however, that these new courses were not regarded as of lower rank than the existing English course. Whether that can be achieved, given the centrality of reading and writing to society's conception of achievement, remains to be seen. Previous official attempts to create 'parity of esteem', where that did not match public perceptions, are not encouraging. However, a contribution to the TESS, 'English-Spoken must not be allowed to fail' (Lawson, October 1994) argued that the new examination gives pupils 'the opportunity to demonstrate, entirely from their own resources, their linguistic competence without the yoke of pen and paper'. Lawson pointed out that:

> They will still be using scribes in other Standard grade subjects where communication elements are not assessed, so that that relationship of trust in and familiarity with a scribe which learning support teachers rightly cherish will be maintained and carried forward into Higher... On the other hand, the demands of the non-mediated 'spoken' course hopefully will enhance the pupil's ability to organise, plan and sequence ideas independently and in doing so complement the use of a scribe.

The debate was continued by Graham Dane ('Pass the keyboard please' TESS 6/1/95) who argued that 'writing' and 'reading' should not be tested as physical processes. The intellectual tasks of creating meaningful text and extracting meaning from text were the essentials; the withdrawal of scribes from S-grade English was 'disastrous', and with advances in information technology, increasingly irrelevant. Weedon (3/10/95) supported Dane's article from the disappointing experience of piloting Standard Grade Spoken English:

in no case do I welcome the prospect of having to dispense with the unique support offered by readers and scribes... we will be closing off more avenues for personal and intellectual development than we will be opening.

Fears were expressed to our research, by both the SEB and regional officers, that opportunities to take advantage of the arrangements were unevenly distributed. In cases where schools were 'clued in' to the system, or middle class parents were motivated to exert pressure, the chances of children benefiting from the scheme were seen as much greater. (We shall be considering the position of parents in chapter 6.)

It was clearly the intention of the SEB that any support received by the child in the context of the examinations would reflect the support which he or she had been regularly receiving in the classroom, quite possibly over a period of years. There was some anxiety that schools might be uncertain about what form that support should take. This research did not include observation of classrooms so we have no direct evidence of the nature of support in typical cases. The next two chapters, however, may provide some indicators of what is going on. They are concerned with questions of how teachers are prepared (pre-service and in-service) to deal with specific learning difficulties, and how learning support teachers perceive the teaching of children with such difficulties.

4 The contribution from teacher education

This research aimed to elucidate policy makers' and practitioners' understanding of the term specific learning difficulties and the strategies they adopted in identifying and meeting the needs of children with such difficulties. However, to go beyond straightforward descriptions and generate explanations of the nature and effects of policy, other kinds of information were needed. In particular, we felt it was important to know something about how beginning teachers were prepared for work of this kind and how, as they became more experienced, the support continued.

We were also aware that the resources of this research did not enable us to penetrate one important area of practice in relation to children with specific learning difficulties: namely the role of mainstream teachers in observing and identifying children's difficulties, initiating appropriate referrals and assisting the child to work in areas across the curriculum while support procedures were taking place. An exploration of this aspect of practice would imply an ambitious observation and interview study with mainstream teachers (we hope this might be accomplished in future research). At this stage, however, we limited ourselves to looking at how beginning teachers were prepared for this work, and how experienced teachers enlarged their knowledge when they moved into the field of learning support.

Three of the project's research questions addressed these issues:

1   How are ideas relating to the nature of specific learning difficulties manifest in pre-service and in-service provision for teachers?
2   What support is offered to teachers and student teachers, in initial training and in-service, on the identification and assessment of pupils with specific learning difficulties?

3   What support for teachers and student teachers in meeting the needs of children with specific learning difficulties is available in initial teacher education and in-service provision?

This chapter presents some findings on these questions. Initially, the interviews with teacher educators offer accounts of the provision in initial teacher education in this area. We go on to report on student teachers' perceptions of this provision and how they construe specific learning difficulties. Finally, we return to the teacher educators' descriptions of some aspects of in-service provision.

Pre-service provision

The teacher educators provided insight into the ways in which their understanding of specific learning difficulties was incorporated into particular courses. Our study focused on two large colleges of education (college A and college B) which train the majority of teachers entering the profession in Scotland and are likely, therefore, to have a marked effect on future practice. We interviewed one lecturer in relation to each of the Postgraduate certificate of education secondary (PGCE) and B.Ed primary courses at both colleges. They were asked to explain the structure of the course, the ways in which learning difficulties were addressed and which parts of their teaching were relevant to specific learning difficulties.

Course structures

The B.Ed and PGCE courses at both colleges were based upon three strands: professional studies, curricular studies and school experience. Preparation for school experience in A was more closely tied to theoretical aspects than in B and the professional studies element was designated *Theory and Practice of Teaching*. In B the decision had been taken to separate out the theoretical parts of professional studies and present these with a wide conceptual perspective. The advantage of this move was that the same tutors would be responsible for presenting practical classroom issues and supervising the students on school experience. College B also had elective elements in both courses where the range of options included learning difficulties (these were reported by the teacher educators as being popular among students). At both colleges, final year B.Ed students carried out a personal project.

Coverage of learning difficulties

Both colleges aimed to develop the professional identity of a good teacher with an emerging awareness of the individual educational needs of all children. Learning difficulties were presented in ways that permeated the courses rather than in discrete units. According to one lecturer in college A: 'Special needs had more discrete input in the old course'. Coverage of learning difficulties arose in workshop sessions in professional studies, and in curricular studies where ways of achieving differentiation were introduced for the particular subject.

The general aims of all courses with regard to learning difficulties were described in college B as:

- promoting an awareness that effective learning is not always happening and a consciousness of the range of learning difficulties;
- building up deeper knowledge by means of elective topics;
- promoting knowledge of how to use support agencies.

In college A direct input on learning difficulties occurred in the student assignments set in connection with school experience. The PGCE students undertook a shadow study of a class in which differentiated learning was a theme; they had worked in a small group with a learning support teacher before going on school placements. The B.Ed students carried out a study of an individual child as an assignment which was built in to the first school placement; they too had previously considered the role of the learning support teacher. The approach to children in general was presented as 'observe, analyse and respond'. While observation and analysis might involve detecting possible learning difficulties (and response might include consulting learning support teachers), the terms 'identification and assessment' of learning difficulties which we used in our survey questionnaire as well as in the tutor interview schedule were perceived as somewhat alien.

Special needs tutors in college B had an input to B.Ed courses, with an introduction on learning difficulties in the first year (focusing on the seeking of help), and revisitation in subsequent years. Discussing the changes in the organisation of school placements, they pointed out that the tutors who supported the students on the school practice were **not** learning support specialists. They might well focus attention on the child by using deficit approaches and normative tests. This was not compatible with the special needs approach of 'observe and interpret', together with encouragement of the student to look at how the child interacts with the curriculum and teaching methods and to form an idea of why the teaching is not working.

Roles of learning support

Both colleges described coverage of the roles of learning support teachers as part of the response of the classroom teacher to an observed learning problem. Special educational needs tutors in college B advocated discussion with class teachers as well as learning support staff where a student teacher was faced with a problem he or she could not handle alone.

The teaching of reading

This was not a part of the PGCE (secondary) course at either college. We decided not to ask pre-service secondary teachers about it in the survey questionnaire and have not addressed the question of whether it is desirable for secondary teachers to understand the processes of learning and teaching reading.

The professional studies staff pointed out that the main responsibility for teaching reading lay with the language programmes in the curricular studies part of the courses at both colleges. The special education tutors in college B expressed the view that it was done very thoroughly, both in the B.Ed and in the PGCE (primary) courses. In the B.Ed it was tackled in three of the four years, with theoretical and practical issues covered and a review of the subject as a whole.

In spite of this coverage, our findings (see next section) suggest that the pre-service primary respondents felt ill-equipped to tackle the teaching of reading. The answers were similar in both colleges: students felt that theoretical aspects of reading had been well covered, but practical aspects less so. This finding has to be considered with caution. To single out for criticism one aspect of teacher education can be dangerous when the research has focused on such a narrow area of student teachers' experience.

Tutors' views on specific learning difficulties

All but one of the eight tutors interviewed agreed that a child may have a specific learning difficulty in reading, writing or spelling, and that their performance in these areas may not accord with general ability. This agreement was expressed in a low key, particularly in the college B: 'It is not surprising that children should vary in literacy abilities'. None regarded children with specific learning difficulties as a discrete group, although one college A respondent referred to advantages in coming down on that side of the debate. The other tutor from this college saw specific learning difficulties as part of a broad range of learning difficulties rather than a discrete group. I dislike the way they are sometimes viewed as entirely separate from the whole range of learning difficulties. Specific difficulty tends to be a high status special need because of its association with middle class status, and may therefore be given too high a profile.

The one tutor who rejected the notion of specific learning difficulty did so on the grounds that she also rejected the notion of general ability, so that ideas of discrepancy in abilities broke down. Admitting only that 'some children undoubtedly have more difficulties than others', the tutor stated that there is no discrete group with 'immutable, permanent' difficulties. Even constitutional difficulties were only permanent obstacles to learning if society failed to make adequate adaptations to allow the individual to experience a full life. However, the term 'dyslexia' had enormous advantages in terms of self-image:

> It is preferable from the point of view of the child and parents, and probably the teacher, that he should be labelled dyslexic rather than thick, stupid or backward at reading. I don't think it has any basis in evidence. There is no group of symptoms that people agree on sufficiently to give a diagnosis. (college B)

Coverage of specific learning difficulties on courses

In college A, the core PGCE course did not cover specific learning difficulties, although they might be mentioned by learning support teachers according to individual interests among a little 'sketchy' coverage of learning difficulties generally. The use of special arrangements for Scottish Examination Board examinations, however, was mentioned. The B.Ed course had always included some work on specific learning difficulties; modules being developed at the time of the research through a secondment funded by the Scottish Dyslexia Trust would enable more coverage by means of permeation. End-of-course projects provided another opportunity for individuals to undertake study of this area.

In college B there was no module or part of the main courses covering specific learning difficulties or dyslexia; but opportunities arose to address the topic during the third year of the B.Ed. An option on learning disability offered a number of topics in which a case study on specific learning difficulties could be undertaken and some students chose dyslexia as a final year project. The PGCE (secondary) students could choose specific learning difficulty within their elective.

In the student survey, students from college A claimed more familiarity with the term specific learning difficulties than did those from B. However, it was the students from B who were significantly more likely to choose the 'discrepancy of abilities' definition which we had identified from the interviews with educational psychologists as the most generally acceptable to the profession. It is to the student survey that we now turn.

Student teachers' perceptions of specific learning difficulties

The structure of the questionnaire

The questionnaire for student teachers began with general questions on their perception of how and at what points in their training learning difficulties were covered. It then probed their understanding of how children's needs were to be met (in particular with regard to the role of the learning support teacher), asked whether the term 'specific learning difficulties' was familiar to them and invited them to select from a range of phrases the one which they saw as the most accurate description of specific learning difficulties. Since most of the college educators had referred to the 'discrepancy of abilities' view of specific learning difficulties, we wished to see what proportion of student teachers showed this preference and how much agreement there was among them in their understanding of the nature of specific learning difficulties. The last question in this section asked them to identify at what stage of their course they had learned about specific learning difficulties.

The final section of the questionnaire was addressed to student teachers of primary education only and concerned the teaching of reading on the course, and aspects of reading difficulties.

Administration and analyses of the questionnaires

Questionnaires were administered to PGCE students at both colleges in June 1991 at the end of their training. In September 1991, questionnaires were administered to fourth year B.Ed students.

Table 4.1 shows the distribution by course and college of those completing the questionnaire. Altogether, 275 questionnaires were returned, 121 from college B and 154 from college A. The chi-square test was used to explore whether there were any statistically significant differences between students from different colleges or between the primary and secondary sectors.

Table 4.1 Distribution of pre-service teachers by course and college

	B.Ed Primary	PGCE Secondary	Total
A	68 (44.2)	86 (55.8)	154 (57)
B	59 (51.3)	56 (48.7)	115 (43)
Total	127 (47.3)	142 (52.7)	269(100.0)

Coverage of learning difficulties on course

The student teachers were asked to identify the part of their course, and the style of teaching, in which most attention was paid to children's learning difficulties. For the majority of students this was in professional studies; and was seen by most people as covered in lectures, tutorials and seminars by most people. Approximately half also suggested these matters were addressed during school experience.

When the results were broken down by college and course, students from A were more likely than those from B to say that learning difficulties were covered in school experience. This may have been a result of the shadow study undertaken by students of this college which was often of a child with learning difficulties. In addition, PGCE secondary were more likely than B.Ed primary students to say that learning difficulties were covered in school experience.

Identification of learning difficulties

Students were asked to consider the course of action they would take if a pupil in their class was having considerably more difficulty learning than other pupils. More than three-quarters said they would consult the learning support teacher and approximately two-thirds said they would attempt to diagnose the problem in the first instance. Differences emerged between B.Ed primary and PGCE secondary student teachers with regard to discussing a child's learning difficulties with the head-teacher or other colleagues (see Table 4.2). This strategy was more strongly favoured by the former than the latter group and perhaps reflects a more collegial atmosphere in the primary school.

Table 4.2 **Primary and secondary student teachers who said they would discuss a child's learning difficulties with colleagues (Result of chi-square test)**

	Yes	No
B.Ed Primary	90 (71.4)	36 (28.6)
PGCE Secondary	73 (51.4)	69 (48.6)

N = 268
p < .01

Students were asked what strategies they would use if they were to attempt to diagnose the nature of a child's learning difficulties themselves. Nearly 85% favoured observation of the child in the classroom and nearly 65% favoured the trial of different teaching approaches to help a child acquire a particular skill or understanding. A relatively small proportion said that they would use tests as a means of identifying learning difficulties.

The role of the learning support teacher

A number of items in the questionnaire probed student teachers' understandings of the role of the learning support teacher. First, they were asked whether the learning support teacher should help **all** children in the class or only those with learning difficulties.

Nearly two-thirds thought the learning support teacher should be concerned with **all** children in the class. This view was significantly more likely to be held by students from A (73%) than B (59%). PGCE secondary students were also more likely than B.Ed primary students to see the learning support teacher as having a whole class remit. Beyond that (see Table 4.3), most students saw the learning support teacher as having a role in co-operative teaching (92%) and providing advice on the preparation of differentiated learning material (72%). Over half (52%) identified direct tuition and withdrawal as a legitimate aspect of that role, with significantly more students from A than from B identifying direct tuition and withdrawal as an important aspect of a learning support teacher's role (see Table 4.4).

Table 4.3   Student teachers' understanding of the learning support teacher's role

Co-operative teaching	Direct tuition/ withdrawal	Consultancy	Other	Total
249 (91.9)	141 (52.0)	196 (72.3)	18 (6.6)	271

Categories are not mutually exclusive
Missing values = 4

Table 4.4:   Student teachers' identifying direct tuition/withdrawal as part of learning support teacher's role (Result of chi-square test)

	Yes	No
A	89 (58.2)	64 (41.8)
B	52 (44.1)	66 (55.9)

$p < .05$

Understanding of the term 'specific learning difficulties'

Student teachers were asked about their familiarity with the term specific learning difficulties; the majority (85%) had encountered it.   A higher proportion of those from A than B, and B.Ed primary than PGCE secondary, claimed familiarity.

The next item on the questionnaire was designed to investigate the extent to which there was a shared understanding of the term among student teachers. They were offered several alternatives including the generally accepted definitions of specific learning difficulties by professionals and voluntary organisations.   Approximately half the student teachers selected this option, which defined specific learning difficulties as 'learning difficulties, usually in reading, writing and/or spelling which do not accord with the individual's abilities in other areas'.   However, of college B students, 70% selected this definition.   About a quarter (including a significantly higher proportion of student primary teachers) suggested that the term implied a visual or auditory

55

handicap; in other words, they adopted a literal interpretation of the word 'specific'.

Students who said they were familiar with the term specific learning difficulties were asked about the source of their knowledge. The majority (75%) said that they had learnt about the term in college classes and just over half that they had encountered it in the course of school experience. Secondary PGCE students were significantly more likely to have learnt about specific learning difficulties on school experience than B.Ed primary students.

Primary student teachers and the teaching of reading

Primary student teachers were asked about their preparation for the teaching of reading, since this aspect of the curriculum is likely to pose particular problems for children with specific learning difficulties. The first question focused on the aspects of the teaching of reading that had been covered on their course. A majority indicated that theoretical aspects of the teaching of reading were included in the course, but less than half that practical aspects had been covered. Just over 10% thought that neither theoretical nor practical aspects of the teaching of reading had been covered (see Table 4.5).

Table 4.5: Primary student teachers' accounts of aspects of the teaching of reading covered in their course

	Theoretical aspects	Practical aspects	Neither	Total
A	54 (87.1)	28 (45.2)	7 (11.3)	62 (49.6)
B	53 (84.1)	29 (46.0)	7 (11.1)	63 (50.4)
Total	107 (85.6)	57 (45.6)	14 (11.2)	125 (100.0)

More than three-quarters of student primary teachers felt that their training had not prepared them adequately to teach reading, the questionnaire findings indicated that they felt in need of more assistance with its practical rather than theoretical aspects. Whereas over 70% of student primary teachers felt that their course had given them insight into possible causes of reading difficulties and 57% felt that the assessment of reading difficulties was covered, less than 30% felt that the remediation of reading difficulties was covered.

In-service provision in colleges of education

Student teachers' pre-service education covers many aspects of teaching and makes multiple demands on their learning and thinking. Learning difficulties (and especially specific learning difficulties) is just one area to which some priority must be given: one which probably only becomes accessible in the light of experience. As the students become qualified and move to work in schools some will develop particular interests in learning difficulties and may even see their careers developing in the context of learning support. One matter which this research addressed, therefore, concerned the provision of in-service courses (such as the Diploma in Special Educational Needs - DipSEN) by the colleges of education for more experienced teachers, and the place of specific learning difficulties within such courses.

Six teacher educators with responsibility for special educational needs were interviewed in the two colleges. In college B, this involved the Head of Special Educational Needs, the DipSEN Course Director, and another member of the department's staff; in college A, the contacts were the DipSEN course leader, the co-ordinator for the primary pathway of the DipSEN, and a seconded member of staff developing a series of modules on specific learning difficulties. The primary objective for these interviews, as with the interviews with the pre-service teacher educators, was to identify concerns to be included in the questionnaires for pre-service teachers and for learning support teachers. We sought data on the following research questions:

1   What is the structure of DipSEN and other courses provided for learning support teachers?

2   What general views of learning difficulties underlie these courses?

3   What are the views of these teacher educators about specific learning difficulties, and how are these difficulties addressed in the courses?

4   What approaches to the identification and assessment of learning difficulties, including specific difficulties, are promoted?

5   In what ways do learning to read and progression in reading feature in the courses?

6   What guidance is given on meeting the needs of children who appear to have specific learning difficulties?

Because the data reported here are derived from only two colleges (albeit the largest in Scotland) conclusions about provision more generally have to be treated with caution.

Structures of DipSEN and other special needs courses

One of the DipSEN courses (available on a full-time or part-time basis in college A) was modular, with four core modules for all students, and 'pathways' with varied content adapted to non-recorded primary and secondary, recorded needs, visually impaired and hearing impaired. The pattern of pathways was being revised for the year 1991-1992; those concerned with non-recorded needs were the most relevant for our research. Most of the work was college-based, but three school placements were undertaken leading to a written assignment as part of the course assessment.

The other DipSEN, in college B, offered separate but overlapping courses for non-recorded needs in the primary and the secondary school. Basic sections such as 'The Curriculum and Learning Difficulties' and 'Matching the Curriculum to Pupil Needs' were common to primary and secondary. Each section of the course incorporated college based and school based periods. In 1992 the course would combine with DipSEN (Recorded) and a module on specific learning difficulties introduced.

In college A, where modules on specific learning difficulties had been developed, a core specific learning difficulties module became compulsory for the DipSEN (non-recorded). Related modules were also offered as optional elements in the PGCE and M.Ed courses in the college. They could be taken singly, or in a combination of four modules to form a specialised Certificate in Advanced Studies: (Specific Learning Difficulties). The certificate was designed to be taken by evening study over one college session. As well as primary and secondary school learning support teachers, who might or might not already be holders of the DipSEN, prospective students could include reading centre teachers, lecturers in FE, speech therapists, psychologists, or teachers undertaking tutoring for the Scottish Dyslexia Association. The DipSEN courses were part-time for two years or one year full time.

Learning difficulties

College B presented a clear philosophy of learning difficulties. The course handbook stated that the course rationale was 'based on the assumption that learning difficulties are caused more by inadequacies in the curriculum than by pupil deficit; that the cure lies in the development of an appropriate curriculum and that the implementation of that approach is the responsibility of the whole school'. This emphasis was borne out by the three interviews with staff members. The HMI report of 1978, *The Education of Pupils with Learning Difficulties*, was referred to as an important statement underlying the aim to 'prepare teachers for the multi-purpose role of the learning support specialist'. The whole of the non-recorded pathway of the course in college A was also stated to be about meeting the needs of pupils with learning difficulties in the mainstream classroom and the five roles of the learning support teacher in the national guidelines (SCOSDE) were taken as the policy basis. There was, however, more of a balance expressed between curriculum deficits and within-child deficits in discussion of the origins of learning difficulties than was the case in college B:

> The document *Ten Years On* (MacLeod 1988) almost overemphasises the curricular sources of difficulty; it falls over backwards not to go into the pupil deficit model. If by putting all the emphasis on the curriculum you ignore the fact that some kids have difficulties which are personal and individual to them, and continue to exist almost regardless of curriculum adjustments, then you are losing something. It is equally true that the whole emphasis on [individual difficulties] is worse. (college A)

Specific learning difficulties

Staff at both colleges agreed that children may have specific learning difficulties and that these formed part of the whole range of learning difficulties. There was a perceptible difference between the two colleges in the ways in which the notion of a continuum of learning difficulties was discussed. In B, the merging of groups of learners was stressed:

> There is not a discrete group; it is a continuum. To pick out a single factor would be against the whole philosophy. We would also consider the interaction of factors such as parental pressure and school context. But teachers should recognise and treat specific learning difficulty as part of the range of learning difficulties ... The focus is on how to help the child rather than focus on the weakness. (college B)

On this DipSEN course specific learning difficulties were not singled out; there were no separate modules, but an educational psychologist with a particular interest in the topic came in as a visiting speaker, and gave guidelines for the identification of such difficulties. The students were told that 'learning support is the initial filter; it is important to refer children with such unexplained difficulties to the psychological service for further assessment'.

In college A, one speaker had 'no doubt at all' that children might have specific learning difficulties, while questioning 'whether this made them a different beast'; the merging of these with other learning difficulties was suggested as being multidimensional, rather than just a linear continuum. 'What marks out specific learning difficulty is its persistence and complexity'. Specific learning difficulties were seen as crossing the ability range, but more readily noticeable with children of average or above average attainments. The member of staff with a specific learning difficulties remit stressed that the perspective offered in the Certificate in Advanced Studies (Specific Learning Difficulties) and in the modules used in other courses did not restrict the focus. It was about any children not responding to normal teaching strategies and showing an unexpected discrepancy in their cognitive profiles. 'They are a discrete group but with shades of grey'. Since the research was carried out, this certificate and its associated modules have moved from support by a charitable trust to a partly government funded Centre for Specific Learning Difficulties within the college.

This represents ground gained by the sponsor, the Scottish Dyslexia Trust, towards their aim of official recognition of specific learning difficulties and its incorporation into the public provision of teacher education. This is especially significant in view of a general shift in SOED funding for SEN training away from colleges towards regions (from providers to purchasers).

The DipSEN staff welcomed the higher profile given to specific learning difficulties by the development of the Certificate and the new modules. The Diploma module had already been introduced and was becoming a compulsory part of the course, even before the appointment of the specific learning difficulties tutor. However, the linkage between work directed towards specific difficulties and the general skills of teaching and learning support remained important:

> Specific learning difficulty merits an increased emphasis: many children with these difficulties have been misunderstood and teachers trying to meet these needs have become discouraged. But I hope that teachers don't imagine that there is a single easy answer. There are a lot of skills in the DipSEN, not in the special module, and even skills in initial training; if teachers have the tenacity to get them all under their belts, hold on to them, draw on them and use them widely and selectively, [they can achieve] an approach matching the child. (college A)

Developments subsequent to the research involve the incorporation of both colleges into neighbouring universities and funding by the new Scottish Higher Education Funding Council (SHEFC). The impact upon modularised DipSEN courses was to sharpen the move towards 'twilight' and 'outreach' courses which could be delivered to serving teachers, eliminating the need to cover for absence. Many regions were reported to be choosing to train more teachers through four or six modules rather than the full course (12 modules and 10 weeks of placement) specified in the SCOSDE guidelines (Closs, 1994); leaving only one college in Scotland continuing to offer the DipSEN as a full time course. Closs identified specific learning difficulties as a market leader in this environment, but feared for the prospect for other types of special need:

> Higher education establishments could, against professional inclination, opt for financial viability by running only core, generic and "popular" specialisms while reducing or eliminating training in non-viable areas. After all, as long as the number of children with emotional and behaviourial difficulties keeps increasing, and as long as parents of children with specific learning difficulties or attentional deficit disorder threaten to sue local authorities for not providing "adequate and effective" education, there will still be some specialist modules which sell and sell.

Identification and assessment of learning difficulties

The main diagnostic technique recommended at college B was classroom observation together with the analysis of pupils' work and the errors they made. Primary learning support teachers were given more information about the use of standardised tests; and of addressing children's difficulties with reading and number. For the secondary DipSEN students, more emphasis was placed on bypassing reading difficulties and facilitating access to the curriculum for all pupils by the adaptation of materials and the use of coping strategies. Assessment of specific learning difficulties was also addressed in the sessions with the visiting Educational Psychologist, who advised referral to the psychological service of any child with intractable unexplained difficulties.

College A also stressed teacher observation in the non-recorded DipSEN course; there was no practical training in administering tests or recommendations for particular diagnostic techniques. Observation was covered as a range of skills, from informal observation in the classroom to information about highly structured observation using any published test. The construction of criterion referenced tests was also included. All these aspects featured in an assessment module, and students were expected to put it into practice in their assignments.

The DipSEN module on specific learning difficulties contained one day's work on identification and assessment particular to that area, and briefly included the use of standard measures such as the Aston Index. It was pointed out that having used such published items, teachers quickly develop the capacity to recognise by observation those characteristics which are measured by the Index. Within a short time the tests are used to demonstrate rather than to discover the kind and degree of difficulty a child is experiencing.

In the specific learning difficulties certificate, one optional module was designed to examine diagnostic assessment and methods of intervention in relation to specific learning difficulties, using recent findings from linguistics.

One tutor discussed the relationship between parents, teachers and local authority services in relation to the assessment of children believed to have specific learning difficulties. Assessment requests from parents were described as 'a real thorn in the flesh' owing to the lack of clear policies among psychological services, either nationally, regionally or even from office to office. Research into the nature of specific learning difficulties was still 'wide open', leading some professionals to conclude that detailed assessment could not be soundly based. Meanwhile parents were eager for action; this teacher educator felt that it was quite unreasonable to stereotype such parents as 'pushy':

> A pushy parent is a parent doing their job when they think their child is not getting a fair deal. I wish that teachers felt more comfortable with parental anxieties. (college A)

Reading

Both colleges considered that there was no place for practical work on the teaching of reading in the DipSEN courses, where all students were fully qualified and experienced teachers. There was work on strategies for dealing with reading difficulties, particularly at the primary stage in college B. In college A a language module formed part of the non-recorded pathway of the DipSEN. This included theoretical content on reading, said to be on a fairly superficial basis, limited by the time available. There were short sections of the pedagogy module covering approaches to reading, and the use of technology in compensatory and remedial programmes for children with reading problems. A former option module on reading had been withdrawn.

Meeting the needs of children with specific learning difficulties

At college B the advice given the learning support teachers, about how to meet the needs of children with specific learning difficulties, was the same as that for any child with reading difficulties: see what works through trial and error, while supporting the child emotionally. Where the difficulties impeded access to the curriculum, the learning support teacher was encouraged to seek ways of bypassing those difficulties. If these measures did not lead to progress, the recommended procedure was to refer to the psychological services. By the end of the course the teacher was expected to have some ability to perform all of the roles of the learning support teacher as outlined in the SCOSDE guidelines: direct tuition, cooperative teaching, consultancy, staff development and temporary support.

Broadly similar approaches were followed in college A, although the phrase 'trial and error' was explicitly rejected by one respondent as implying the lack of a sound theoretical basis: 'It is not just a bag of tricks, or trying this and that'. The main focus was on learning support for the child with specific learning difficulties in the mainstream classroom, with a wide range of books and materials displayed and discussed in relation to the appropriate methods for using them. Many of the approaches were suitable for other kinds of learning difficulties; for example, multi-sensory teaching, often advocated for specific learning difficulties, was also in use for moderate and severe learning difficulties. The emotional side of learning support, combining an optimistic view of the learner, the encouragement of self esteem and positive work with the family, was particularly appropriate to specific learning difficulty, but again, was not peculiar to it.

While all five learning support roles were taught in both colleges, it was in college A that more emphasis was given to the role of direct tuition, both in the classroom and by withdrawal. One tutor enlarged upon changing perceptions of the role of withdrawal, particularly in relation to specific learning difficulties:

There was a generation of teachers with some kind of socio-economic bias against the label 'dyslexia', or who believed that some children had vocal parents who might hi-jack scarce resources at the expense of a greater number of children from a different background with more generalised learning difficulties ... Elements of this outlook led to a bias against what was perceived as a war-cry for withdrawal. But individual or small group work by withdrawal is one of the roles of the learning support teacher, though wherever possible the child is kept in touch with the class curriculum. The more pronounced the difficulties, the greater the need for withdrawal. One group for whom I have sympathy is where the needs are very much out of sync with the child's age and ability grouping; the work they need to do could be a source of mockery to their peers. (college A)

63

This tutor referred to the persistence of specific learning difficulties, and emphasised that any means of meeting the childrens' needs would provide coping mechanisms, not cures.

Summary

Most of the eight pre-service teacher educators we spoke to in two colleges of education supported the view that some children experienced specific learning difficulties, described as an unexpected discrepancy in levels of achievement in different areas, usually with regard to literacy and general measures of intelligence. However, alongside this view they also favoured a continuum model of learning difficulties, suggesting that in practice it would be difficult to separate out children with specific learning difficulties from others with more global difficulties.

Both colleges were more concerned with conveying basic insight into the needs of all individual children, rather than with focusing on particular manifestations of learning difficulties such as specific learning difficulties. Their priorities were for student teachers to develop some understanding of differentiation and be aware of the need to provide curricular materials at appropriate levels for individual children. Furthermore, they believed it important to develop an understanding of the role of the learning support teacher as consultant and individual tutor. It was policy at both colleges that learning difficulties should permeate all the programmes as well as featuring in distinct inputs on particular matters in professional and curricular studies and school experience.

In so far as some of these opportunities to study particular issues within the general area of learning difficulties were available only as electives, guided reading or research projects, it is likely that not all students develop a deeper knowledge of this area. However, in both colleges developments were afoot to provide students with the chance to study specific learning difficulties in more depth. In college A, a tutor who had joined the college as a seconded educational psychologist had developed modules in specific learning difficulties. The modules were primarily intended for those wishing to gain a Certificate in Advanced Studies (Specific Learning Difficulties), but elements were to be incorporated into pre-service teacher training courses. By 1994 there was a graded input on specific learning difficulties for each year of the B.Ed course. The former options on reading and writing difficulties had been incorporated into the language core.

At college B, the new B.Ed course provided an elective on learning difficulties in the fourth year which would take a broader view of the area and cover aspects such as specific learning difficulties. Demand outstripped places for this element by 1994. Collaboration with college A enabled some SpLD modules to be delivered at B, and some B students to take the specialist Certificate.

It was clear that learning difficulties were recognised by student teachers as permeating elements in the courses, cropping up in both school-based and college-based components. They appreciated the idea of pathways for the identification of learning difficulties, beginning with observation of the child, through discussion with colleagues (particularly in the primary sector), to liaison with the learning support teacher. They also had a relatively sophisticated view of the broader role of the learning support teacher as meeting the needs of all children rather than those defined as having learning difficulties, one of the messages of the 1978 HMI Report. The co-operative teaching and consultancy roles were recognised by a large number of students but fewer referred to the importance of individual pupil tuition.

There was some confusion among the student teachers over the definition of specific learning difficulties. Whilst most claimed familiarity with the term, only slightly more than half selected a definition based on the concept of discrepancy of abilities (the definition most commonly held by the profession).

Not surprisingly the student teachers had a general grounding in the area of learning difficulties, but had sketchier knowledge of specific learning difficulties. Both colleges were in the process of reviewing their programmes at the time of our study and it appeared that more detailed inputs on specific learning difficulties were likely to appear in the future. They pointed out, however, that there is a potential danger in focusing too narrowly on one particular area in an initial teacher education programme. As one teacher educator noted, if some areas receive greater attention than others, it may distort beginning teachers' abilities to make a balanced assessment of a child's needs and difficulties.

One area of education, however, which is important in any approach to teacher education (particularly in the primary sector) is the teaching of reading. Again we have to remember that this research was not designed to explore this matter but it has been raised in a variety of contexts. The college staff viewed their treatment of reading as thorough and satisfactory, but the primary student teachers were concerned that although they were well versed in theoretical aspects of the teaching of reading, they lacked practical knowledge. This is, of course, an area which is particularly important in meeting the needs of pupils with specific learning difficulties.

The colleges' provision in the in-service area, designed for experienced teachers, displayed some differences between institutions. In one case, the DipSEN was entirely composed of modules; several of these were concerned with specific learning difficulties with one, compulsory for the course, which focused on children without a Record of Needs. Versions of these modules were available in PGCE and MEd courses or grouped as a Certificate in specific learning difficulties. The staff of this college were more likely than those from the other one to see learning difficulties as likely to arise from problems within the individual child as well as inadequacies in the curriculum.

They were also more likely to see specific learning difficulties as a distinctive category of learning difficulties, which included particularly persistent and complex problems. While staff from the other college appeared to advocate the continuum concept of learning difficulties, those involved in the modular course seemed to adopt a multidimensional view where one of those dimensions was distinctively characterised by specific learning difficulties. In other words, children with specific learning difficulties do form a discrete group but with a range of severity of problems and some variety in the discrepancies shown by individuals in their cognitive profiles.

This perception of specific learning difficulties, which accepts the location of the problem to be largely in the child, appears to have led this college to place more emphasis on systematic consideration of assessment with a repertoire of measures. It has also accepted the importance of direct tuition and withdrawal of individuals from mainstream classes where there are pronounced problems. Multisensory approaches, attention to emotional factors and the need to work with the whole family have all been endorsed. These strategies were not seen, however, as necessarily exclusive to children with specific learning difficulties; those with more general problems might also have their needs met in this way.

The other college, which was more reluctant to distinguish children with specific learning difficulties as a discrete group, was firmly within the camp which believes that 'learning difficulties are caused more by inadequacies in the curriculum than by pupil deficit'. Observation and testing for the identification of individual's problems were subsumed within the process designed for the whole population of learners. There was, perhaps, more of a sense in this college that the teacher should set out to meet the needs of all children with whatever means available, support each one (emotionally as well as cognitively), endeavour not just to resolve problems but, if necessary, take steps to bypass difficulties, and if the outcome remains unsatisfactory, refer the child to psychological services. This approach does not, of course, deny the existence of specific learning difficulties, but it does use a different strategy which may well affect the stage when such children get singled out.

5 The perceptions of learning support teachers

In chapter 4 we commented that, had the research had more resources, it would have explored mainstream teachers' views about practices in schools in relation to children with specific learning difficulties. We chose instead to give priority to a survey of learning support teachers in the light of their particular responsibilities for all children with learning difficulties. As in the other parts of this study, the broad research questions to be addressed were:

1 To what extent are these pupils recognised as a group with distinctive needs and how is the nature of their difficulties perceived?

2 Where specific learning difficulties are recognised, how are they identified?

3 How are the needs of these pupils met and their identified difficulties remedied?

A questionnaire was devised within that framework with emphasis on learning support teachers' views about

- definitions of specific learning difficulties and dyslexia
- the identification of pupils experiencing specific learning difficulties
- teaching methods and teaching materials used to meet the needs of such children
- regional policy
- the learning support teacher's role
- communication with other professionals, voluntary organisations and parents
- the Scottish Examination Board regulations and their use.

(The last of these was reported in chapter 3.)

Administration of the questionnaire

Names of learning support teachers were obtained from each Region and respondents were selected randomly on a one in ten basis. A total of 400 questionnaires were issued, representing 9% of the 4373 teachers in the whole of Scotland giving learning support in primary or secondary schools (1990 SOED Schools Census). There was some variation in the sampling in different regions or divisions. The questionnaires were distributed to a proportion of the learning support teachers in the region on a basis ranging from 5% to 16%. Part of this variation arose from the fact that the Census totals were expressed in teacher FTE rather than individuals. Of 400 questionnaires issued, 206 completed responses were received which together with thirty blank returns gave a response rate of 59%. All but one of the seventeen regions and divisions were represented. The response rate was somewhat disappointing despite efforts within the limits of the resources of the research to 'chase' people. We can offer three speculative explanations for the low rate of return.

First, we suspect that the 'anti-categorisation' view of specific learning difficulties is under-represented in our data, and those with that perspective were reluctant to take the time to complete a questionnaire about something which they saw characterising a quite different conception of learning difficulties. Two large authorities from which only 30% and 36% of responses were received were among those where opposition to the labelling of particular difficulties was most strongly expressed in our earlier interview study (reported in chapter 2).

Secondly, we gained the impression from some comments that less experienced and unpromoted teachers may have been put off by the length of the questionnaire and the difficulty of the subject. There was a sense that an element of 'testing' was involved. Some people were apparently unaware of our interest in finding out how common it would be for experienced learning support teachers to be lacking in knowledge and considered opinions, about specific learning difficulties.

Thirdly, we have reason to believe that promoted teachers may be over-represented in the sample. For example, one region's sample was arranged in separate sections for principal teachers and others. Those sent to principal teachers were all returned; while this Region had a higher than average total response (70%), the unpromoted teachers were less likely to complete the questionnaire. A greater response rate might have been achieved, therefore, it **promoted** learning support staff had been targeted. Our problem then would have been that the sample would not have been representative of the learning support teachers encountered 'on the ground' by pupils with specific learning difficulties. Unfortunately, although we asked respondents about their qualifications and length of service (in learning support and teaching generally), we did not ask what post they held. In developing our initial research plan we had no reason to believe that variable would be important.

This discussion about the response rate has made it clear that we cannot claim to be representing the views of all learning support teachers in Scotland. We do have a relatively large data set and we believe it provides some valuable insights, but the findings have to be treated with caution.

Characteristics of sample

52% of the total responses were from primary teachers and 42% from secondary teachers; 10 teachers worked in both primary and secondary. A large majority of the respondents (87%) were women. The sample were **highly experienced** teachers. Only 19 of the 206 had less than 10 years' total teaching experience; 98 had from 10-19 years and 89 had over 20 years. Length of experience in learning support was much more evenly spread: 53% had worked as LS teachers for less than 10 years.

Turning to relevant qualifications, 36% held the Diploma in Special Educational Needs; these were significantly more likely to be secondary than primary teachers. Other, often older, qualifications in special educational needs were held by 44% of the sample and 33 of these were listed. Only 6 people listed items overtly focused on specific learning difficulties and one respondent held the Dyslexia Institute qualification.

Understandings of specific learning difficulties and dyslexia

In response to the open-ended question, 'What does the term "specific learning difficulties" mean to you?', some teachers suggested several possible definitions and all responses were coded. Rather unexpectedly the responses of 37% were very general and suggested that almost any learning difficulty could be described as a specific learning difficulty. Typical answers of this sort included: 'any specific factor preventing full access to the curriculum'; 'a continuum of learning disabilities'; 'problems due to medical, cognitive, developmental or acquired difficulties'; 'some learning problem that can be identified and worked on'. The most common view expressed, however, by 40% of respondents was that specific learning difficulties were characterised by literacy difficulties and by a discrepancy between attainment in this area and general ability (a further 5% and 2% identified only one of these characteristics). Numeracy difficulties were cited by 19% and other problems by 7%. It would appear that on the whole our respondents used the term 'specific learning difficulties' in a broad way and there was little general agreement on a precise definition.

Respondents were asked whether they would ever use the term 'dyslexia' to describe a learning difficulty and 70% indicated that they would, although many of these expressed strong reservations about using it. The teachers with ten or more years of experience in learning support were significantly more likely than less experienced teachers to use the term. The majority of those who used the term (86%) defined it as involving difficulty with decoding symbols or print, 29% as involving memory/sequencing difficulties and 35% as a discrepancy in abilities. (The total is more than 100% because many respondents offered multiple definitions.) Clearly, the definitions of dyslexia which the learning support teachers offered were more precise than those relating to specific learning difficulties and there was greater agreement. Learning support teachers who used the term dyslexia had a number of other characteristics, including a greater degree of confidence in their ability to identify children with specific learning difficulties.

Teachers were asked with whom they would use the term dyslexia and Figure 5.1 indicates that they were likely to use it with colleagues and the educational psychologists; fewer would use it with parents and an even smaller number with the child. Where the respondent did not use the word with everyone, varied explanations were given. Some suggested that other professionals would understand the implications, while parents might be misled and children frightened by it. Alternatively, it might be seen as a 'lay' expression, known to parents through the media but highly offensive to, for example, psychologists. A small number of the teachers only used 'dyslexia' if the child had been officially diagnosed as such. Of the 83 who did not use it at all, no one explanation held sway, but a feeling that it was misleading was the commonest (34). Answers coded as misleading included all those rejecting it as too wide, including: 'blanket term'; 'too generalised'; 'many difficulties, not one'; 'too convenient a label'. A number of these answers conveyed irritation with parents 'latching on to the word' and 'wanting to call every learning difficulty dyslexia'. One teacher called it 'too emotive and political'. Other reasons included not using the term because it was against regional policy, or too medical or the teacher did not feel qualified to judge which children were dyslexic.

Figure 5.1 People with whom learning support teachers would use term 'dyslexia'

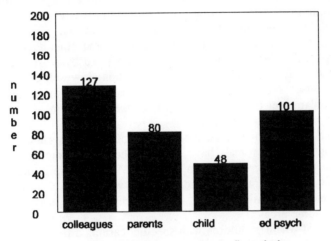

Note: Categories are not mutually exclusive

Some expressed the view that neither specific learning difficulties nor dyslexia could be used without reservations. One commented:

> I dislike the term specific learning difficulties; it is unwieldy, vague and nobody else understands what it means. Having used it, you have to launch into further explanations. I actually prefer 'dyslexia' but only use it with qualifications because of people's varying reactions. Learning support colleagues are aware of the ambiguities and controversy surrounding the word. However, I find it a very helpful word to use with other colleagues, parents and children, though I am always wary of using it, and only do so if it is going to aid a positive approach.

A minority (75) of respondents agreed with the statement that children with specific learning difficulties have higher than average achievements in other areas. They cited many oral and non-verbal skills, artistic, practical and sporting achievements. 'They can shine where their intelligence is not hampered by their specific learning difficulties'. Some referred to character traits, the development of exceptionally strong determination and other coping strategies. A larger group, however, disagreed with the statement; 117 or 57% of responses. The supporting comments of this group varied widely and the statement was dismissed entirely by only a small number. About 30 comments stressed that specific learning difficulties covered the entire range of ability, with several pointing out that specific learning difficulties was very difficult to identify if the child had no 'higher than average' achievements.

The interaction between the basic learning difficulty and other factors was mentioned: 'A specific learning difficulty may be masked by all-round poor performance due to frustration', lack of concentration, low self-esteem, or inability to organise; some children, indeed, have multiple disadvantages. 'Language is fundamental to nearly all aspects of the curriculum and to self-confidence'.

Several teachers rejected the statement on grounds of precision: children with specific learning difficulties may have many higher achievements than in literacy, without these being higher than average. A few answers turned the issue to the child with general learning difficulties, who may well have some higher achievements. 'All children given a chance will show higher achievements in some areas'.

On the question of whether children with specific learning difficulties form a discrete group, 60% agreed, and 40% disagreed. One answer drew the distinction between a discrete group of difficulties, which did exist, and a discrete group of children, which in the respondent's opinion did not, as specific difficulties could be present alongside other types of learning difficulty. Other teachers commented that specific difficulties were harder to identify where children also had more general difficulties, including those arising from family circumstances. One respondent who agreed that there was a discrete group commented that this was not a static situation:

> They tend to be taught in the same way as others with reading/number problems; as they get older the gap does widen and this tends to result in them becoming a discrete group requiring extensive modifications to the curriculum.

We then asked teachers about the relative priority they attached to meeting the needs of children with specific learning difficulties. Just under half (48%) indicated that they gave a high priority to the needs of such pupils. Only 6% chose the answer 'low priority'; the remaining large group (46%) found it impossible to say, commenting on their commitment to tackling the needs of individual children which presented themselves on a basis which varied from year to year. This group included a few who drew a distinction between provision for specific learning difficulties and for other learning support: 'I have a particular interest in specific learning difficulties but try not to prioritise different needs;' 'setting up individual work for a child with specific learning difficulties takes time but the child with general difficulties may need more sustained input'. Practical problems also arise: 'very few with specific learning difficulties - many social problems and other difficulties'; 'should be high but for lack of staff'. This situation is also expressed by two of the 'low' respondents: 'numbers of slow learners and behaviour problems is so high'; 'only pupils with the most severe difficulties of any kind receive support'.

The teachers according a high priority to specific learning difficulties explained their position for the most part in terms of the needs of such children for individual teaching on a daily basis outwith the mainstream class. The class teacher also needed more help from the learning support teacher to assist such children. A small number had a particular responsibility for specific learning difficulties. Another common comment referred to the teacher's satisfaction in unlocking the capacity of the pupil to achieve 'so much more' in place of the frustration they have experienced.

Identification of pupils with specific learning difficulties

The next group of questions asked teachers about policy and practice for the identification of children with specific learning difficulties. Although 42% were confident that they could identify children with specific learning difficulties, the majority were more cautious. Those who used the term 'dyslexia' were more confident about their ability to identify children with specific learning difficulties (Table 5.1) as were more experienced learning support teachers.

About 60% of the respondents were prepared to estimate the percentage of pupils with specific learning difficulties in their schools. Their estimates ranged from less than 1% to a startling 60% and varied sharply according to the definition of specific learning difficulties held. Figure 5.2 summarises the estimates which were given. Comments on this included 'More than I know; only the obvious ones are known'; one teacher offering the estimate 5% suspected that many more were undiagnosed as they were 'coping on an average level'. The modal estimate appeared to be around 4% of the population, though there was considerable support for about 1%. The latter appeared to be appropriate for the clear examples of literacy problems and discrepancies with other abilities.

Table 5.1 **Confidence in identifying specific learning difficulties reported by learning support teachers using term 'dyslexia' (Result of chi-square test)**

	Confident	Possible	Impossible to say	Total
Use term 'dyslexia'	69 (50.0)	63 (45.7)	6 (4.3)	138 (70.4)
Do not use term 'dyslexia'	15 (25.9)	38 (65.5)	5 (8.6)	58 (29.6)
Total	84 (42.9)	101 (51.5)	11 (5.6)	196 (100.0)

p < .01
Missing values = 10

Figure 5.2   **Estimate of percentage of children with specific learning difficulties**

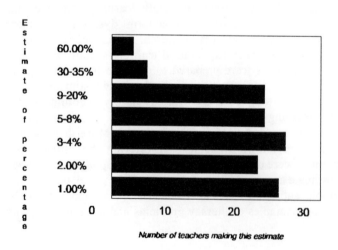

Number of teachers making this estimate

Figure 5.3 Person responsible for identifying specific learning difficulties

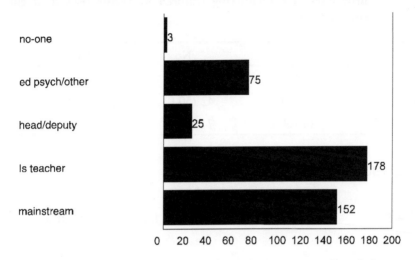

Note: Categories are not mutually exclusive

Perceptions of the onus of responsibility for identifying specific learning difficulties are shown in Figure 3 with 86% suggesting the learning support teacher and 74% the mainstream teacher. There is evidence of the existence of different pathways for identification in the primary and secondary sectors. In secondary school, learning support teachers were more likely than those in primary to see themselves as having major responsibility for identifying such pupils. Conversely, more primary learning support teachers described the mainstream teacher and the head or deputy head as having this responsibility. The comments which included the learning support teacher. Data on identification come from the 60% of teachers who reported that their school had such procedures (Table 5.2). Primary teachers were significantly more likely than secondary to say that this was the case.

Table 5.2   Learning support teachers reporting school has systematic procedures for identifying children by sector (Result of chi-square test)

	Yes	No	Total
Primary	72 (69.2)	32 (30.8)	104 (55.3)
Secondary	42 (50.0)	42 (50.0)	84 (44.7)
Total	114 (60.6)	74 (39.4)	188 (100.0)

p < .01
Missing values = 18

Figure 5.4   Stage at which children most likely to be identified

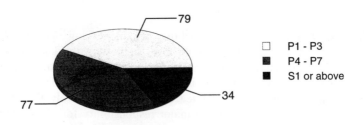

Figure 5.4 summarises the perceptions of the stage at which children are most likely to be identified as having specific learning difficulties. Comments were added by several: 'secondary is too late'; 'recently more recognition in primary but only in obvious cases, most still in S1'; 'the problem is identified in P2/3 but confirmed in P4 when it becomes obvious that it is not just late development'. Overall it appeared that identification took place in the primary school and that this was fairly evenly divided between the early and later years.

About three quarters (154) of the 206 teachers named at least one means of diagnosis of specific learning difficulties that were in use in their schools.

Informal tests and observation were described by 68, most of whom also cited particular tests. One teacher stated that all responsibility for testing was passed on to the educational psychologist: 'Highly unsatisfactory but we simply do not have the time to do it'. Others indicated that the more specialised individual tests were the province of the educational psychologist, a situation that they accepted.

A total of 50 different tests were named, twelve items by 10 people or more. Those named the most frequently were:

Aston Index	60
Neale Analysis	44
Bangor Dyslexia Test	37
Quest screening	32
Quest diagnostic	30

Delivery of the curriculum to children with specific learning difficulties

The Scottish HMI report of 1978 recommended that pupils with learning difficulties 'should be taught *as far as possible* by class and subject teachers' (SED 1978, para 4.11 p25). As we described in chapter 1, the report considered that separate remedial departments were at odds with the acceptance by subject departments of full responsibility for what came to be called learning support. The lack of explicit guidance on the limits of support in the mainstream classroom has contributed to the uncertainties found by the research. Some recent writers including Moses et al have found a level of disapproval of withdrawal tuition which they described as 'a new orthodoxy' (Moses et al 1987).

In Scotland, learning support teachers were officially expected to be able to offer specialised help to children with specific learning difficulties (SCOSDE 1990) but the nature of this help was not spelled out. Our questionnaire therefore provided an opportunity to explore the ways in which schools and teachers interpreted official guidance which was at least vague, and potentially contradictory.

Figure 5.5 Where children receive education

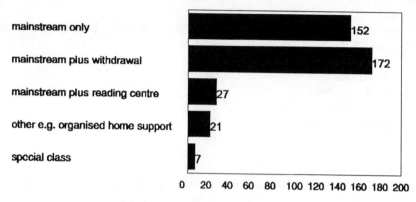

Note: Categories are not mutually exclusive

Figure 5.5 illustrates where the learning support teachers indicated children with specific learning difficulties received their education. By far the most common provision at all stages was in mainstream classes, often with some withdrawal support (83% of cases). 46% were taught within the mainstream class only; 13% had the use of reading centres. Only 3.4% were in special classes. More than one form of provision existed within many schools, and was used as appropriate for different children. 10% cited some form of other provision, including various means of organised home support. Paired reading was also offered in lunchtime groups by senior pupil volunteers, reported in two schools. Special provision in the option column of the secondary school was offered in one place.

Different patterns of provision were evident in the primary and secondary sectors, with secondary learning support teachers more likely than those in primary to report that children with specific learning difficulties were taught in mainstream class only (Table 5.3). Primary learning support teachers were more likely than those in secondary to report that children with specific learning difficulties were likely to be educated in the mainstream class but, in addition, be withdrawn for individual tuition (Table 5.4).

Table 5.3 Learning support teachers reporting child likely to receive education in mainstream class only by sector (Result of chi-square test)

	Yes	No	Total
Primary	39 (36.1)	69 (63.9)	108 (56.5)
Secondary	48 (57.8)	35 (42.2)	83 (43.5)
Total	87 (45.5)	104 (54.5)	191 (100.0)

p < .001
Missing values = 15

Table 5.4 Learning support teachers reporting child likely to receive education in mainstream class plus withdrawal for individual tuition by sector (Result of chi-square test)

	Yes	No	Total
Primary	99 (91.7)	9 (8.3)	108 (56.5)
Secondary	63 (75.9)	20 (24.1)	83 (43.5)
Total	162 (84.8)	29 (15.2)	191 (100.0)

p < .001
Missing values = 15

In response to the question of whether the identification of specific learning difficulties led to the opening of a Record of Needs, 15% suggested this was usually the case but the majority (61%) said it was only sometimes the case. Where a Record of Needs was opened, 47% believed it led to different provision with additional resources.

Advice and materials for teaching children with specific learning difficulties

Our respondents were asked whether they had any guidelines on appropriate teaching methods for children with specific learning difficulties. Overall, approximately 60% said that they did. Learning support teachers who used the term 'dyslexia' were more likely to report the existence of such guidelines than those who stated that they would not use the term. The guidelines come from various sources: 82 teachers cited guidelines from the region, 37 from voluntary organisations and 53 from commercial publications. Primary learning support teachers were more likely than their colleagues in the secondary sector to be aware of regional guidelines on teaching materials. With regard to guidelines from voluntary organisations, secondary learning support teachers were more likely to report having these than those working in the primary sector. Several teachers referred to internal school policy guidelines as their main source of advice.

Almost 70% of respondents had teaching materials designed for tackling specific learning difficulties, although only around a quarter of the whole sample regarded these as being significantly different from those recommended for other learning and literacy problems. The minority who did find a difference in the materials cited structured approaches; repetition; breaking down outcomes into manageable sections; use of phonics; visual or auditory targeting; emphasis on hand-eye coordination; multi-sensory methods. The interest level of the materials was often aimed at an older age group than the reading content. A slightly larger number of respondents, 36%, disagreed that the specific learning difficulties materials were distinctive; many children, it was argued, need a structured approach and could benefit from the listed items, while multi-sensory materials also suit slow learners in general. Some commented that methods may vary in using the same materials, and anyway it is the method which is crucial: 'the cost of supplying special material would be prohibitive. It is the teacher's approach that makes the difference'.

The listed materials covered a wide variety of readers, word schemes and spelling materials, number work and oral or visually based items. Over fifty titles were cited, very few by more than ten people. Twelve teachers described home-made materials and 11 referred generally to material from the teacher resource centre. The most frequently used titles, including series titles, were:

Alpha to Omega	50
LDA	34
Fuzzbuzz reading	22
Starpol Readers	11

Learning support teachers were asked to comment on their degree of confidence in assisting pupils with specific learning difficulties. Just over a third said they were confident and 57% said they felt they could sometimes be of assistance. Only 7% lacked confidence in being able to help. Those with more experience were more likely to report confidence in offering assistance.

A similar pattern was evident in learning support teachers' view of their ability to advise other teachers; those with longer experience were more likely to express confidence in being able to do this.

Learning support teachers' perceptions of regional policy

The majority of learning support teachers reported that their region did have a policy on specific learning difficulties. Those working in primary were more likely to indicate that this was the case than those employed in the secondary sector (Table 5.5). Figure 5.6 illustrates their perception of the effectiveness of regional policy, with about 36% of those responding regarding it as very effective or effective and 33% considering it not very or not at all effective. Primary learning support teachers judged regional policy more favourably than those in the secondary sector.

Table 5.5   Learning support teachers reporting awareness of regional policy on specific learning difficulties by sector (Result of chi-square test)

	Yes	No	Total
Primary	77 (75.5)	25 (24.5)	102 (56.4)
Secondary	46 (58.2)	33 (41.8)	79 (43.6)
Total	123 (68.0)	58 (32.0)	181 (100.0)

$p < .05$
Missing values = 25

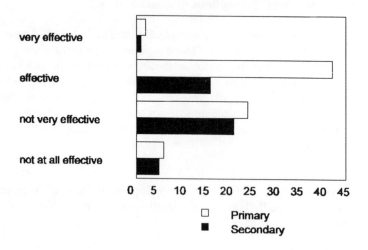

Several comments on this section qualified the writers' perceptions of the effectiveness of policy: 'I am optimistic that it will be effective when established and resourced'; 'Effective where staffing is available'; '... if there is good continuity'; '... where there is pressure by articulate parents'. 'Inevitably it varies: it provides effective help for some children'. Two teachers who gave negative answers commented that their region's policies were good on paper but not in practice. 'It does not deliver on resources, money or staff'; and 'I could write a book'.

Although perceptions of the use of Records of Needs did not reveal any statistically significant differences from region to region, it was highlighted in a number of respondents' final statements. Two teachers from the same region reported that specific learning difficulties were not regarded as an adequate reason for recording in that authority. Some additional factor had to be present, such as physical handicap, or prior placement in a special unit. In two further local authority areas, widely separated geographically, respondents stated that pressure from concerned, articulate parents could be instrumental in achieving recorded status for a child with specific learning difficulties, but that other children with needs which were just as severe might be omitted. There were still further comments giving the opinion that Records of Needs should be more widely used; a few respondents thought that they detected some attempt to ration their use because of shortage of resources.

Learning support teachers' view of their role

A group of questions invited learning support teachers to reflect upon the aspect of their role which they regarded as most important. This was felt to be worth investigating in the light of parental anxiety that the amount of individual tuition which their children were receiving was inadequate. Figure 5.7 shows the number of learning support teachers who regarded particular aspects of their work as being of prime importance. Whereas co-operative teaching is ranked first by 42% of teachers, less than 20% regard individual tuition as being the most important. This coincides with pre-service teachers' perceptions of the importance of the various aspects of learning support teachers' work. Primary learning support teachers appeared to attach more importance to withdrawal of children for individual tuition than did secondary teachers (Table 5.6).

Table 5.6 Learning support teachers' views of the importance of individual tuition outwith the class by sector (Result of chi-square test)

	Rank 1	Rank 2	Rank 3	Rank 4	Rank 5	Total
Primary	29 (27.6)	28 (26.7)	21 (20.0)	22 (21.0)	5 (4.8)	105 (57.4)
Secondary	8 (10.3)	14 (17.9)	20 (25.6)	16 (20.5)	20 (25.6)	78 (42.6)
Total	37 (20.2)	42 (23.0)	41 (22.4)	38 (20.8)	25 (13.7)	183(100.0)

$p < .001$
Missing values $= 23$

Figure 5.7: Learning support teachers' view of the most important aspect of their role (numbers)

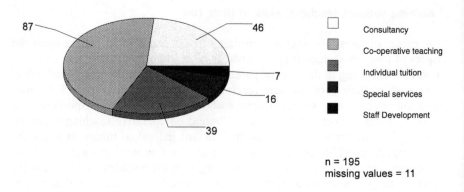

87   46
7
16
39

☐ Consultancy
▨ Co-operative teaching
▨ Individual tuition
■ Special services
■ Staff Development

n = 195
missing values = 11

Although, as we have already noted, respondents generally indicated their belief that children with specific learning difficulties need specialised tuition, a number questioned the reliance on the expertise of the learning support teacher:

> The emphasis in the region is currently on one to one teaching and on removing responsibility for children with specific learning difficulties from class teachers. In my view this is very wrong. A child with any learning difficulty should be entitled to support and understanding from the class or subject teacher.

Another teacher stressed maximising opportunities to include children with specific difficulties in mainstream activities; yet another distinguished beneficial tutorial methods in class from harmful extraction. Some teachers simply rejected the one to one approach ('I have no time or inclination to tutor') but this was a minority view. One whose rank ordering of the learning support teacher's various roles placed 'individual teaching outwith class' last in order wrote of 'a constant anxiety' as to whether this aspect should be promoted to greater importance.

Communication with parents and other professionals

Given the general level of dissatisfaction expressed by parents with regard to communication with teachers, we were interested to see what learning support teachers had to say on this subject. A high proportion of learning support teachers reported that they spoke with parents on parents' evenings (91.3%) as well as participating in individual consultations (85.4%).

The comments of a minority of respondents stressed the openness of schools and learning support teachers to informal contacts: 'They can pop in any time; or make contact by telephone or letter', 'We have an open house policy'. Particularly in small communities, teachers and parents might meet outside the school, or may chat about a child's progress at informal school events. There were a small number of organised channels of communication: homework jotters which were countersigned; paired reading sessions in three places; home visits in a further three schools; an open meeting on learning support run by the guidance staff; a parents' support group; and a successful three-week parent course on learning support services with a community 'outreach' worker involved. However, these positive comments were from no more than twenty responses; it would appear that while the great majority of the teachers met parents at parents' evenings and individual consultations, these relatively formal channels did not necessarily provide occasions when parents felt that their concerns were listened to.

Learning support teachers were asked whether they had had contact with voluntary organisations on specific learning difficulties and 40% indicated that they had. Teachers who used the term 'dyslexia' were more likely to have had contact than those who did not use the term. Similarly, secondary school teachers were more likely to have had contact with voluntary organisations on specific learning difficulties than primary colleagues (Table 5.7).

Table 5.7 **Learning support teachers' contacts with voluntary organisation by sector**
(Result of chi-square test)

	Yes	No	Total
Primary	35 (33.0)	71 (67.0)	106 (55.8)
Secondary	41 (48.8)	43 (51.2)	84 (44.2)
Total	76 (40)	114 (60)	190 (100.0)

p < .05
Missing values = 16

Figure 8 summarises the numbers of learning support teachers indicating that they had collaborated systematically with other professionals. The most frequent collaboration was with educational psychologists, reported by 73%. About 30% reported collaboration with speech therapists and special needs advisers; the first of these was reported more frequently by primary than secondary learning support teachers. Contact with medical officers was reported much less frequently. Comments about the collaboration were few; one teacher described contact as 'regular rather than systematic' another suggested 'discussion but not collaboration' and a third made the judgement that, 'On paper collaboration exists, in practice not'. One primary teacher of 20 years' experience focused on this point in her final statement:

> In the area of specific learning difficulties I have been given help by the School Medical Officer; school nurse; physiotherapist from the regional child development centre and speech therapist; but I have only got this help by my own efforts. I have had little or no support from the psychological service or the region generally ... Unfortunately the general feeling of learning support teachers in this area is that help is unavailable; the onus is on them to cope with the difficulties.

Figure 5.8 Learning support teachers collaborating with other professionals on special learning difficulties

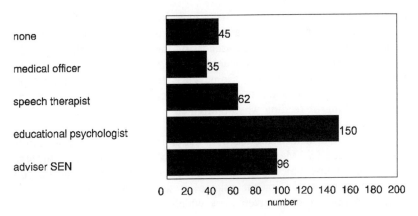

Note: Categories are not mutually exclusive

Final comments

Seventy of the 206 responses added additional comments in the space at the end of the sheet. These conveyed a strong impression of committed and perceptive teachers who identified and worried about gaps in provision and who were eager to contribute to improved understanding in the light of their own experience. The aspects of the questionnaire that most statements focused upon were the nature of specific learning difficulties and the terminology for discussing them, perceptions of the provision needed, the task of learning support services as a whole and the place of specific learning difficulties within this context. Above all, there were pleas for more resources.

A number of teachers commented on how their views had evolved over the years:

> As a classroom teacher of English for eleven years I was completely ignorant about specific learning difficulties. I don't think I was unusual; I would guess most teachers don't recognise it and have a very low tolerance level for pupils with the problem. It is invariably put down to one of the following: laziness, carelessness, stupidity, thrawnness.

A principal teacher had moved from a school in an area of multiple deprivation to one in an average socio-economic catchment. He felt that observation of the differing patterns of learning difficulties in the two schools had enlarged his understanding of the existence of specific learning difficulty, of which he was now convinced.

Perceptions of necessary improvements included earlier identification, based in the first instance on perceptive and informed observation in the classroom. This would require much greater awareness on the part of mainstream teachers than currently exists: 'Classroom teachers have no opportunity to learn about specific learning difficulties' and 'Some class teachers are still unwilling to accept the existence of specific learning difficulties'. The importance of competent teaching of reading was highlighted:

> I do wish that mainstream teachers understood more about how children learn to read ... Many teachers appear to just push children through a reading scheme which they cannot cope with, or give P1 and P2 pupils a reading book just for the sake of it which they cannot read at all. Older pupils are often given work which is too difficult.

Many learning support teachers felt that they too have limited knowledge of the best means of helping children with specific learning difficulties. They commented that teachers involved in learning support were 'mainly without extra qualifications' and in some places often on temporary contracts where a lack of continuity inhibited improvements in practical knowledge. One such teacher regarded herself as 'fortunate to be working with the same children over three years: continuity is vital'. The holder of a DipSEN stated that only one day of that course had been devoted to specific learning difficulties; even this input was not pre-planned, but was in response to student requests.

The difficulty of meeting the needs of children with specific learning difficulties in the context of the overall task of learning support services was emphasised, especially by teachers from urban areas. A response from an area of priority treatment spoke of being 'overwhelmed with numbers especially social problems; swimming against the tide'. From another such school came the comment 'Only one child in the school is diagnosed as having specific learning difficulties but there are many slow learners who must have priority'. The obvious demands from the kinds of problems indicated here might well be obscuring the need for learning support directed towards specific learning difficulties. As one teacher wrote:

> The problems are also found in a much larger group of children [than those diagnosed specific learning difficulties] who do not have 'higher

than average achievements in other areas'. These pupils often benefit greatly from a structured individual approach but rarely get it ... They have not the necessary pre-reading skills before they are required to begin learning to read and write .... These children often come from language-deprived homes and live in socially deprived areas. Children who are diagnosed as having specific learning difficulties are almost always in my experience from socially advantaged backgrounds with parents who can effectively ask for help. Children from disadvantaged backgrounds with similar difficulties are unlikely to get specific help; the difficulties are blamed on their home background and lack of parental skills; schools and education authorities seem to think there is little they can do.

The battle for resources for all kinds of provision for learning support was a constant theme. 'One learning support teacher in a school of 400 children is insufficient in a deprived area. One to one teaching is impossible'. The varied roles of the learning support teacher were enthusiastically undertaken but this summary outlines the pressure felt by one respondent:

I am sole learning support teacher in a school of just over 600 pupils. 11 children with Records of Needs, 9 for specific learning difficulties. Various other pupils with less severe specific difficulties not recorded. 2 pupils with severe specific learning difficulties have Reading Centre help two periods a week; the rest are the school's and my total problem. We also have traditional slow learners, a boy with muscular dystrophy and a boy with moderate learning difficulties. We rely on whole staff awareness and push to support these pupils. I am also involved in Staff Development and curriculum development. A tutu and fairy wand definitely required.

Summary

It was apparent that the term 'specific learning difficulties' was used in very different ways by the teachers in our survey. For some, it had a very precise meaning and was synonymous with dyslexia, whilst for others it was used to refer to any learning difficulty. The term 'dyslexia' used by over two thirds of teachers on at least some occasions, was defined more tightly than specific learning difficulties. The majority of teachers used to it refer to problems with decoding written symbols. There was an association between the use of the term 'dyslexia' and confidence in identifying children with specific learning difficulties and awareness of school guidelines.

Despite some uncertainty over terminology, most teachers felt that they were able to identify pupils with specific learning difficulties. Primary learning support teachers expressed greater awareness of and confidence in systematic identification procedures than their secondary colleagues. It may be that this confidence arises from a collaborative approach to the identification of problems alongside the mainstream teachers. All primary teachers see themselves as having responsibility for the development of basic literacy and numeracy and for being alert to difficulties in these areas. By way of contrast, in the secondary sector responsibility for identification was more likely to be seen as the sole responsibility of the learning support teacher; secondary subject teachers seldom see themselves as having a significant role in the development of basic skills among their pupils. Given the lower awareness of and confidence in systematic identification procedures in secondary, there appears to be a strong argument for greater co-operation between subject and learning support teachers in monitoring children's performance.

The findings about provision from this questionnaire confirmed the earlier indications that most children with specific learning difficulties were educated in mainstream classes with some withdrawal for individual support. Withdrawal was more common in practice in the primary than the secondary school and in their ranking of the roles of the learning support teacher, withdrawal for individual tuition was rated higher by primary than secondary learning support teachers. In the secondary sector, there appeared to be more concern that if children were withdrawn they would lose touch with the mainstream curriculum. There was also a sense of acceptance that learning difficulties which persist to the secondary stage may be less amenable to remediation.

Primary teachers were more likely than their secondary colleagues to be aware of school and regional guidelines on teaching methods for children with specific learning difficulties. Secondary teachers, on the other hand, expressed greater awareness of voluntary organisation guidelines. Although a majority of teachers had teaching materials for children with specific learning difficulties, in most cases these were no different from those which would be used with any child with learning difficulties. This reflected the view of most education professionals that there is not an absolute demarcation between children with specific learning difficulties and other children with more global learning difficulties.

Although learning support teachers met parents at parents' evening, discussion with individual parents about their child's progress appeared to be less common. This suggests that the Warnock ideal of partnership had not yet been achieved and that closer liaison is required. Warnock also placed great importance on inter-professional collaboration in meeting the needs of children with learning difficulties and this also appeared not to be happening in any great measure.

A number of learning support teachers expressed the view that they themselves required more training in the area of specific learning difficulties if they were to fulfil adequately their educative role (only a third of those in our survey held the DipSEN). Some questions, however, were raised concerning the extent to which the diploma addressed adequately the area of specific learning difficulties. In our survey, possession of the DipSEN was not associated with confidence in assisting children with specific learning difficulties or advising other teachers, whereas experience as a learning support teacher and acceptance of the term 'dyslexia' were.

The overall impression from the learning support teachers' comments was one of them seeing themselves to be the victims of excessive expectations by the educational establishment and parents: they were having to deal with too many children and fulfil too many different roles. Where they felt they could not meet the needs of all children, they established their own priorities and for some it was clear that children with specific learning difficulties might not feature prominently in the hierarchy of demands. While none discounted the needs of this group of pupils, the needs of others were seen as even more dire within a context where there is intense competition for resources. We should, perhaps, bear in mind the cri de coeur of the teacher quoted earlier who suggested that only those blessed with supernatural qualities could fulfil her job description, and the warning offered by another:

My personal fear is that with the pressure from national testing there will be a return to the cheap alternative: streamed classes, with all the vicious categorisation which that entailed.

6 Parents of children with specific learning difficulties

Any consideration of how the education system is meeting, or could meet, the needs of children with specific learning difficulties has to take detailed account of parents' views. It is not just a question of parents' rights in the matter, it is also to do with the impact which parents may have on the effectiveness of the provision. In all cases of special needs there are likely to be tensions: parents clearly have the concerns of their child at the forefront of their priorities, but education systems have to provide as best they can for **all** children. In the area of specific learning difficulties the tension may be exacerbated by conflicting conceptions of the nature of specific learning difficulties and the effects these have on priorities for provision. And further to complicate matters, this is an area which may have contributions, from funding sources and from professionals, coming out of two different budgets: health and education.

In this part of the study, therefore, we set out to investigate parents' conceptualisation of specific learning difficulties and their perceptions of the provision made by schools using the following research questions:

1   Among parents who believe their children to have specific learning difficulties, how are the difficulties and abilities of the children perceived and how do these compare with the views of educational and health professionals, involved in making provision for these groups?
2   Is there an effective dialogue between professionals and parents/voluntary organisations?
3   What are seen as appropriate formal and administrative procedures to ensure the identification and assessment of children with specific learning difficulties?

4   How do parents view current practice in the identification of specific
     learning difficulties and what suggestions have they for changes in
     practice?
5   What are the views of parents on the attempts made by schools to meet
     the needs?

The parents' questionnaire

The first phase in the process of constructing the questionnaire involved pilot
interviews with parents, which used the following headings: parents' definition
of specific learning difficulties; identification and assessment; provision;
voluntary associations; satisfaction. Key concerns were identified from these
interviews and used as the basis of the questionnaire.

Most of the questions were closed (to facilitate analysis), but a number of
open-ended questions were also included to allow parents to tell us about their
experiences in their own words. Many parents wrote at length in the space left
for additional comments and these proved particularly illuminating; they are
included in the following analysis.

Sampling procedure and administration of questionnaires

The interviews with local policy makers had suggested that we were likely to
encounter difficulties in drawing up a sample of parents of children with
specific learning difficulties because:

- There was no agreed definition of specific learning difficulties across
  different authorities nor, in certain instances, within the same authority.
- Some authorities had adopted what we have termed an 'anti-
  categorisation' approach to learning difficulties. In these authorities, the
  emphasis was on meeting the needs of individual children rather than
  classifying them according to the nature or origin of their learning
  difficulties.
- In some authorities, a degree of hostility was evident to the use of the
  term 'specific learning difficulties'. We suspected that these authorities
  were unlikely to be enthusiastic in assisting us in compiling a sample.

On the other hand, the Scottish Dyslexia Association and local branches
indicated that their members would be very willing to co-operate with the
researchers. Although we recognised that parents affiliated to the Association
should form part of our sample, it was unlikely that they would be typical of

all parents whose children might be identified as having specific learning difficulties. In order to achieve a more representative sample, it was important to include parents identified by the psychological services, despite the difficulties anticipated in contacting such parents.

We decided on a sample size of 200, divided equally between parents contacted through the voluntary associations and the psychological services. The covering letter sent out to the voluntary organisation sample pointed out the possibility of two survey forms being received. Parents were instructed if this occurred to return one form blank and mention the circumstances. Only two blanks were sent back on this basis. As expected, members of the voluntary organisations were keen to participate and branch secretaries undertook the task of distributing questionnaires to members selected on a random basis. Forty questionnaires were sent out by the largest dyslexia association and ten or less were distributed by each of seven other dyslexia associations.

Constructing the psychological services' sample was less straightforward. We asked principal educational psychologists to draw up lists of parents of children with specific learning difficulties. The ease with which they were able to do this was indicative of the extent to which they recognised such children as a discrete group, distinguishable from other children with learning difficulties. We explained that we wanted to target the parents of children for whom a discrepancy had been identified between general ability and performance in certain areas, particularly literacy. Finally, however, the basis of the selection was left to the discretion of the principal psychologist; it was already clear that the samples of parents, particularly those from the local authority contacts, would be illustrative not representative. The following two statements indicate the nature and variation of the strategies agreed with the psychologists:

I have sorted our database of pupils with Records of Needs, and extracted the names ... of all those with Records of Needs as a result of specific learning difficulties. Although we have other children with more moderate specific learning difficulties it is much more difficult for me to compile a list of these, and would take several weeks because of the number of individual learning support teachers I would need to contact.

Our method of identifying SpLD pupils would target:
(a) past and present Learning Unit clients;
(b) other pupils, both at primary and secondary levels, who have similar problems

(c) (possibly) children known to learning support teachers and diagnosed by them as SpLD but not referred to the psychological service - although these should not, one would hope, be a large number.

Ultimately, principal educational psychologists in seven regions and three divisions of a large regional authority compiled such lists and distributed questionnaires to the parents whom they had identified. The number of questionnaires distributed in each region/division ranged from 3 to 18, depending on the size of the region and the estimate of the number of children with specific learning difficulties. Some principal psychologists, even though they found the survey form and the premises of the research to be ill-matched with their own conceptualisation and procedure, went to considerable trouble to be of assistance and to ensure that their standpoint was represented in the research. One psychologist, after consulting the region's adviser for special educational needs, wrote, 'We are agreed that the way learning support is delivered here simply does not fit the bipolar structure you offer'. However, this psychologist did choose a small number of names from the region's submissions to the Scottish Examination Board for special examination arrangements. He commented

Interestingly enough, only two out of 100+ submissions unambiguously mention the word 'dyslexia'; but the terms 'specific learning difficulties' and 'specific learning difficulties of a dyslexic or similar nature' are used. In neither of these two large categories is there any indication that these formalisations have been talked through in any detail with parents.

This psychologist expressed concern at asking parents to take part unless there was some pre-existing evidence that their child had the difficulties we were investigating and that this had been discussed with them. In the case of children receiving learning support in the primary and lower secondary school, such labels had not been used.

Another psychologist who did not provide any part of the sample wrote explaining the position:

The psychological service and learning support do not dichotomise youngsters as having specific or general difficulty in learning. In each instance the most appropriate strategy for responding to the youngster's educational needs is developed and a detailed description ... is kept for that purpose. The categorising you requested would require reconsideration of individual pupil records; [and could not be made without undue] investment of staff time.

Thus two regions and three divisions of another region did not contribute to the local authority parent sample. Since the sample turned out in any case to be an opportunistic one, the matter was not pursued further. The nature of the sample, however, precludes us from drawing conclusions about the regional distribution of parental views and experiences. Despite not being able to claim that our sample is representative of a given population, we believe that it does cover the broad spectrum of parents who define their children as having specific learning difficulties. There were some significant differences in the responses of the parents contacted through the voluntary organisations and through the psychological service, and these are identified in the fundings. There was also some overlap in our two populations - 40% of parents whom we contacted through the psychological service indicated they had been in touch with voluntary organisations.

The questionnaires were distributed in February 1992 and reminders issued in March. One hundred and fifty three were returned, an overall response rate of 77%. The responses to the questionnaires were analysed using SPSSX. A separate analysis of the additional comments written on the questionnaires by parents was also undertaken.

The characteristics of the sample

The response rate from parents contacted through voluntary associations was 83% and from those contacted through psychological services was 70%. The sample included the parents of 114 boys (76.5%) and 39 girls (25.5%). It is a well known phenomenon that boys outnumber girls in the group of pupils identified as having special educational needs of all kinds, and a 3:1 ratio is not unusual. There is a continuing debate about whether the incidence of learning difficulties is really greater in boys than in girls, perhaps due to underlying physiological causes, or whether this is a gender-related artefact of the ways in which society recognises such difficulties.

The ages of children whose parents responded to the survey varied from 6 to 23. Ninety-three (60.8%) of the children whose parents responded were in primary, 56 (36.6%) in secondary and 4 had left school and were either working or in further or higher education.

About a third of the sample of parents were working class and about two thirds middle class (see Appendix B for definition of social class). This is the reverse of the distribution which one would expect to find in the general population. Table 6.1 shows the proportion of parents in each class and among

96

those contacted through the voluntary organisations and the psychological service.

There were significantly more middle class parents among the voluntary organisation sample and fewer working class parents. In the sample of parents contacted through the psychological services, the reverse was true, with a significantly larger proportion of working class parents and a significantly lower proportion of middle class parents. Although the overall proportion of working class families represented in the whole sample is less than that for the general population, it is clear that children identified as having specific learning difficulties are by no means restricted to the middle classes.

Details of school attended (Table 6.2) indicated that 22(14.4%) of the sample were in private schools and 131(85.6%) in state schools. There was, not unexpectedly, an association between method of contact, type of school attended by child and class of family. Parents contacted through voluntary organisations were more likely to use the private system. All of the children of the working class sample were in state schools, whether or not the parents were contacted through the voluntary organisations.

Table 6.1 Social class of family by means of contact
(Result of chi-square test)

	Working class	Middle Class	Total
Voluntary organisations	17 (20.5)	66 (79.5)	83 (54.6)
Psychological services	38 (55.1)	31 (44.9)	69 (45.4)
Total	55 (36.2)	97 (63.8)	152(100.0)

p < .001
Missing values = 1

Table 6.2 Method of contact by type of school attended

	Private	State	Total
Voluntary organisations	21 (95.5)	62 (47.3)	83 (54.2)
Psychological services	1 (14.5)	69 (52.7)	70 (45.8)
Total	22 (14.4)	131 (85.6)	153 (100.0)

p < .0001

The age when the child's learning difficulties were first identified ranged from 3 to 14 with a modal age of 7 years. (Figure 6.1). This suggests that learning difficulties tend not to be identified until it is clear that the child has failed to master early steps in reading and writing.

Figure 6.1 Age when learning difficulties first identified

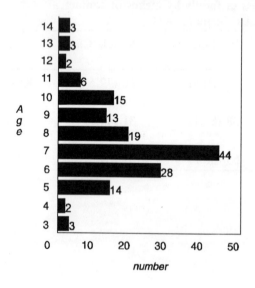

98

Parents' assessment of child's ability and perception of child's difficulties

Parents were asked to estimate their child's ability. The majority (almost 60%) were described as average in ability, about a third as above average, and approximately 10% were described as of below average ability. This suggested that almost all parents in the sample considered their child's difficulties to be qualitatively different from those of children with more global learning difficulties. There was an association between parents' assessment of child's ability, method of contact, social class and type of school. Parents identified through voluntary organisations, middle class parents and parents of children at private schools were all more likely to assess their child as being of above average ability.

Parents were asked to describe the nature of their child's learning difficulties; the question was open-ended in order to collect information on the range of difficulties which parents believed their child to experience. Figure 6.2 illustrates the range of learning difficulties which were named. Almost all parents said that their child experienced difficulties with reading, writing and spelling.

Figure 6.2 Parents reporting child experiences particular difficulty

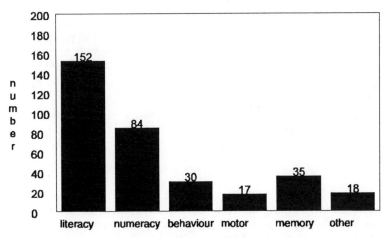

Note: Categories are not mutually exclusive

Numeracy difficulties were indicated by just over half our sample and Table 6.3 reveals that a higher proportion of children in primary than secondary were believed to experience such difficulties. This may be an indication that some of these difficulties are resolved in the later stages of primary. Numeracy problems were associated with specific learning difficulties by a substantially larger proportion of our parent sample than of our education managers, advisers and psychologists (chapter 2) or learning support teachers (chapter 5). Almost 20% of parents listed behaviour and emotional problems and a similar proportion said that their child experienced memory and concentration difficulties. There was an association between parents' assessment of child's ability and memory/concentration difficulties. Of those who believed their child to be of above average ability, 40% felt that memory and concentration was a problem area, whereas in the average and below average categories these proportions were only 17% and 14% respectively. Approximately 11% of parents reported that their child experienced co-ordination or motor difficulties, and the same proportion named other difficulties such as physical or sensory problems.

Table 6.3 **Parents' account of whether child experiences numeracy difficulties by sector**
(Result of chi-square test)

	Yes	No	Total
Primary	55 (59.1)	38 (40.9)	93 (60.8)
Secondary	25 (44.6)	31 (84.7)	56 (36.6)
Other	4 (100.0)	0	4 (2.6)
Total	84 (54.9)	69 (45.1)	153 (100.0)

p < .05

The complex intertwining between learning difficulties, social and emotional problems and physical illness was referred to by many parents. One primary school child, who was seen as lazy and a daydreamer by the school, developed stress-related migraine. His parent commented:

His dislike of school grew to such an extent that every other morning he was in tears before going to school and on many occasions was too unwell to attend.

Another child was reported as having been operated on for a suspected twisted bowel before specific learning difficulties were identified.

The implications of learning difficulties remaining undiagnosed over a long period were described by a number of parents. The example of one girl in secondary school was a case in point:

We feel that the help J is being offered now has come too late as she is extremely embarrassed by her problem. She feels that her friends will laugh at her and that any help she accepts will make her stand out. She refuses to accept that there is any need for help and is doing her best to be expelled from school.

A high proportion (90%) of parents said that they would use the term 'dyslexia' to describe their child's difficulties. However, as Table 6.4 indicates, parents contacted through voluntary organisations were more likely to use the term than those contacted through the psychological services, as were middle class (95%) than working class parents (78%).

Table 6.4   Parents reporting use of term 'dyslexia' by method of contact
(Result of chi-square test)

	Yes	No	Total
Voluntary organisations	80 (96.4)	3 (3.6)	83 (54.6)
Psychological services	55 (79.7)	14 (20.3)	69 (45.4)
Total	135 (88.8)	17 (11.2)	152 (100.0)

$p < .01$
Missing values = 1

Parents' comments were most illuminating in explaining why the use of the term dyslexia was considered to be important. First, they felt that if their child was identified as dyslexic, then this legitimated their claim for additional educational resources. In the eyes of one parent, the use or rejection of the term dyslexia was essentially a political decision and associated with provision of access to resources.

> Up until last year no one at my son's school would agree that he was dyslexic. I have since found out that once they agree he is dyslexic they have to provide help with teaching and in this area they don't have either the resources or the know-how. They are forced to make political judgements about the children and not look at what the problem is. You shouldn't have to fight to have your children properly educated and look at private education just to achieve this!

A second reason for favouring the term was the distinction it implicitly drew between their child and others experiencing more global learning difficulties:

> There is a comparison/lumping together of dyslexic children and those who are mentally retarded. Dyslexic children are NOT MENTALLY RETARDED!

This parent's views implied that there was a social stigma attached to being mentally retarded which she did not wish to be attached to her own child.

Parents did not necessarily all concur, however, in their views on the nature of dyslexia. For some, it appeared that dyslexic children were considered to be 'of a kind' and hence required similar educational provision. This view was implicit in the comment:

> I would like to see special units or schools for dyslexic children. C was never happier than when he was being educated by teachers who understood his needs and children who were the same as he was.

Precisely the opposite view was expressed by another parent, who saw dyslexia as a broad term covering a wide range of difficulties which would require different types of educational provision:

> A lot of people do not realise that all dyslexic children are different and the help when given should be rationed to suit that particular child and not treated as a blanket issue for all children.

Identification of learning difficulties

Parents were asked a number of questions about how they saw the various stages in the identification and diagnosis of learning difficulties. More than half of parents reported that they themselves pointed out to education professionals that their child was experiencing problems with schoolwork. About a quarter of parents said that primary teachers first suggested that the child might be experiencing learning difficulties. A significantly higher proportion of parents contacted through the psychological service reported that the primary teacher was the first to identify learning difficulties (see Table 6.5). Parents contacted through the voluntary organisations were more likely to say that they were the first to suggest that their child was experiencing a problem with learning.

Table 6.5   Person who first suggested child had learning difficulties by method of contact (Result of chi-square test)

	Self	Primary Teacher	Other	Total
Voluntary Organisation	52 (62.7)	12 (14.5)	19 (22.9)	83 (54.2)
Psychological Service	31 (44.3)	29 (41.4)	10 (14.3)	70 (45.8)
Total	83 (54.2)	41 (26.8)	29 (19.0)	153 (100.0)

$p < .001$

Note: The category 'other' includes nursery teacher, primary learning support teacher, secondary teacher, secondary learning support teacher, educational psychologist, voluntary organisation and medic.

Parents appeared far from happy in cases where they perceived the onus was on them to draw the school's attention to the child's problems.

My main complaint about the education system/school is that from primary 2 onwards at class teacher/parent interviews I pointed out my son had difficulty in decoding unfamiliar words, splitting words into syllables and particular difficulty with vowel sounds. If my husband and I had not taken the initiative to get him assessed, the school would still be happy to classify him as a slow reader.

I feel very bitter about the time it has taken for my son to be recognised as dyslexic. I suggested to the school when he was 5½ that he showed all the signs of being dyslexic. I was told that everyone was climbing on the dyslexic bandwagon and basically to mind my own business.

Figure 6.3 summarises parents' views of who first carried out a test to ascertain the nature of the child's learning difficulties. Overall, the regional educational psychologist was the most likely (50%) followed by a medical officer (18.6%), a learning support teacher (16%) and a voluntary association psychologist (11%). Interesting differences between parents contacted through the voluntary organisations and the psychological services are also shown. The former were more likely to report that a medical or a voluntary association psychologist was the first to carry out tests, whereas the latter group were more likely to indicate that a local authority educational psychologist was the first to test the child.

Figure 6.3   **Person who first carried out test to identify learning difficulties by method of contact**

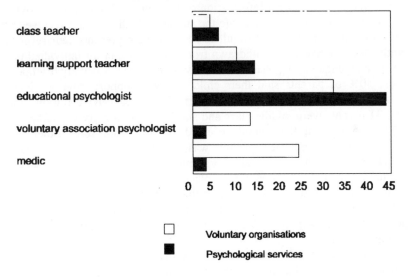

class teacher

learning support teacher

educational psychologist

voluntary association psychologist

medic

0   5   10 15 20 25 30 35 40 45

☐   Voluntary organisations
■   Psychological services

Parents' written comments also conveyed dissatisfaction with assessment arrangements, especially the amount of time it took to arrange for some children to be tested by the regional educational psychologist:

> It took one whole school year before the child was assessed by the educational psychologist after the head had requested an assessment. A whole year wasted.

One parent was not aware that she could request a referral to the regional psychological service and since the school was reluctant to do this, she had arranged an assessment through the Dyslexia Association. Others reported problems in getting schools to acknowledge the validity of assessments carried out by psychologists contacted through the Dyslexia Institute or the Dyslexia Association.

Provision of support

A series of questions sought information on the nature of educational provision. First, parents were asked to indicate the support which the child received after the identification of learning difficulties and Table 6.6 presents their responses. Slightly less than half were withdrawn from the classroom for individual tuition and written comments suggested that this was often for a relatively brief period. Almost 40% of parents said their child received support from the learning support teacher in class. About a quarter indicated private tuition, and of these, 31 parents were middle class and six were working class. Rather fewer (18%) reported that their child received support from some other source (written comments indicated that this was usually in the form of occupational therapy or speech therapy), and 14% identified tuition in a special school or unit (this included children who were placed in one of the reading units run by a number of authorities). It was clear that very few children were placed in special classes. About 10% of pupils (more secondary than primary) were reported as receiving no additional support after the identification of their learning difficulties.

Again, there were differences in the accounts of provision given by parents contacted through voluntary organisations and those contacted through the psychological services (Table 6.6). The former were more likely to indicate that their child received private tuition and that no additional support was available in school, and the latter that their child was placed in a special school or unit. The form of provision could be influenced of course, by the apparent severity of the learning difficulties. We do not have the information to enable us to test out a hypothesis of that kind. Our analysis suggested that there was an association between receipt of help from a learning support teacher and both the type of school attended and reported ability. Children attending maintained schools were more likely to receive assistance from a learning support teacher than those in independent schools, and children who were judged to be of high ability were less likely to receive learning support than those reported to be of average or below average ability.

There are marked differences between the levels of provision reported by parents and those in the learning support teachers' accounts. Generally higher levels, both of withdrawal tuition and of co-operative teaching support in the classroom according to the teachers reflect the fact that teachers were asked to list all provision in use in their schools. The parents' accounts provide an indication of provision actually experienced by an individual child.

106

Table 6.6 Type of support received after identification of learning difficulties by method of contact (Results of chi-square test)

	Withdrawal for individual tuition	Support in class from l.s. teacher	Placed in special class	Placed in special school unit	Private tuition	Other	No additional support
Voluntary Organisations	35 (42.2)	27 (32.5)	1 (1.2)	6 (7.2)	32 (38.6)	16 (19.3)	13 (16.0)
Psychological services	38 (54.3)	31 (44.3)	1 (1.4)	16 (22.9)	5 (7.1)	12 (17.1)	1 (1.4)
Total	73 (47.7)	58 (37.9)	2 (1.3)	22 (14.4)	37 (24.2)	28 (18.3)	14 (9.3)
	$p < .01$	$p < .01$					

N = 150
Missing values = 3
Categories are not mutually exclusive.

Parents with children at secondary school were more likely than parents of primary school children to report that their child received no additional support after the identification of learning difficulties.

Parents were asked whether their child had a Record of Needs; rather more than a third of parents reported that they did. Proportionately children with Records of Needs were from the psychological services and working class groups of sample families. Lower proportions were from the voluntary organisation/middle class groups (Tables 6.7 and 6.8). This could have been an artefact of the sampling procedure described above. The age at which a Record of Needs was opened ranged from 6 to 15. More records were opened for children at 11 than other ages, just before transfer to secondary.

Table 6.7 **Parents reporting that child has Record of Needs by means of contact**
(Result of chi-square test)

	Yes	No	Total
Voluntary organisations	20 (25.0)	60 (75.0)	80 (54.1)
Psychological services	37 (54.4)	31 (45.6)	68 (45.9)
Total	57 (38.5)	91 (61.5)	148 (100.0)

p < .001
missing values = 5

Table 6.8 Parents reporting that child has Record of Needs by social class
(Result of chi-square test)

	Yes	No	Total
Working class	34 (64.2)	19 (35.8)	53 (35.8)
Middle class	23 (24.2)	72 (75.8)	95 (64.2)
Total	57 (38.5)	91 (61.5)	148 (100.0)

$p < .001$
Missing values = 5

A further question explored parents' overall satisfaction with services provided by the school and Table 6.9 presents these findings. There was a roughly equal split between those who were satisfied (37.2%) and dissatisfied (41.9%) with 20% unsure. A number of parents who indicated that they were satisfied at the time of the survey reported that at an earlier date they had been dissatisfied. Those contacted through the psychological services showed a higher level of satisfaction than those contacted through the voluntary organisations, and middle class parents were less satisfied than working class parents (Table 6.10).

Table 6.9 Parents reporting satisfaction with school support by means of contact
(Result of chi-square test)

	Satisfied	Unsure	Dissatisfied	Total
Voluntary organisations	20 (24.7)	12 (14.8)	49 (60.5)	81 (54.0)
Psychological services	35 (50.7)	19 (27.5)	15 (21.7)	69 (46.0)
Total	55 (36.7)	32 (21.3)	63 (42.0)	150(100.0)

$p < .001$
Missing values = 3

Table 6.10 Parents reporting satisfaction with school support by class of family
(Result of chi-square Test)

	Satisfied	Unsure	Dissatisfied	Total
Working class	29 (53.7)	11 (20.4)	14 (25.9)	54 (36.0)
Middle class	26 (27.1)	21 (21.9)	49 (51.0)	96 (54.0)
Total	55 (36.7)	32 (21.3)	63 (42.0)	150(100.0)

p < .05
Missing values = 3

When asked to explain the reasons for their view of the quality of educational provision, many parents wrote at length about their struggle to secure provision for their child. It was noticeable that parents who were unhappy with provision generally had more to say. The major complaint voiced by almost 50% of parents was that tuition in school was inadequate. Relatively small proportions (less than 20%) of parents cited failure to diagnose, misdiagnosis of the learning difficulty and apparent ignorance on the part of teachers about specific learning difficulties. However, a third commented on the high quality of learning support in school and just over 10% mentioned their high regard for the work of reading units. Significantly more parents contacted through voluntary organisations commented on teachers' lack of knowledge of specific learning difficulties, whilst parents contacted through the psychological services were more likely to commend the reading units. More middle class than working class parents reported that the school had failed to identify their child's learning difficulties and that school tuition was inadequate. The number of working class parents who considered school tuition inadequate was the same as the number of working class parents in the voluntary organisation sample. (Table 6.11)

Table 6.11 Parents reporting school tuition inadequate by class of family (Result of chi-square test)

	Yes	No	Total
Working class	17 (31.5)	37 (68.5)	54 (35.8)
Middle class	59 (60.8)	38 (39.2)	97 (64.2)
Total	76 (50.3)	75 (49.7)	151 (100.0)

$p < .001$
Missing values = 2

Once again, parents' comments conveyed something of the reasons underlying their perceptions of the quality of educational provision. For those who viewed tuition as inadequate, it appeared there was dissatisfaction with the amount, the quality and the nature of the provision. A number of parents were critical of the teaching methods used by the mainstream class teacher, particularly for the teaching of reading:

> Whoever thought up the look and say method (otherwise known as glimpse and guess) should have been shot. Had my son been taught at school by phonics, sounding, spelling rules etc his problem would have been minimised instead of maximised. By using computers, tutoring etc we are now attempting to round up the horse and put it back in the stable.

One parent argued a very different case, suggesting that there was already an over-emphasis on the acquisition of basic skills:

> The state school places so much emphasis on the 3Rs rather than educating the whole child. The current system does not produce socially sensitive individuals.

He went on to quote Rudolph Steiner in support of the view that education should be about enhancing individual creativity. We should make it clear, however, that this parent's views were shared by few others in our sample.

There was disagreement about the type of learning support which would be of value. Most parents favoured individualised tuition to address their child's particular problems. The co-operative teaching approach was clearly rejected by one parent:

> I certainly do not agree with the learning support teacher working in the class situation as I feel these children need to have their confidence built up so that they can cope with the class work and this can only be done on a one to one basis.

However, parents were also well aware that it was not enough just to withdraw the child for individual or small group instruction; the nature of such tuition and the way in which it was handled within the social context of the classroom were of great importance. The potential for stigmatisation if learning support was handled insensitively was apparent in the comments of these parents:

> He was removed from the class at the primary school for better teaching. This was inadequate and did more harm than good. He was treated as stupid by both the remedial and class teachers which in turn affected his relationship with his peers.

> After many unhappy weeks we withdrew her from learning support because we felt that the humiliation she felt as a very bright child being singled out to work with children with totally different problems, who were perhaps not very bright, totally outweighed any help she was given.

There was some tension between, on the one hand, the view that the function of learning support was to keep the child up to date with the mainstream curriculum and, on the other hand, that it should focus on the acquisition of basic skills. In support of the latter, one parent stated:

> I feel that the remedial teaching offered is insufficient. There is no work programme and the support given is to keep the child abreast with classroom work.

Other parents, however, argued that too much time was spent practising basic skills which the child would always find difficult. More attention should be focused on assisting children to circumvent their problems, through the use, for instance, of word processors, spell checkers, calculators and scribes. Clearly, assisting a child with individual problems and helping him or her to gain access to the wider curriculum were not mutually exclusive. Nonetheless, parents tended to emphasise the importance of one or the other and some criticised the learning support programme offered by the school.

The criteria for assessment were also seen as disadvantaging children with specific learning difficulties. Particularly in English, parents felt that too much emphasis was placed on handwriting and spelling. One parent who had two dyslexic children said that at primary school they had been placed in the bottom group for everything because judgement of academic potential was based on reading ability. At secondary school, while most teachers had been helpful:

> the English department have torn sheets of work from their jotters, covered their work with red pen, written 'spelling' over everything and told them to use a dictionary. It's really constructive, positive help.[sarcasm]

Some parents complained about the diagnosis of specific learning difficulties: they suggested the children were labelled as slow, lazy and disruptive and this was likely to have a negative effect on the child's self-confidence. Schools were perceived as regarding the parent as neurotic or incompetent, and hence responsible for the child's problems:

> H's learning difficulties have been put down by the school and the psychological service to my single parent status and having a stressful job. The Education Authority will not consider that it is inappropriate teaching methods which have led to her difficulties.

> At a meeting attended by 'dignitaries' when he was 7 the reason he couldn't read was recorded as poor self image due to dog hairs on his clothes. One of the 'dignitaries' was extremely scruffy, unpressed, unkempt etc.

A number of parents suggested that the reason teachers tended to pathologise children with specific learning difficulties and their parents was that they lacked the knowledge and skill to assist:

> Schools tend to be very ignorant about dyslexia. Teachers tend to dismiss the problems of dyslexic children because they are unable to help them. They also tend to view the parents of dyslexic children as 'neurotic' or 'troublemaking' causing great distress to families who have to fight for their children's right to be educated.

Contrasting experiences of different phases of a child's educational career were described by some parents. For instance, although some parents felt trepidation at the approach of transfer from primary to secondary and feared that learning support would be less readily available, others expressed the view that learning support at secondary had been much better. A number of parents spoke of the improved support their child received in an independent school after an unsympathetic response to their needs in a maintained school. It was evident from other comments, however, that private schools also could be unresponsive. This parent described how her son had been diagnosed dyslexic at age 14, after 5 years at private school:

> The school would not endorse the psychological investigation or result. Dissatisfaction with the level of assistance/understanding encountered at the school, coupled with a series of petty infringements of school rules, led me to remove my son from private school at age 15. He now attends my local state run high school where the level of understanding and support is infinitely better.

Two parents reported their experience of moving from England to Scotland. They both commented on the superior level of identification of difficulties in Scottish schools:

> L had three years of education in England with no suggestion of any learning difficulties. We moved to Scotland and after only three days in Scottish education a problem was detected. The only unfortunate thing was that it took three years for it to be considered bad enough for her to receive the specialised help from the reading unit.

Although those who were critical of educational provision tended to be more voluble, some very positive remarks were made about the support they received.

> My daughter has been given lots of support from her school. Her guidance teacher pushed and prodded other teachers if they were uncommunicative in giving help.

> It took a long time to get support but we now have a place in a reading unit. The staff are wonderful. Reading age up two years. Spelling improved. Now mixes with other children. Confidence up 100%.

Helped greatly by place at special unit. Motor learning difficulties largely resolved through physiotherapy both during school visits and regular appointments at hospital occupational therapy unit.

Her Record of Needs for the moment ensures that she is getting taught in the way that suits her needs and not that of her peers. It is only 30 minutes a day but it is making a difference both to her confidence and her learning.

Parents who wrote positively about learning support provision described a coherent programme which they felt was targeting their child's particular problems and bringing about improvement both in skills and self-confidence. All the comments made about reading units were positive and parents whose children were receiving occupational therapy also spoke positively of the contribution this had made to the child's development. In addition, the attitude of the class teacher was seen as important. One parent, describing the damage done by a teacher who had 'pushed the top group and left the rest to muddle along' commented:

Children with specific learning difficulties not only require good learning support but also good class teachers and good teaching.

Parents' general comments on child's learning difficulties and help provided

At the end of the questionnaire, space was provided for parents to make general comments. Many wrote extensively and two key themes emerged. The first concerned perceptions of the availability of resources, which, in the words of one parent were not adequate to 'match the size or scale of the problem'. Some felt that the situation was worsening:

The economic climate of cutbacks in the Region is very depressing. When my son was first diagnosed, I was told of the availability of a place at a special reading unit once he was in P6. Now that time is nearing, places in the unit are scarce.

One solution to the scarcity of resources was for parents to seek private tuition; however, having to pay for a service which they felt the school should be providing was not an attractive proposition.

Two years ago in the same school our daughter, who is only mildly affected, got 6-8 hours learning support a week. Our son, who is badly affected, gets 1 hour per week. We feel he does not get the learning support which his problem requires and there seems to be no way of obtaining that support without resorting to a private tutor outwith normal school hours.

Another solution was to pressurise the system to make better provision, working collectively with other parents. A number of comments suggested that parents of children with specific learning difficulties were likely to compare the support received by other children with disabilities and protest if they perceived an imbalance:

A deaf child has been given extra support by a 2:1 ratio since day one. This, in my view, is not equal opportunity.

Furthermore, it was apparent that parents had a sense that learning support was the right of every child and parents should not have to struggle to procure it. It was also clear that at least some parents were conversant with their rights under the terms of the 1981 Act and were prepared to take legal action if necessary. One commented:

From the discovery of dyslexia it took two years to get any qualified help. This involved making an appeal, then the appeals committee passing on the case to the Secretary of State. We did eventually win, but two very precious years were wasted in the battle.

Another parent, whose child was transferring from primary to secondary, described the process of ensuring that his son received adequate learning support in the secondary school. Having been told by the head teacher that the secondary school would not be able to supply the same level of learning support as the primary, the parent explained:

So I shall be writing back to the educational psychologist asking what provision they can supply. It depends what he replies how far we shall take it. If we have to go to court we shall. Under the 1981 Act, the Region must provide educational facilities no matter what your child's difficulties.

Information from the SOED during the course of the project supported the view that parents have become increasingly confident in using the legislation.

The numbers of appeals have been small, but many official complaints are received under Section 70 of the Education (Scotland) Act 1981. For instance, a significant number of parents of children with specific learning difficulties have complained that speech therapy has not been provided when this has been listed in the Measures Proposed section of the Record of Needs.

Although most parents would probably wish to pursue their claim for improved provision without recourse to the courts, among our respondents there was a general feeling that appropriate education should be available as of right rather than at the whim of the education authority. Dissatisfaction with the lottery aspect of provision was evident in this parent's comment:

> Whereas some teachers and educational psychologists recognise dyslexia quickly and provide the limited resources they can, as there is no policy statement issued by the authorities parents have to rely on being 'lucky' and not fall into the category of either being over-anxious and fussy or liking 'trendy' labels.

The second major theme to emerge from parents' written comments was the key role which effective communication between professionals and parents plays in reassuring parents that their child is receiving appropriate help. A commonly expressed view was that parents were not listened to by the professionals and their anxieties were dismissed as ill-founded. One parent whose child had experienced both physical and emotional problems after a difficult birth described her dissatisfaction that no formal assessment was carried out until the child was 9:

> I am quite satisfied with the help that he is now receiving, but feel that, had I been taken more seriously from the start, then a lot of these problems could now be under control, and I wish that, when parents have concerns about their children, people would listen. We are the ones who know our children and our opinions should be listened to with sympathy, instead of condescension.

It was also evident that the use of different terminology by professionals dealing with a particular child caused considerable confusion:

> Meetings with the educational psychologist and learning support adviser have been frustrating because I feel these people don't really know my son yet are the people who make provision in terms of resources available. Despite my son being labelled dyslexic by the adviser, the psychologist told me at our last meeting when we were pressing for

resources that he had never been labelled as such. He only had 'dyslexic tendencies'.

The need for sensitive discussion with parents of their child's difficulty is clearly evident from this parent's experience:

> Her class teacher, when asked at a parents' evening what my child was good at said she could not think of anything. This was **totally devastating** to me. This teacher was not interested in slower children, could not find the time for them and **shattered** my confidence in my child .... Schools must listen to parents. I always regret not standing by my feeling that she was too young for school.

These accounts of the breakdown of communication were balanced by other parents who spoke of the excellent rapport between the learning support and the class teacher. One parent wrote:

> The school has been very good with support and explains and discusses everything with us.

Finally, parents were asked about how well their child was progressing. Almost two thirds reported that their child was making good progress, almost a quarter were unsure and 15% reported little progress.

Communication: learning support teachers' views

Chapter 5 reports what learning support teachers had to say on the subject of communication between schools and parents. The great majority of the teachers met parents at parents' evenings and individual consultations, and the twenty or so teachers who added additional comments emphasised open channels of communication with parents. Not surprisingly, no learning support teacher reported unwillingness to hear parents' views. However, comparison of the two surveys reveals a wide gap of perception between parents and learning support teachers abut the adequacy of home-school contact where specific learning difficulties are concerned.

Summary

Approximately half of the sample of parents was drawn from psychological service records and half from the membership of local dyslexia associations in

Scotland. Most children were described by their parents as being of average or above average ability and experiencing literacy and a range of other difficulties. Social and emotional problems were often seen as resulting from unrecognised learning difficulties. Most parents were strongly in favour of the use of the term dyslexia in order (i) to draw a distinction between their child's difficulties and those experienced by children with more global learning difficulties and (ii) to secure additional resources.

More than half the parents were themselves the first to draw attention to the child's learning difficulties and many felt that schools had been unduly slow in recognising the problems. About half said that a regional educational psychologist was the first to undertake an assessment, and again comments indicated that many parents felt they had had to fight for a referral. Some arranged to have an initial assessment undertaken by a medical officer or by a psychologist contacted through a voluntary organisation. They were likely to take this course of action if they felt that the school was failing to act sufficiently quickly in making a referral.

With regard to the type of learning support which parents believed their child received after the identification of learning difficulties, about half were withdrawn for individual tuition, approximately 40% received support from the learning support teacher within the mainstream class and 10% were perceived as receiving no additional help. Parents were almost equally split on their overall level of satisfaction, with over a third expressing satisfaction, a similar proportion voicing dissatisfaction and 20% unsure. Parents' dissatisfaction focused on inadequate tuition, lack of recognition or misdiagnosis of the child's learning difficulties and lack of expertise among teachers. Parents who were satisfied reported the provision of a programme tailored to the child's particular needs and a generally supportive atmosphere within the school.

Throughout the analysis, it was apparent that there were some significant differences between the experiences of parents contacted through the voluntary organisations and those contacted through the psychological services. The former group were more likely to perceive their child as being of above average ability; use the term 'dyslexia' to describe their child's difficulties; be the first to draw attention to the existence of learning difficulties; use a medical officer or a psychologist contacted through a voluntary organisation for an initial assessment; use private tuition after the identification of learning difficulties; express dissatisfaction with the services provided; and be middle class. Parents contacted through the psychological services were more likely to have a Record of Needs for their child, report satisfaction with services and be working class.

Two themes emerged strongly from parents' general comments on the help provided to resolve the child's learning difficulties. The first suggested that a feeling of parents being listened to by professionals was an important element in maintaining confidence in the system. The second was that parents had a strong sense that resources were limited and that they were prepared to struggle to achieve the level of learning support they considered adequate, even if this entailed making formal complaints to the authority.

7 The voluntary organisations and specific learning difficulties

We have concentrated so far upon policies and provision in the public sector of education. In the voluntary sector, the dyslexia associations (by this we mean the branch associations of the national organisation - the Scottish Dyslexia Association) have had a high profile, and in our various surveys we asked regional officers, learning support teachers and parents to comment on the part played by these associations. A wide variety of views, both positive and negative, were expressed. In this chapter, we describe an investigation of the voluntary organisations' own perspectives on specific learning difficulties, and report on how the role they have adopted was perceived by parents and those who work with the education system.

Data for the investigation were collected through interviews, carried out in September and October 1991, with the national chairperson of the Scottish Dyslexia Association, the administrator of the Dyslexia Institute, Glasgow, and spokespersons from the eight branch dyslexia associations in Scotland. Three of the interviews were carried out face to face, the remainder by telephone. The informants received copies of the interview schedule in advance and, in some cases, consulted other members to provide a consensus response rather than a personal view. The broad agreement on most issues among this group of informants demonstrates the close liaison that exists between the branch associations and the national organisation.

The objectives of this series of interviews were contained in the following research questions:

1   What definitions of specific learning difficulties are held by these organisations, and what terminology do they use in discussing them?

2   How do the organisations describe their own role and function?

3   What are their experiences and views with regard to local authority provision for children with specific learning difficulties?

4   How do they consider that provision could be improved?

Terminology and definition

All the voluntary bodies used the term 'dyslexia', in their titles and in general discussion of the learning problems relevant to our research. They were aware of the controversy which it frequently aroused, and all were prepared to use the term 'specific learning difficulties' with those to whom it was more acceptable. They suggested, however, that 'dyslexia' was strongly preferred by the parents who consulted them, and by adults experiencing learning difficulties of this kind. 'Specific learning difficulties' was accepted as synonymous for the purpose of the interview, but was generally seen by this group as an umbrella term covering a wider range of difficulties. Some dismissed it as 'jargon' and argued that parents were unhappy with it as it appeared to promise that the child's difficulty could be specified, while in fact this was not possible.

A particular problem with the expression 'specific learning difficulties' was its similarity to 'learning difficulties', which was regarded as

> a euphemism for mental handicap. People could make assumptions that the young person with specific learning difficulties was mentally handicapped; I don't want to look down on mentally handicapped people, but these young people could be of the whole range, it is nothing to do with their intelligence. They have one problem and they don't need to be saddled with another one.

Agreement was not unanimous; one speaker suggested that dyslexia was a wider term than specific learning difficulties, given the variety of difficulties it covered. These difficulties were enumerated by the speakers as difficulties with words (especially the written word) involving reading, writing and spelling; sometimes difficulties with numbers, especially the written parts of mathematics; some sequential, directional and organisational difficulties; and problems with short term memory and hand skills. It was stressed that a group of difficulties were involved (though not always all those mentioned above) which might occur in any combination or degree of severity. The mildest, for example, might present an intractable spelling problem only.

Five of the ten respondents referred to a discrepancy in abilities as a characteristic sign of specific learning difficulties:

SpLD is a learning difficulty that is a surprise in the child; there is no obvious reason for it.

These individuals ascribed specific learning difficulties to a constitutional condition which was lifelong; the problems which it caused, however, could be seen as amenable to being alleviated and even overcome in practice, given appropriate teaching and sympathetic support. All of the group regarded children with specific learning difficulties as a discrete group who did not respond to 'ordinary remedial teaching', although several expressed some caution on this point, and pointed out their lack of expertise with regard to the whole gamut of special educational needs.

The policy of the Scottish Dyslexia Association was not to hazard a guess at the incidence of specific learning difficulty in the school population, as there was no Scottish research on this, and figures from England came from a study nearly twenty years old. The English research (Rutter et al, 1976) provides the basis for the figures quoted by the British Dyslexia Association estimating that between 4% and 10% of children are affected. Figures like these were quoted by several respondents, who referred to the upper figure as a blanket estimate including those only mildly affected. The lower figure, variously given as two, three, four or five per cent, was suggested as the proportion requiring particular help; the speculative nature of the estimate was mentioned by most of those who attempted to answer the question, though one person referred to the experience of the local tutor-organiser, and another to figures suggested by the education authority. One person went on to say that such figures made it probable that there would be a child with specific learning difficulty in every class.

One respondent referred to increasing incidence. When asked how what she had called a constitutional condition could be becoming more common, she explained that on the one hand there could be increased awareness leading to the identification of more children with specific learning difficulty, but on the other hand, trends in classroom methodology based on learning by inference or absorption represented the wrong approach for such pupils. Such approaches allowed problems which would resolve themselves with more structured step by step teaching, to develop into intractable learning difficulties.

Role and functions of the voluntary organisations

The Scottish Dyslexia Association described itself as operating at a national level within and beyond Scotland to raise public awareness, speak to government and work with the British Dyslexia Association at a UK level. The

Dyslexia Institute was presented as an independent body which acts to provide psychological assessment and teaching in relation to specific learning difficulty, and also fulfils a counselling role. The eight branch associations described their roles as support, advice and information for parents; raising public awareness by means of meetings, conferences and local pressure group activities; and catering for adults with specific learning difficulty. Parental support was seen as the most important function. The provision of information and awareness was addressed to the public at large, but very particularly to teachers. One association had supported a small number of teachers to take the British Dyslexia Association qualification, and the national association had initiated the formation of a Trust which supported the development of the Centre for Specific Learning Difficulties at a college of education.

Assessment and tuition were generally provided privately with the associations acting to arrange contacts between families and chartered psychologists or teachers. Only one branch association ran its own tutor service directly; as another argued, 'If we began a tutor service we would be letting the authorities off the hook.' All the associations made a point of advising parents to go through the school system in the first instance, and of indicating the most effective ways of doing so. Most reported that the parents who approached them had usually already tried asking the school for help, and were often disillusioned by the experience. It was realised that parents who successfully consulted their child's school about learning problems would be much less likely to go to an outside group, and to that extent the voluntary bodies' membership was a self-selected dissatisfied sample. However, where parents expressed a wish to have a private assessment of their child, two speakers said they pointed out that the school would be under no obligation to take any notice of a private report, and that 'many in the local education authorities are quite sceptical of outside assessment.' Parents did not generally realise that they had the right to approach the educational authority or psychological service themselves if the school was unwilling to refer the child for assessment. Information from the local dyslexia association about this right could be the first step in getting action taken.

Two of the smaller, largely rural associations had no network of tutors, but one had run a one-week summer school for three years in succession, catering for twelve children. Another association serving a large rural area had tutors who in effect worked on a voluntary basis; the fixed fee paid by parents only covered their travelling expenses (except in the main population centre). The regional education authority had provided premises in a primary school twice a week for the association to run its town tutoring sessions.

All the tutors on the associations' contact networks or working in the tutor services were teachers registered with the General Teaching Council for

Scotland, who broadly agreed with the view of specific learning difficulties held by the associations. In some places their expertise rested upon general professional or learning support experience, experience of the diploma course of the British Dyslexia Association, or a variety of SEN qualifications. Tutors included both retired and serving teachers.

One to one teaching was a common feature of the teaching provided. The tutors were described as devising individually tailored programmes. A variety of published materials were mentioned, including the Kingston Manual, Alpha to Omega, and Kathleen Hickey materials. Computer equipment and software were also cited, and several of the associations had raised funds for extending its use. Some informants had no knowledge of the teaching, as the association's role was restricted to putting parents in contact with tutors.

The effectiveness of the teaching was reported on the basis of the reactions of parents and tutors. A high level of parental satisfaction was claimed, but this was based on impressionistic evidence and no attempt was made to quantify outcomes. The strongest claims for success were in all cases in relation to children's self-esteem and confidence:

Parents feel there is a dramatic change in the child's conception of himself.

The child is encouraged because he is no longer being dealt with as stupid.

Claims in relation to literacy skills were very cautious: 'Perhaps they get to grips with one or two basics.' Those children taking private lessons with tutors or attending the organisations' teaching centres commonly took one lesson a week for up to an hour, depending on the age of the child. This might be continued over a two year period, but wide variations were reported.

The concerns of the parents approaching the organisations were described in graphic terms. All the speakers had become involved in the organisations through their own experience as parents of children with specific learning difficulties, and they identified strongly with inquirers. Parents were said to be 'desperately worried', giving 'a cry for help', often feeling a sense of guilt and failure themselves at letting their child down. The happiness of the child was seen as the major concern, rated well above academic success, although fears for the future and stress upon the essential role of literacy for participation in modern society were also described. Relations with schools had sometimes become fraught with difficulty: 'they feel they have been fobbed off'; 'they are told they are neurotic or the child is simply immature by schools'; 'concerned parents who go up to the school are perceived as more interfering than caring.'

125

Uncertainty about handling the child was another feature: 'Homework always creates heartache, you are torn between letting the child off and keeping the household peace or insisting that they do it when it takes forever and is very trying.'

The associations lent a listening ear, advised the parents to speak to the teachers and to read as much as possible of the material on dyslexia provided or recommended by the organisations, and informed them of their rights in relation to the education authority under the legislation of 1980-1981. Discussion of the problem could help parents to express their worries to teachers in a non-aggressive way. One speaker had formerly worked as a local government officer, and was in the habit of reminding parents of the problems of those providing public services. It was not the policy of the Scottish Dyslexia Association to give specific recommendations about the provision the child required; the Institute, as a business concern, took a different stance, and explicitly recommended a structured multi-sensory approach as practised in their own teaching and teacher training. Some of the branch associations did advise parents of self-help steps which their members had found useful, such as making tape recordings of the child's own classwork or passages from course books.

Perceptions of local education authority provision

All those interviewed said that they were aware of the provision for children with specific learning difficulties offered in their areas, but most considered that there was a wide gap between the official policy statements of provision and the actual help on the ground. Four respondents, however, spoke of improving recognition and provision for specific learning dificulties over the past year or two. More than one region was said to have marked variations in provision between different divisions of the psychological service. Only one regional authority was very warmly regarded by the local dyslexia association, although helpful individuals within authorities were mentioned by most. The respondents referred to scarce resources, and guessed at linkage between reluctance to recognise learning problems and the impossibility of providing effective help, either within the schools or staff development for teachers.

Even the most sympathetic accounts of the local authorities' provision did not rate at all highly their success in identifying children with specific learning difficulties. Many learning problems regarded by the respondents as specific learning difficulties were seen as missed altogether or not recognised early enough; generally, if the parent asked for the child to be assessed and the class teacher thought it not justified, nothing was done. 'Only those who shout the loudest get any recognition.' It was said to be rare for the teacher to recommend assessment without a parental request. Where a referral was made, the time between referral and assessment was too long, six or eight months being mentioned in several areas:

Referral once took six weeks, now it is six months or more; one girl who was sitting Highers that May had taken a year to be seen.

The assessments themselves were described by one speaker as 'cursory'; the same person deplored the fact that in her experience no written report was given to parents.

A questionnaire survey was undertaken by the Scottish Dyslexia Association in 1989, another by a branch association in 1990. The researchers had access to some of the findings. We hesitated to report on these as we knew very little about how the samples of parents were drawn or how the investigations were conducted. The returns seemed to reveal considerable dissatisfaction with local authority provision on assessment, responses to parental demands, keeping parents informed and offering written reports. However, the sample of parents, who were all in touch with the voluntary organisations and were motivated to return the questionnaire, was likely to overrepresent negative experiences.

Impressions of professional groups

The speakers were asked about the impressions they had of the different professional groups' helpfulness with regard to children with specific learning difficulties. Individual variations were mentioned in all cases. Educational psychologists were fewer in number than learning support or mainstream teachers, and were more influential as individuals, so that the provision could depend on having an educational psychologist who was 'good' in the associations' terms. Being 'good' entailed recognising dyslexia or specific learning difficulties as a discrete group of learning problems, to be tackled in the ways in which the associations had confidence. One respondent said, 'I don't know any good ones'; another spoke of 'pockets of excellence' in an authority which was otherwise designated 'ineffective and incompetent' in relation to this problem. Another referred to what she saw as 'heavy pressure on professional staff to toe the authority's policy line' which was opposed to any categorisation of learning difficulties, and rejected the notion of dyslexia.

Positive views on learning support teachers were given in four of the ten cases. Two cited 'wonderful' learning support teachers at secondary school, one individual being described as 'very much in the know, teaching other teachers in the school.' A general response of 'excellent, very conscientious' came from a single speaker, the remaining positive view being the more guarded 'willing.' The other six answers were not without praise for able individuals and for effort and commitment, but these speakers focused on what they saw as a worrying lack of knowledge and training: 'They are sympathetic but largely ineffective'; 'I am aghast at some who phone having been engaged as learning support teachers with no advice or resources, they are on their knees'. In another region there was poor continuity, and the association knew of a number of learning support teachers on temporary appointments having been moved arbitrarily to accommodate staffing needs.

Mainstream teachers, one respondent commented, 'may be wonderful and observe the child accurately', but the balance of views was much harsher, to the extent of including the terms, 'diabolical' and 'pathetic'. Two informants suggested that mainstream teachers interpreted a parent's enquiry, or even a child's persistent failure to learn to read, as a slight on their professional competence. In such circumstances, the teachers tended to respond with hostility. Lack of knowledge and training in recognising specific learning difficulties was mentioned by the majority of respondents. Two were particularly critical of the secondary schools in not alerting subject teachers to learning problems identified by the primary school, so that

> they just put a red line through [a piece of written work that they can't read], and 'sp', and at the end 'this is dreadful work, see me.' This is criminal, frankly.

One positive experience was that of a girl who had been assessed privately whose teacher not only read the assessment report but was prepared to read books on specific learning difficulties provided by the parent, and said that she was able to use the experience in later years when she encountered other dyslexic pupils. This prompted the observation: 'It takes a very good teacher to be prepared to accept help from outside.'

Satisfaction with provision

No dyslexia association respondent felt that current provision for children with specific learning difficulties was satisfactorily effective, although there were good aspects in various places. One region's special units were highly praised and some secondary learning support services, run on a 'drop in' basis, were seen as good. One respondent praised the co-operative learning support in class, but regretted the lack of one to one teaching to overcome particular problems. In general, the amount of learning support provision was felt to be inadequate: 'one learning support teacher to four hundred pupils'; 'peripatetic learning support is of little use'; 'learning support is allocated but dwindles away by the end of term'. Furthermore, the associations tended to regard the approach to learning support since Warnock as antipathetic to their views:

a lot of learning support went off the rails when it was put into the mainstream.

Voluntary bodies' members were reported to believe that withdrawal teaching for learning difficulties is now officially discouraged; the respondent who was prepared to praise co-operative learning support was atypical. A number of educational psychologists in the earlier part of the research had described children with specific learning difficulties as 'children who have not responded to normal learning support teaching'; it is not altogether surprising, therefore, that some parents of these children and the organisations which look to their interests were inclined to reject the learning support as unhelpful.

When local authority provision was contrasted with the help provided through the dyslexia associations, some mentioned particular methods and materials. In general, however, the perceived superiority of the tuition arranged through the dyslexia association was described in terms of one to one teaching, a structured programme pitched to the level and pace of the individual, and a positive attitude, accepting the child's learning problem as unrelated to intelligence, effort or behaviour.

Recommendations for improving local authority provision were numerous, the most favoured being in the areas of training, and early identification of specific learning difficulties. Five speakers put the highest priority on initial teacher training so that every teacher would be aware of specific learning difficulties and the best approaches of resolving or managing them. Additional training and induction programmes for learning support teachers were also suggested. A focus on the early primary years was seen as important, both for identifying incipient learning difficulties and preventing the behaviour problems that arose when specific learning difficulties went unrecognised. Two respondents suggested that the dyslexia association's preferred multi-sensory teaching would be generally beneficial to all children at the P1-P2 stage. Changes in learning support policy were suggested by others to provide facilities for withdrawal, one to one teaching, more specialised reading units and the continuation of learning support beyond S2.

The Record of Needs system was well known to the associations, and the respondents regarded it as useful; but it was considered to be a last resort, and should not be a requirement for obtaining appropriate provision for a child with specific learning difficulties. Parents needed to be informed about it, however,

129

and of their rights in relation to it if the procedure was started. One association had found parents who were anxious that 'having a Record' had a derogatory sound. In another place, parents felt it would be beneficial, and were keen to ask for one to be opened. However, the association speaker here held that a Record should be a mechanism to deal with an exceptional case; provision for specific learning difficulties within a district should already be in place, ready to be used as occasion arose:

> Since the incidence of this problem is relatively high, it should be possible to provide adequate support for the expected number of children.

Links with the education authorities generally consisted of occasional meetings, mainly with the psychological service; just one association described as a 'positive long term relationship'. The majority of the voluntary organisations, however, felt that they were not welcomed by the education authorities, who were reported as perceiving 'no need for the dyslexia association', which made 'unrealistic demands'. Among the areas where better relationships existed, one authority had given the association the use of premises and a computer, and in another, computers had been given by the association to some schools where there were pupils with specific learning difficulties. Speakers for meetings had been provided in a similar two-way exchange. One association reported a successful meeting with elected Council members as well as with regional officials. With their aim of raising awareness of specific learning dificulties, the associations tended to welcome stronger links with the education authorities; but at the same time they wished to maintain their independence and 'not get over-committed with the bureaucracy'.

When asked to nominate the developments they would most like to see in relation to meeting the needs of children with specific learning difficulties, the dyslexia association representatives proposed:

•   early identification, possibly by means of a screening programme

•   tackling specific learning difficulties by means of individual or small group teaching in units or by withdrawal from class, rather than in mainstream classes only

•   improvements in teacher training so that all teachers knew much more about learning difficulties in general and this area of difficulty in particular

130

- increased public awareness and a change in attitudes towards people with specific learning difficulties.

Employers and youth organisers were among those for whom a better awareness was seen as likely to benefit the young people affected. Several respondents finished by expressing the hope that at least as far as organising teaching and assessment was concerned, the voluntary organisations eventually would be 'done out of a job': 'the public sector should meet all the needs for the education of children'. That is a sentiment with which few would disagree. Achieving it within the resources of eduction authorities is, however, quite another matter as we saw in chapters 2 and 5.

We now turn to the ways in which others, parents and education professionals, view the voluntary organisations.

Parents' contact with voluntary organisations

In the survey reported in chapter 6, one group of questions asked parents about their links with voluntary organisations. In addition to those we had contacted directly through the voluntary organisations, 28 (41%) of those contacted through the local authority psychological services had also been in touch with voluntary organisations.

The dyslexia associations and the Dyslexia Institute were by far the most commonly named voluntary organisations. One parent mentioned having contacted Aphasia, an organisation aiming to assist children with language problems. There was an association between contact with a voluntary organisation and class of family, with middle class parents more likely to report such contact. However, over half of the working class families in the survey had been in touch with one of the organisations. All but one of the 22 parents whose children were at a fee paying school reported contacts, while nearly a third of the parents of children at state schools had taken no such action.

With regard to the type of support offered by the voluntary organisations, two thirds of the parents in our sample said that they had received general advice on coping; this was seen as the way in which the associators had helped them the most (Table 7.1). Parents contacted through the voluntary organisations were more likely than those contacted through the psychological services to name advice on teaching methods, contact with other parents and help with finding a tutor. The two last named items were also regarded as useful, especially by the voluntary organisation sample.

Table 7.1 Types of support provided by voluntary organisations which parents found useful (Result of chi-square test)

	Assessment of learning difficulties	Advice on teaching methods	Contact with other parents	Help with finding private tutor	General advice on coping	Other
Voluntary organisation	47 (56.6)	40 (48.2)	45 (54.2)	45 (54.2)	58 (69.9)	12 (14.5)
Psychological service	9 (36.0)	7 (28.0)	5 (20.0)	1 (4.0)	16 (66.7)	5 (20.0)
Total	56 (51.9)	47 (43.5)	50 (46.3)	46 (42.6)	74 (69.2)	17 (15.7)
	n.s.	n.s.	p < .01	p < .001	n.s.	n.s.

N = 108

Categories are not mutually exclusive

Most parents were satisfied with support offered by the voluntary organisation, although those contacted through the psychological service were less likely to be satisfield and more likely to be unsure. There was an association between class of family and level of satisfaction, with working class parents more likely to be dissatisfied. Again these findings can to some extent be explained by our system of sampling parents.

An open-ended question gave parents the opportunity to explain the reasons underlying their satisfaction or otherwise with the voluntary organisations. Reasons for dissatisfaction included geographical distance from the organisation, the expense of assessment by psychologists contacted through the voluntary sector and that those working for the associations were well-meaning but amateurish in their approach. More critical views included the following:

> Too expensive and too far to travel.

> The association appeared to be wary of the education authorities and vice versa.

> Run totally by enthusiastic amateurs. No direction, accountability.

Those contacted through the organisations were more likely to mention their appreciation of the support for parents which they offered. The following provide a flavour of the positive opinions expressed:

> Been involved with the local branch of the voluntary association since its inception. Delighted with the apparent softening of the attitude of the Education Department. Work remains to be done.

> After years of being told there was nothing wrong with my son but knowing myself that there was, the association gave me the strength to go on and fight for my son's rights within school as well as being very supportive.

> The response was fast, and regular newsletters are most informative. Provision of a tutor at low cost has seen a big improvement in writing.

> The association was very helpful as regards the assessment and very encouraging to my son when they explained to him that he was not stupid, he just had a problem, which cheered him up as at

that time he felt he was too stupid to live. This was a very distressing time for him.

Views of voluntary organisations from within the education system

In the survey of regional officers, psychologists and special needs advisers (see chapter 2) those interviewed were asked about their views of the role played by voluntary organisations in relation to specific learning difficulties. Some officers expressed positive responses to the publicity surrounding the activities of the dyslexia associations and felt that raising the profile of these children had highlighted their difficulties and helped get special provision. In about half of the regions there were some links with the local dyslexia association, the principal educational psychologist or education officer occasionally attending meetings to give a talk.

The bulk of the views, however, were negative. Parents were described as taking their child to a dyslexia association or the Dyslexia Institute when they were not satisfied with local authority provision. The problems arose from the paid assessments carried out by independent psychologists and the recommendations that ensued. The assessments were criticised as 'old-fashioned', 'deficit-focused' and ignoring contextual and emotional factors:

> We believe [in terms of theory] that the dyslexia association are peddling an outmoded concept of learning difficulties ... The psychometric model is wrong. The assessment techniques are wrong - we abandoned that approach years ago. (Psychologist)

Some interviewees claimed that 'false positive' identification was common:

> Any child that goes to the [a voluntary body] for assessment is automatically diagnosed as dyslexic. This is not right in our experience. The definition [of dyslexia] is so broad as to be meaningless. (Psychologist)

Issue was also taken with the British Dyslexia Association's claim up to that dyslexia is a congenital neurological problem affecting 10% of the population, and disbelief was expressed at the coincidence of this proportion living exclusively in certain middle class areas. It was said that local dyslexia associations were not dealing with the most needy cases, just those who could afford a £100 assessment. On the basis of the report saying their child had 'severe dyslexia' parents would demand special educational resources from the psychological services. In one case it was argued that

> Children whose educational age is six months below their intellectual age are being defined [in private sector reports] as having severe dyslexia. Very often these children should be left alone. (Psychologist)

Much of the concern from the point of view of the authority in this particular region appeared to be that the recommendations made by the Dyslexia Institute or dyslexia associations would result in a selected group of people (the most articulate) requesting Records of Needs for children who were not those with most prominent needs, thus deflecting resources away from others with greater difficulties. The demands of 'sectional interest' sat ill with regional policies which were opposed to identifying categories of children. For this reason a minority of authorities found it difficult to have any meaningful dialogue with the voluntary organisations. In one of the larger regions there was an explicit policy *not* to recognise 'dyslexia' as a separate entity and liaison with the dyslexia association was reported to be actively discouraged. This situation was regretted by several individuals:

> Voluntary organisations come about because the system is not providing for children, either in terms of not recognising their needs or providing adequate input. I might not agree with how they go about things but there is a degree of expertise there which we should listen to. We ought to open the door to them and should enter into some discussion with them. We can't just dismiss them out of hand saying we don't agree with their views. We have to talk to them. (Adviser)

One of the consequences of lack of communication causing problems was that an area learning support teacher might arrive at school to see a child with specific learning difficulties and find him or her away for tuition at the Dyslexia Institute. Even in regions where the lines of communication were more open, some regional authority interviewees felt that there was a fundamental difference in viewpoint which could not be bridged. This difference centred round the perceived emphasis of the dyslexia association on the deficit within the child rather than the whole environment of the child and the curriculum:

> They don't really understand our arguments about learning support and the curriculum. They're still looking for 'the cure' therefore

they feel we're not giving them what they want. They really want the child to have his own teacher and we can't produce that. (Adviser)

The meetings between parents and education professionals were frequently described as strained or confrontational. This was attributed to parents' 'unrealistic demands' and the 'false expectations' raised by the Dyslexia Institute and dyslexia associations.

Parents can become quite embittered. It's a big shock when their child is not performing well in one area. They get false expectations from the Dyslexia Institute. 95% of the children that go there are positively diagnosed. They make parents feel that there are other things available, that they can do the magic on their children and we can't. There's no evidence that the independent sector makes any better progress than we do, yet they say they can cure the child. (Psychologist)

One local authority interviewee described problems arising from the view that a 'special kind of teacher' is needed:

[The dyslexia organisations] give parents the impression that the only teaching that is worthwhile is by Dyslexia Institute-trained teachers. Parents then try to ask for the Record of Needs to specify teaching by Dyslexia Institute-trained teachers. Their teaching methods are very thorough and children who go for tuition twice a week have improved. But it's wrong to create this mystique that only they know how to teach these children, whereas it seems that all they do is good commonsense old-fashioned teaching. (Psychologist)

The Education Officer, usually the last line of defence when parents were not satisfied with provision, would try to put the authority's position across:

[We are] recognising individual needs on their own merit and responding to them in that way as opposed to recognising a generic term to characterize a range of disorders. (Education Officer)

In this view a single term, be it specific learning difficulties or dyslexia, 'may provide a crutch for parents', but it was seen as doing nothing to help the child. There was some feeling that the educational services needed to counter the publicity given to the dyslexia lobby by putting their own message across more forcibly:

> As a national service the psychological services are still losing the media battle in terms of the dyslexia question. We are still regarded as the people who are not dealing with these children and withholding resources and not understanding them. (Psychologist)

The questionnaire survey of learning support teachers (reported in chapter 5) touched on their contact with voluntary organisations. At this 'grass roots' level less than half (40%) indicated such contact. Among these, there were significantly more teachers who used the term 'dyslexia' than those who did not. Such contacts were also more likely to be reported by more experienced than less experienced teachers, and by secondary rather than primary teachers, as Table 5.7 shows.

Summary

The voluntary organisations' clear preference for the term 'dyslexia' rather than 'specific learning difficulties' reflected their determination that individuals with such problems should be distinguished from those with more global learning difficulties. The variety of difficulties encountered in this area was acknowledged, but difficulties with words were seen as central. About half of those interviewed acknowledged a likely discrepancy between the child's abilities in the problem area and those apparent in other aspects of his or her learning. Estimates of the incidence of such problems in the general population of children varied from between 1% and 4% for those who need special help, to 10% who may experience the difficulties in a mild form.

The role of the organisations was primarily one of parental support. This included general advice on how to cope with the problems of dyslexia, arranging contacts for the private assessment of children, advising on appropriate teaching methods, helping to find a suitable tutor and putting parents in contact with others in similar circumstances. A clear rationale for putting in place a programme of this kind arose from the accounts of anxious, guilt-ridden parents who perceived the public system of education as ignoring their well-founded concerns about their children. Helping such parents to become better informed about their rights and the alternative courses of action open to them was the main interest of the organisations' work.

There was concern that the education system failed to identify a substantial proportion of children with problems and that identification was often too late

137

in the school career. In those circumstances, the direct effects of the difficulties could lead to unnecessary deterioration in learning and to behavioural problems. In particular, delays between initial recognition of difficulties and subsequent referral for formal assessment were criticised. Dissatisfactions with such delays were exacerbated by what was seen as poor communication between local authorities and parents. A strong recommendation was made for local authorities to focus on the identification in the *early* stages of primary schools of those children who might be dyslexic, and to make strenuous efforts to keep parents informed and reduce their anxieties. There was evidence of a consensus that dyslexic children would not respond to ordinary remedial teaching and a clear preference for a one-to-one approach and withdrawal from mainstream classes as necessary. Some specific materials and technological aids (e.g. computers and software) were recommended. Multisensory approaches were also given considerable attention. Evidence for the effectiveness of these measures, however, was impressionistic and based on parents' apparent satisfaction with the outcomes, especially in terms of children's confidence.

Provision in the public sector for problems of dyslexia was seen as patchy. A variety of very positive judgements, particularly about individual psychologists and learning support teachers, was expressed, but there was an awareness of the pressure 'from above' on such staff to implement policies which were opposed to singling out those with dyslexia for special treatment. Even more concern was voiced about teachers' lack of relevant training and how this, on occasions, led them to adopt a defensive and even hostile stance in their dealings with parents. The general run of learning support in mainstream classrooms was seen as both inadequate and inappropriate. Increased withdrawal from class, specialised reading centres and general support beyond S2 were called for.

The opening of Records of Needs for children with specific learning difficulties was not the area of greatest consensus. While the benefits to be gained in special provision were recognised by some, others saw some stigma attached to children involved in such a process. The preferred approach would be one where provision for such children's needs was automatically in place and brought into play as the need arose.

In the survey of parents, in addition to the parents contacted through the voluntary organisations, 41% of the local authority sample had had contact with these organisations. Overall, such contact was more likely among the middle class parents and those with children in independent schools. Satisfaction was expressed by a substantial number for the material and moral support offered by the associations and the incentive they provided to press on and find ways of resolving or managing the problems. It was clear that in many cases they were perceived as having helped to effect improvements in children's performance and self-esteem. Dissatisfactions appeared to arise from the geographical remoteness of the associations from some people, the expense of private assessments and the lack of professional expertise of the organisers (as perceived by several parents).

Statements of dissatisfaction from local authority officers were more strident. Although some had positive comments to make, others expressed adverse criticism of the voluntary organisations on the basis of perceptions of:

- their 'old-fashioned' notions of deficits within children

- high rates of false positive indentification of dyslexia

- the correlation between high rates of dyslexia and middle class areas

- their encouragement of parents who were thought to pursue high levels of scholastic attainment rather than the resolution of their child's difficulty

- the deflection of resources from the broader population of children with special needs

- the disruption caused to peripatetic learning support programmes when individual children are, without warning, taken out of school

- their supposed search for a 'cure' for specific learning difficulties

- unrealistic expectations raised in the minds of parents

- their success in the 'media battle' to discredit the psychological services.

At the level of learning support teachers, there was less awareness of the voluntary associations. Under half of the sample in the survey (see chapter 5) had had contact with the associations.

These findings have presented something of a contrast. Whilst at least some local authority professionals held distinctly unfavourable views of voluntary organisations, this negative stance was not reciprocated by the voluntary organisations. There was no significant embattled hostility to local authority provisions, but rather a keenness to help make the system work effectively and provide appropriate education on the basis of individual needs. As with many pressure groups, office holders of the associations tended to be middle class. They did not conform, however, to the caricature of privileged people wishing to hijack scarce resources for their children at the expense of others more deprived. These interviewed showed appreciation of the resource problems encountered by local authorities as they endeavoured to meet the needs of children with specific learning difficulties as well as fulfil all their other commitments. The allegations that a 'cure' is expected and that the voluntary organisations encourage parents to pursue high scholastic attainment above all, were not borne out in our interview data from the organisations.

The tension in this area can be thought of as arising in two ways. First, there is the matter of inadequate resources to provide for all children with special educational needs. The public demand for high quality services to meet those needs is increasing. The educational legislation of recent years has raised expectations and made parents more aware of those rights. We can expect, therefore, that they will increasingly demand the services they believe they should have, and that some will form more effective pressure groups than others. All this will put the providers of education, who see their resources as static if not dwindling, on the defensive. It is always easier to make a convincing and well-heard case if you are a pressure group with a single area of priority than if you are the agency which has to carry the responsibility for the whole of educational provision.

Secondly, there are tensions which might be thought of as conceptual and ideological in nature. Specific learning difficulties or dyslexia may or may not be conceptualised as a distinctive set of problems which sets apart a discrete group of pupils from the general run of those with learning difficulties. Even if the discrete group model is accepted, however, there is a second question of whether such a group should have a special share of the resources available.

We shall discuss these matters further in chapter 10.

8 Illustrations of provision and practice

The emphasis in this research was on the collection of the views of different groups (regional officers, learning support teachers, teacher educators, student teachers, parents, voluntary organisations and professionals in the health service) about policy, provision and practice in relation to specific learning difficulties. It could be argued, however, that we have reported very little about **practice**. Most practice relevant to the support of pupils with specific learning difficulties is carried out in mainstream settings, and in any given setting such pupils form a tiny minority of the total. Observation of such practice in schools and classrooms to provide representative information would have to be, therefore, both detailed and carried out in a large number of locations. Such a study was beyond the resources of this project.

There were, however, several examples of practice in which substantial numbers of children with such difficulties were offered special provision. These examples provided **convenient** opportunities to look at practice; not only did they involve reasonable numbers of pupils, but also the teachers had concerns which were much more focused on specific learning difficulties than were those of the general run of learning support or mainstream teachers. The provision was, furthermore, **important** in two senses. First, all the examples reflected arrangements which had been carefully thought through, offered specialised support and displayed a commitment to individualised tuition (though not necessarily to withdrawal from mainstream education). Individual provision is, of course, in tension with some philosophical stances of the public sector, though it is preferred by many parents and the voluntary organisations. The second (and related) reason for the importance of the examples of practice was that they reflected the kind of provision which was highly regarded by those parents whose children had received support of that type; for example, although as a proportion of all parental respondents to our survey, the number praising reading centre provision was small, they represented almost **all** those with experience of such centres.

Although the examples we offer here were, we believe, both convenient and important, they were certainly **not** typical. The provision described served only a minority of those pupils regarded as having specific learning difficulties and a lot of it was expensive (perhaps unrealistically so if equality of opportunity across the country were to be envisaged). We would also wish to stress that there is very little hard data on its effectiveness (though softer data like parental satisfaction was often evident).

Of the four examples of provision for children with specific learning difficulties described here, two were reading centres in different local authorities, one was a dyslexia unit within an independent school and the fourth was a paired reading scheme in a secondary school, run by the learning support department. By definition, the first three examples were based on the assumption that specific learning difficulties exist as an identifiable, if not necessarily discrete, area of difficulty for which certain forms of targeted provision are appropriate. The fourth example provided for a continuum of reading difficulties which included some specific learning difficulties. Brief outlines of the four studies are given below, followed by a report of the evidence collected in each case.

Outlines of the four studies

The first study was based on a local authority reading unit catering for around 20 pupils with specific learning difficulties at the P6-P7 stage. All pupils travelled to the centre from their mainstream schools. The sole teacher in charge of the centre used phonic-based methods adapted to individual pupils who attended in groups of four or five. Selection of pupils from a referral list always longer than places available was a recurring problem, although all the potential unit pupils received learning support in school. The principal objective was to enable the pupils to address the secondary curriculum; but the minimal explicit liaison procedures and absence of provision at the secondary stage were seen as weaknesses.

A much larger reading centre with five primary and three secondary teaching staff was the context of the second study. Teaching was provided for primary pupils either at the centre or in their own schools, much of it one to one. Secondary provision was all by peripatetic teaching. Phonic methods based on the Letterland System were the foundation of a varied programme, individually adapted to each child. There was strong involvement by parents. Identification of pupils could be from P1 onwards, with most pupils starting in the middle primary years; a wait of up to two years for admission was, however, not uncommon.

An independent day school with a dyslexia unit as part of learning support provision was the focus of the third study. It was located in the secondary department of the school, with six pupils each year being admitted specifically to the unit. Learning support in the primary department was offered from P1; if primary pupils were identified as dyslexic, the nature of this support was adapted appropriately. We were interested to see if any differences in provision were apparent in a context where the difficulties were conceptualised as 'dyslexia', rather than the more general 'specific learning difficulties'. This did not appear to be the case. There was less stress on phonic teaching than in the reading units, but as the latter dealt largely with primary pupils this was not necessarily an important distinction. The involvement of volunteer pupil help and close daily contact with subject teachers were features of interest.

The final example was provided by a learning support department in a secondary school which set up its own paired reading scheme, to enable pupils in S1 or S2 experiencing severe reading difficulties to be paired with pupil volunteer tutors from S6. The study was based upon the guidelines produced by the department, interviews with the principal teacher of learning support, and a selection of pupil evaluations of the scheme by the S6 tutors.

1.   A 'travel-to' reading unit

The first reading unit was visited and teaching observed for one morning and one afternoon session. The teacher in charge and the area principal psychologist were interviewed.

The work of the unit

This reading unit was one of three run by a city division of an education authority. It was situated in a reasonable residential area, but a wide range of socio-economic conditions existed within the section of the authority which it served, and some of the local primary schools were in poor and disadvantaged catchment areas. The unit was accommodated in a hutted classroom block forming part of the premises of a large, modern well-kept primary school; it occupied one classroom, with a second room, largely unfurnished, available for individual tape recording and the use of a computer trolley.

The unit was staffed by one full-time teacher, who had been in charge of it for several years. She was previously a primary learning support teacher. All the teaching took place at the unit; groups of four to six pupils attended, mostly travelling by bus from their own primary schools. Four out of five groups

143

attended for two half days per week, and the fifth for half a day only. The pattern of work had been organised to minimise the time lost from the school day in travelling; journeys almost all took place before or after school or in the lunch hour. The teacher regarded the necessity of travelling independently as an element of the experience offered by the unit, emphasising trust in the children and in their personal competence. The three reading units in the authority were responsible for their own timetabling, and another teacher might well have preferred more frequent shorter attendance.

The pupils were almost all from P6 and P7 classes. They were identified and selected for the unit in P5 or P6, and all left the unit upon transfer to secondary school. The teacher and the psychologist discussed the stages served by the unit in somewhat different terms. Both agreed that the main objective was to equip pupils who had specific difficulties in reading, writing and spelling so they would be better prepared to cope with the secondary curriculum. The psychologist had inherited the existing system, was clear that it met a genuine need quite effectively but considered that earlier intervention might well enable particular children to achieve more. The teacher felt that the maturity of the child aged ten or eleven was needed to make full use of the special provision of the unit. Both pointed out that the unit was just one aspect of learning support, which all the pupils had been receiving before admission to the unit. The principal teacher of learning support, attached to the area psychological service, played a key role in linking school-based learning support and the work of the Reading Unit.

Identification and selection of pupils

The question of identification of pupils to take up unit places was one of the most difficult parts of the work, as described by both informants. There was always a waiting list, with more names on it than the places available. The names of children in P5 or P6 who were thought likely to benefit from the unit were placed on the list during the course of the year; they were identified by schools in the first instance and referred to the area psychologist or principal learning support teacher. The main criterion as described by the principal psychologist, was that 'they become stuck; they are causing concern to their learning support teacher as they are not making progress. The staff are not looking for specific learning difficulties or dyslexia as such.' The PEP held a meeting in May of each year to discuss which children from the list should be offered the places that would become available as P7 unit pupils left. The P6 unit pupils would automatically retain their places as they moved into P7.

They have had on-going difficulties for some time, so progress is not

144

usually so dramatic that they are able to discontinue on grounds of having made so much progress (Teacher)

With a total of just over twenty places in each reading unit, the number of new placements varied according to the balance of P6-P7 children in a given year.

The two criteria for placement on the waiting list were:

- Lack of progress in school although receiving learning support
- The child's difficulties appear to be specific rather than global

Priorities for selection from the list for admission to the reading unit focused on factors enabling the child to make best use of the help. Three such factors emerged from discussion:

- motivation
- home support
- signs of discrepancy between current attainment and potential ability

In illustrating the requirement for **motivation** the teacher indicated that 'they have to be willing to accept the help and to work'. The psychologist qualified this: 'Motivation is not a given quality, it can be created. There are many examples of children battered by failure who come into the unit and find they can do well'.

Home support was something of a double-edged criterion. Selecting unit pupils on grounds of good home support raised the possibility that certain kinds of homes were favoured. The psychologist hoped that that was not the case but admitted that if the intake were scrutinised it might be. No scrutiny was carried out by this study, but the four boys attending the observed morning group all came from two primary schools in relatively advantaged areas; three were due to move into two secondary schools with fairly high proportions of middle class pupils, and one was going to go to a private school. The teacher suggested that it was generally the case that reading unit pupils came from the better-off parts of the division. She had no ready explanations for this, and ruled out any intention on the part of those carrying out the selection. Among the suggestions advanced tentatively were:

- higher parental expectations
- any discrepancy in abilities might be seen more easily in the context of higher achievement within the class as a whole as well

as the child
* the reading and writing of some unit pupils would be considered acceptable progress in a poorer area
* learning difficulties in poorer areas are more likely to be interpreted as global difficulties.

The third criterion, discrepancy in abilities, for selection of pupils for reading unit places, was seen as an important indicator of specific learning difficulties. However there was no narrow focus on potential high achievers. One of the other reading units had assembled information of tested IQs of its pupils over a five year period; a range of IQ 80+ to IQ 120+ was found. A majority of pupils in the reading unit were boys: seven of the eight pupils attending on the observation visit. The teacher felt sure that this reflected the incidence of specific learning difficulties among boys and girls, and rejected the possibility of any bias in the selection process.

The problems addressed by the reading unit

Both informants stressed the notion of a discrepancy in setting out to define specific learning difficulty: 'a child showing abilities in some way out of keeping with functioning in reading, spelling, writing' (Psychologist); 'seem to be seriously underachieving in relation to their aptitude and ability as it is perceived by the school.' (Teacher). The psychologist went on to say that while there were some 'glaring cases', the type of difficulty shades into others, and in certain circumstances is hard to identify:

> The child who is unstimulated, who comes from a poor background or where the school is not supportive, it is a brave thing to say one has a specific difficulty and another has not.

The teacher pointed out that the less intelligent child can have a specific difficulty, although it might be more difficult to detect and less likely to lead to a reading unit place. The psychologist suggested awareness of the patterns of test profiles could point towards identifying specific learning difficulties.

> However much one struggles with the concept it does exist, I am quite convinced of it.

The term specific learning difficulty was helpful in separating the problem from the child, but did not, in the psychologist's words, solve the dilemma of finding language which is not derogatory. Information is perhaps lost by abandoning categories, but it forces you to think in a different way about the child's difficulty.

Both used the term 'dyslexia' on occasion, but reserved it for the 'glaring cases'; the teacher considered that it was only appropriate for a sub-group of all the children with specific learning difficulties. She mentioned just one of the four pupils in the observed morning group as possibly dyslexic, but could not be certain, as it happened that the pupil was from a bilingual family background and English was not his mother tongue.

The problems experienced by the reading unit pupils included reading, writing and spelling, with certain pupils being selected for help in a group focused on spelling only. Difficulties with mathematics and number work varied; in some cases it was not a factor, in others there were problems with mathematics going beyond those arising from difficulty with reading the text of mathematics tasks. Some behavioural difficulties were quite common, particularly in the context of the mainstream school rather than that of the unit. Children sometimes became disruptive and aggressive, or alternatively withdrawn. There had been occasional instances of children being removed from the unit because of behavioural problems; in these cases, the impetus had come from the mainstream school or the parents. The psychologist mentioned an example of a boy who was very able and needed help, but felt so embarrassed and miserable at being in the unit that staff were unable to overcome his reluctance.

Provision made by the unit

The reading unit was described as tackling specific difficulties in literacy skills by means of phonic-based methods used in a fairly traditional style but adapted to individual children. This was consistent with the teaching observed. The raising of self-esteem and motivation and the development of study skills were secondary objectives; it was felt that these could be best achieved as a side effect of the improvements in literacy skills rather than by any direct means.

The first observed group of four P7 boys began with a ten minute check of individually dictated spelling words, from lists compiled by the teacher during the pupils' last session of work and from Blackwell's Spelling Workshop. As the answers were marked, the teacher focused the discussion principally upon sounds and letter combinations, e.g. aunt/ant, trepass/trespass. A few discussion points were about meaning, e.g. port/starboard, and some tips were given such as '"every" is just "very" with "e" in front'.

Thirty minutes of individual work followed; the boys continued with tasks started on an earlier occasion and the teacher had short individual discussions with each as they settled down. Subsequently she moved among them observing and supporting. When reflecting on her methods, she said:

> Every reading unit teacher has her personal style; [what I did this morning] is typical for me. I like to give them success whenever possible. I try to get them to think it out, and always give praise for any success and point out anything they can do which they could not do before. J. has made a lot of progress; he is still very slow but he works out most of the words given time. You have to be patient; it does much more for his self-esteem to work it out than to be constantly given a word. He knows if he makes a mistake, because he can see it doesn't make sense ... Many of them have problems with short term memory so you have to do things over and over again, 'overlearning' ... You have got to reinforce the process in as many varied ways as you can think of.

The first part of the morning was completed with a group task on listening comprehension and writing. The boys took notes as the teacher read out a short factual story about an oil-rig rescue. They produced individual written accounts from their notes by the end of the morning in addition to undertaking a new individual task chosen (within guidelines) from among:

- a taped story

- helpspell minicomputer exercise/ phonic crossword

- written work on a previously-heard taped story

- a word exercise, chosen by the teacher as the pupil had spent some time reading a youth newspaper but had not chosen a 'work' task.

The pupils' work for the morning was entered on personal checklists, and the teacher discussed with them the extent to which they had achieved personal targets. Cartoon-style achievement stickers were attached to their checklists when they had achieved certain negotiated rates of task completion. Some pupils preferred to set themselves a high target to aim for; others felt safer if they knew they could reach the target every day, or see by how much they could beat it. The targets were for numbers of tasks, and did not depend on obtaining 'marks' for work done. Discussing her approach to the correction of errors, the teacher said:

> If they have written something and the object was not to improve spelling

I certainly don't go over every spelling mistake, but I pick on one they might remember. I sometimes correct written work that they have done on the computer and give them a print-out, so that they have the original and the corrected version. I try to change it as little as possible in structure so that it is their story, unless the structure just does not make sense.

As well as the target incentives for the pupils, the daily checklist enabled the teacher to ensure a balance of tasks and complete coverage of planned programmes.

The second observed group of three boys and one girl worked along similar lines. One individual task was a map exercise, following instructions using compass points. The boy had some problems finding N,S,E, and W on the map, although apparently able to read the instruction sheet. The last part of the afternoon was spent as a group playing a card game of phonic rummy with the teacher. The pupils, who had been working diligently, were all keen to play and did so with signs of enjoyment.

Progress of pupils in the reading unit

The reading unit teacher took measures of pupils' reading level, comprehension and spelling attainment upon admission and at the end of each school year. (The psychologist used British Ability Scales and WISC tests as part of the referral process when the children were placed on the waiting list.)

Standard tests usually bear out what we have discovered ... progress tends to be relatively slow ... You can expect to see progress by half way through the session, but sometimes schools may say they see a difference earlier ... You have to think back to what they were when they first came, because you do not see progress from week to week, and there will be plateaus rather than a regular pattern. (Teacher)

The psychologist summed up the progress made by the children attending the unit as 'fairly good'. In a five-year study in another reading unit almost all the pupils involved were found to have made substantial progress while attending the unit and a few had made spectacular gains. However, five or six over the five years 'had made nothing of it. They all turned out to be very able, with IQs of 120+'. The psychologist could not explain the factors inhibiting the progress of this 'maverick group'.

The progress of the observed reading unit pupils is illustrated by three examples. The first of these children was intelligent, articulate and well motivated but with severe reading difficulties. In two years, his reading age (which on entry was more than four years below his chronological age) had improved by little more than six months, though his comprehension score had improved by a little more than a year. He had reached a point, however, where he began to communicate his ideas in vivid and varied vocabulary.

1a) November 1989, aged 9y 2m

```
     Change

The way I have chaje ov the yis is I gron and I dot sleep

in.  A cot enemore.  A I drnk milk from My mum and I eet

big pees and los mor food.
```

1b) February 1992, agend 11y 5m
Tape recording transcribed by teacher

```
So the arguments went on for years and years.  They never

tired of it.  The woodsman came along with some wood to put

on the fire, so they put their problem to him.  He was as

baffled as they were
```

1c) February 1992

Uncle an aunt citshun was fool of food I thort. Mums cltshun was emty. I slept in the bedroom nest to the ottic I am a havy sleeper. I was spris to hire a dor clos foot steps and low wispre. In the morning I told Dan. we trid the attic door it was lokt. The old gardner was

150

The second example was a child with epilepsy and emotional and behavioural difficulties. Over a period of eight months his reading age (which on entry was just over three years behind his chronological age) had improved by six months, reading comprehension by a little over a year and spelling by six months. His progress was certainly not striking but comparisons of stories written at an interval of ten months showed an increase in length and fluency.

2a) February 1991, aged 10y 2m

2b) December 1991, aged 11y

Finally, the third example was a younger child, with a weak short-term memory and formerly a poor attitude to work, who within six months had provided evidence of dramatic progress in writing. (Example 3a, b and c)

3a) September 1991, aged 8y 7m

<u>a tree</u>

12.9.91

my frencl cam to play and I went
to gat a coner and the bransh
and I was I hotol to dary 3. noot
and 3 fillms.

3b) February 1992

```
mountain and sulda it staert to rain for six holl day and

nits and then a lightning bolt cracs the ice the uglais

moster the moster sed I am gaing to eay yoo and Trog grass

a stig?
```

3c) February 1992

at two o'clock thea hard six mor bag har
reads he is on black delt in care jumps dune
kis theom and gets the pleam and paul gets
rewd of six hundred pound. and her get
a <u>TV</u>.

While each example had, no doubt, some heartening aspects, it is clear that the progress being made by these children was such that they were generally falling further behind their contemporaries. They are victims, perhaps, of our society's obsession (not shared by all cultures in the world) that all children of the same chronological age must be at the same stage in school.

Transfer to secondary school

The psychologist expressed some doubt about the extent to which children's improvement was maintained after they left the unit and started secondary school.

> So much depends on whether and how they continue to be supported in secondary. I don't think there is sufficient learning support in secondary; it is quite patchy, very good in places but with some big schools having only 1.5 learning support teachers. The nature of the support changes; it is a much more complex exercise to cover the whole curriculum.

The psychological service attempted to alert the secondary schools to the needs of the reading unit children, with written reports to the receiving schools following a meeting about the unit leavers between the principal learning support teacher, psychologists and reading unit teachers. The reading unit teacher attended liaison meetings with secondary learning support and sometimes guidance teachers, and might also visit the secondary schools discuss the progress of pupils now in S1; but such visits encroached on the teaching time for the new session's unit pupils. The visiting reading unit teacher has no authority over the secondary school or its learning support department, and the visits were sometimes replaced by telephone calls, or omitted altogether. The psychologist acknowledged that he lacked data on follow-up procedures or subsequent progress of pupils.

> There is a handing over process, but there may be a washout effect by S3 ... Liaison with the secondary school is probably our weakest point. (Psychologist)

The teacher considered that entry to secondary school was probably the right time to discontinue provision, as it would be difficult to arrange unit provision without leaving gaps in the timetabled curriculum. Children might be less willing to attend a unit from secondary school; and she too mentioned 'manpower problems' affecting the varied level of learning support in different secondary schools. However, a number of former unit pupils 'cope better than adequately without any learning support in secondary school. Some have gone on from strength to strength'.

Relationships with parents and other outside bodies

There was a discussion with parents when pupils started at the reading unit.

> Quite often the parents have been aware of the child's problems since very early in the child's school career ... They often say they know he's not stupid but he's certainly got problems. They are very happy for anything extra that is going to help the children. (Teacher)

Parents were encouraged to make contact at any time; quite a lot of them telephoned from time to time, and if there was any problem regular contact was invaluable. A parents' evening was held in June and most attended. They were said to be keen to support the unit, so that keeping them abreast of what was happening was not an onerous task.

Relations with other professionals were seen as presenting few problems. The primary schools provided background information when a child's placement was arranged, and the reading unit teacher maintained regular contact at least once a term. The three reading unit teachers undertook staff development together, arranging it amongst themselves. The learning support adviser was always in the background, and contact with the psychologists, although not frequent, was a two-way process. Sometimes reading unit teachers were asked to take part in in-service days for other staff. Not many unit children were involved with speech therapy or other specialist provision; liaison with such services would be with the child's school rather than the unit.

Voluntary bodies, in particular the Scottish Dyslexia Association, were not seen as having a role in the work of the unit. The school would provide copies of any report about a child's contacts with the voluntary organisation. Occasionally children attending the reading unit had gone to the local branch dyslexia association for additional help; the teacher regarded this positively if the child accepted it happily, but felt that a further source of teaching could become a burden. She received information about the association's conferences and meetings, and attended from time to time.

Recommendations for provision for children with specific learning difficulties

Both informants favoured the reading unit provision backed by general learning support in schools. The existence of the waiting list suggested a need for more such places; the psychologist felt that one more unit might make the difference and avoid 'the agony of the selection process and having to justify the selections to parents'.

If a child has difficulties that are serious enough for him to be put on a reference list as not being helped adequately by learning support, there should be something for him.

Even if resources for an additional unit were available, the decision to take that way forward would not be clearcut. It is possible that a further unit would simply fill up the following day, returning to the old system of taking all the learning problems out of schools. That was not wanted by either of those interviewed. They explored the possibility of more input into schools so that expertise and knowledge of learning difficulties could reach 'outwards and downwards' to the mainstream teacher as well as learning support staff.

2.   A reading centre: 'travel to' and outreach

Another local authority reading centre was visited for two school days. This centre gave tuition both on its own premises to children travelling from their primary schools by taxi, and in primary and secondary schools by visiting staff from the reading centre. Examples of the teaching provision were observed both at the centre and in schools; informal discussions with individual teachers and psychologists attached to the centre were held, and a special staff meeting was convened at which the researcher put the interview questions to the staff as a whole for collective discussion.

The work of the centre

The centre was located in a purpose built psychological service centre in an urban area. It occupied a large room crammed with every kind of colourful teaching material, both published and home made, and a variety of equipment including BBC and Macintosh computers. A photographic display of children, dressing up materials, children's art work and collages give a bright and comfortable impression. Another small room was shared between the reading centre and speech therapists. The centre was staffed by five primary and three secondary teachers, all qualified and experienced learning support teachers who had specialised in teaching children with specific learning difficulties. Two teachers held the qualification of the British Dyslexia Association. Another small reading centre had been established in the same division of the local education authority, with 1.5 teaching staff.

The centre specialised in provision for children with specific learning difficulties, identified as showing a marked discrepancy between tested reading level and tests of general ability. Although, in principle, specific learning difficulty as defined by the centre could occur at any level of general ability, the centre catered for those in a broad band of average or above average attainments, and did not take children below an IQ of 82.

A primary school was visited with a reading centre teacher, and individual teaching observed with three pupils: A and B in P6 and C in P4. In the afternoon, four further primary pupils attended the centre in two paired groups: first D, P6 and E in P5; secondly F and G. All were boys except pupil E. This was the usual pattern; the overall balance of the centre's pupils was 10:1 in favour of boys. On the second day two different secondary schools were visited with another reading centre teacher; individual teaching sessions were observed with H and J, both in S1. When the centre began, all pupils travelled to it from their own schools. By the time of the research, that was true of less than a third of the primary pupils; travel was by taxi at the region's expense. All the secondary teaching took place in the pupils' schools.

Identification took place initially in the child's own school, with referral to the psychological service for further assessment; this might result in the child being placed on the reading centre waiting list. Although time on the waiting list was commonly 18 months to two years, the learning support and class teachers were often able to start some help for the child right away, with advice from the psychologist who carried out the assessment, and a review by the new area learning support teacher at least once a term.

The earliest identifications of the most severe cases took place in P1 or P2; in such a case, a Record of Needs might be in place by P3. P3 was a common stage for identification, although a substantial number were picked up later, including some at the secondary stage. Children moving schools could be overlooked and the centre staff considered that there were still some missed by class teachers. 'They look upon it as a slight upon themselves to have to refer to an outside agency' (Teacher). Patterns of referral varied sharply between schools and some schools never referred any children. Where a school already had been through the procedure of opening a Record of Needs for a child they were more likely to start proceedings for another.

Criteria for reading centre placement were said to be arbitrary, decided by individual areas but limited by available resources. A gap of around 2 years between the reading age and chronological age when a child is ten years old and within the average ability range was one basis for the decision; although the problem had been increasingly recognised as occurring across the whole ability range, the focus was still on the identification of a **discrepancy**. If such identification was delayed until secondary school, the gap had widened.

The teachers and two psychologists at the staff meeting debated the nature of specific learning difficulty and the terminology in use with vigour. While there were no instances of outright rejection of each others' perceptions, the search for precise concepts and descriptions was very open and indicated varied shades of meaning between individuals. 'Specific learning difficulty' was the generally preferred term; it was considered to be an umbrella under which both 'dyslexic' and certain other specific difficulties could be found. At least one teacher rejected the abbreviation SLD, as too easily confused with 'severe learning difficulty'; even the apparently innocuous 'learning difficulty' has its dangers since the abandonment of 'mental handicap', from which parents in particular wish to dissociate those of their children with specific learning difficulties. All the staff agreed that stigmata of this kind were keenly felt, and although this might apply with more force in middle class districts, it was also felt in the poorer urban areas.

There was a feeling that 'specific learning difficulties' was unfamiliar terrain for most people, even teachers and especially secondary subject teachers: 'staff tend to home in on the learning difficulties and equate that with not very bright'. 'Dyslexia' was seen as having a much more positive image in schools, especially secondary, and appeared to be preferred by almost all parents.

> Our parents see themselves as the dyslexia support group; 'reading centre support group' was suggested but they wouldn't entertain it.

The centre staff themselves were likely to use the term 'dyslexia' at least on occasions and one teacher preferred it. It had the advantage of being a clearly recognisable term, avoiding the vagueness of specific learning difficulty:

> I have heard a teacher tell a parent that their child had a specific learning difficulty when they meant that the child was having difficulty with subtraction that week.

The group were asked what difficulties were under the 'wider umbrella' of specific learning difficulty; mathematics difficulty was the main area identified. When one member suggested that specific difficulty in mathematics applied to a very small group, strong dissent was expressed. 'People thought that dyslexia was a small group'; 'maths difficulties should be addressed in early primary, the same as language'. The fact that many primary teachers were 'uncomfortable' with mathematics made it more likely that early difficulties would be missed. The topic was regarded as having lagged behind language because the social stigma was less, but 'avoidance of it won't be an option for much longer' (Psychologist).

The relationship between specific and global difficulties was also discussed. While it was accepted that specific difficulties occurred right across the spectrum, there was seen to be an overlap:

> You reach a point as you go down the intelligence scale where general difficulties come in as well. For prognosis, the fact that the child is generally slow becomes of more importance than any dyslexic difficulties they may have. (Psychologist)

Provision: methods and materials

The work of the reading centre was built around the Letterland system of phonic-based materials. This was described as a very structured, cumulative multi-sensory programme; in these respects it was similar to the Hickey programme favoured by the Dyslexia Institute, but the reading centre teachers described Hickey as more abstract, less suitable for young children. However, Hickey and many other materials were also in use; the centre was well resourced, the staff looked at materials as they were published and a wide variety of useful items were selected to build up individual programmes for each child: 'no one scheme is the answer'. Spelling problems in particular required individual adaptation of published schemes of work.

Emphasis at the primary stage was on strategies to enable children to link sounds and symbols in decoding and encoding. It was designed to complement the programmes followed in the schools where the children were receiving their education, and was said to be based on a shared understanding of the philosophical underpinning from the literature (eg Bryant and Bradley). The description was borne out by the teaching sessions observed. The children's folders were divided into sections for reading; phonics; word attack and spelling. A typical pattern involved the child in reading aloud pages prepared at home; new pages of the reading book were then tackled by paired reading with the teacher; and a set of words focusing on a particular phonic pattern were worked upon, possibly with reference to the Letterland cartoon stories and memory devices. Word attack consisted of another prepared set of words with a particular pattern of syllabification: one child might tackle 'e' prefixes, and another have words with two middle consonants (for example, 'blanket'). Spelling was generally approached by means of 'look, cover, write, repeat'.

The teachers were asked about the balance of phonic and semantic emphasis.

> the more intelligent the child the more attention you give to meaning;

158

there is no point in getting them just to articulate a word; it might as well be nonsense syllables.

However,

most reading centre children have reasonable listening comprehension and understanding of language; the emphasis at the primary stage is on the decoding side. If he could read it he wouldn't have any difficulty; that is why the emphasis is on the structural side.

The balance shifted towards the semantic in the secondary school, where the child was 'faced with the printed word day in, day out. The end goal here is to make sense of the text' in order to make sense of the curriculum. The conscious teaching of alternative coping strategies was also a feature of the reading centre work with secondary pupils:

One of the objectives in secondary is to raise the awareness of subject teachers, an ongoing battle in some schools. We get learning support staff to make subject teachers aware that the reading centre children must have specified forms of assessment where it is necessary; most need unit tests read to them. They dictate answers on to tape or a teacher scribes, which is highly staff intensive. We can provide the material ready on tape, so that the pupils can do the test at the same time as the class. Often the test requires selecting an answer to tick; our pupils can do it provided the questions are read. Staff do try; it varies from school to school, according to the credibility of learning support in the school, as well as that of the reading centre.

Where alternative assessments could be built in to the pupils' school work they were able to experience success and were considered by the reading centre staff to have become more motivated to make an effort.

At the time of the research, an experiment was being undertaken in which two boys had been given the use of lap-top computers at home, initially for a three week trial to see if they would find it helpful. (Later information was that this provision was expanded and was extremely popular, with demand always outstripping supply). It was planned to include the requirement for provision of a lap-top computer in the Records of Needs of appropriate cases. Interest was expressed in the PAL software developed at Dundee University; this went beyond spelling checks and generated words from the first few letters typed in by the user. As word recognition is much easier than spelling, the child had a chance to select a suitable word from those the programme suggested.

The variation in children's problems and progress was exemplified by the teachers' descriptions and observed responses during teaching of some of the pupils A - J who were seen during the visit:

A: Almost dysgraphic at the start, he had great struggles to hold a pencil. By P6 in his third year of reading centre support, he had made great strides; the teacher described him as motivated and keen.

B: From pre-school to P3 he attended the divisional language unit part-time, receiving speech therapy for articulation and meaning. By the time of this research study, his spoken language had been sorted out. He began the reading centre programme with pupil A, but had not made such rapid progress and so was being taught individually. He often felt tired and needed pushing, but on the day of the researchers' visit apparently made an extra effort.

C: He had been seen for eighteen months, since the beginning of P3. The youngest of his family, he had a heart problem at birth. For a time the home support for his reading centre work was interrupted, and behaviour problems developed in class. His progress stopped, but a letter home had produced improvement. When reading aloud to the teacher his posture, half standing against the edge of his chair, suggested tension, but when he discussed the story he relaxed and chattered fluently.

F: As well as difficulties in sequencing, this P5 pupil had some hearing impairment, and was said to show considerable frustration; he could not concentrate or sit still. His general knowledge was considerable; reading centre staff were trying to build up his study skills. He and his partner wrote words containing 'ow' as they were spoken by the teacher; he commented that an owl is 'a bird that's nocturnal, it comes out at night and looks for its prey'. The other pupil was unable to give the meaning of 'a bird of prey'; F continued, 'His prey is his food, mice . . . and there are other ones, barn owl'.

H: This S1 pupil was a very conscientious boy with severe dyslexia and language difficulty of an aphasic type. He was receiving one hour per week peripatetic reading centre teaching, and had three full years in the reading centre twice a week from P5 to P7.

Strong parental support for the centre gave rise to some worry that possibly unrealistic ambitions for higher education might place too much pressure on H.

J: This mature intelligent boy in S1 had difficulties with processing and retrieval of words which were masked by his own coping strategies. He was only identified as in need of help in P7. His discussion of character and motivation in his reading book was well up to the level expected for his age group, and he was able to prepare questions on the story by means of silent reading; but his reading aloud was given with evident strain and errors.

Relationships with schools, parents and voluntary organisations

The centre aimed to maintain close relationships with **schools**. The pupils' progress was regarded as a team effort in which the reading centre teacher, the child's own school and the psychologists played their parts:

> The strength of the reading centre methods and materials is that they are related directly to school work. It is a flexible programme, based on the needs of the individual. Each child has a homework package which is a variation of the reading or spelling pack of the primary class teacher or learning support teacher; they consolidate the work we are doing. (Teacher)

One instance was described where the primary head teacher had taken an interest in reading centre methods and materials, and decided that they could be of general benefit, while their use by the mainstream teacher would enhance the integration of the child with specific difficulties.

> They have been using some reading centre Letterland sheets in the classroom. At the head teacher's wish, I am planning to do a whole class lesson in the class including the reading centre pupil. They are starting to do our writing and spelling. The little girl gets the same work as the others, and others in the class will benefit. The plan is to go right through P4 to P7; it will be interesting to see how it will turn out. (Teacher)

Such close collaboration was difficult to achieve in the secondary school, where the children had subject homework and the reading centre demands could not be too onerous. Although the relations between the reading centre's peripatetic secondary teachers and the learning support staff in schools were described as good, teachers pointed out that in the secondary school there was nobody who could spend ten minutes a day on a regular basis reinforcing the reading centre work. 'We are very much aware that we are the only ones to take these children on their own for this very intensive programme'. Contact between the reading centre and subject teachers was usually indirect, by means of the learning support department.

Building closer relationships between the centre and schools had been enhanced by divisional initiatives on staff development; each school had had the opportunity to send a member of staff for a session at the centre. All the centre teachers and psychologists gave talks in schools and for planned activity time sessions quite frequently, at schools' request. The centre staff were often invited to address school parents' evenings, and had given in-service training sessions to psychologists. One member was a visiting speaker on a college DipSEN course, and teachers taking the Diploma, as well as other individual teachers, often requested to see the centre's work and talk to staff. Other visitors had included senior officers from the region and elsewhere.

In spite of the admirable aims and practice of promoting close working relationships with schools and teachers, the outcomes were not uniformly good. The existence of schools which never referred any pupils, in spite of all the efforts at raising awareness that were made, was regretted. Not all the schools where the reading centre teachers worked were equally welcoming: in places

> the reading centre teacher is perceived more as a threat than a help (Teacher);

> sometimes teachers misunderstand; they say, 'why help X? I have ten worse', and feel the child is being rewarded for bad behaviour. (Psychologist)

The new role of area learning support teacher was apparently a problem in places:

> We used to be consulted over materials and tests, together with the psychologist. Now area learning support have taken that role leaving the reading centre teacher with very little credibility; you are just another nuisance to come in and give them more work. (Teacher)

Cries of 'no, no,' greeted this opinion, however, and the advantages of the area learning support teacher in taking a burden from psychologists was mentioned. As it became established with schools, area learning support and

162

reading centre support were complementary. One teacher explained the flawed relations with some schools by the increasing demands placed on schools and teachers from many quarters: 'It is not just us; teachers are scunnered'.

The reading centre also aimed to involve **parents** actively with their child's programme of work. Individual discussions were held when the child was admitted and there was an annual parents' evening at the centre, as well as a general invitation to make contact whenever parents desired to do so. Parents were encouraged to join the support group. This was run by parents themselves to their own agenda: fund raising, mutual support, discussion and social activities and talks by the teachers, psychologists and occasional outside speakers were the main elements in their programme. Staff suggested that the 'Dyslexia Support Group', the parents' preferred name for the group, did not always follow the course most convenient for the staff; in particular, they were inclined to encourage each other to resist recommendations that a child's reading centre work be discontinued, perhaps at the end of S2. With such a long waiting list, parents might suspect tension between the centre's commitment to the individual child's programme and the planning of a vacancy for the coming year; they were less likely than the reading centre staff to accept that in-school learning support was the answer. The centre tried to steer a course between an inadequate individual programme and on the other hand over-dependency on the part of the child. One example of parents resisting the advice of the centre had been over Records of Needs. Most of the centre's pupils were recorded, especially in the secondary schools; the only secondary pupils without Records were three whose parents were unwilling to proceed with them. A ten- page booklet of information and advice was issued to all parents, describing the centre's work, outlining homework policy and the ways in which parents were asked to help the child, describing a technique of paired reading for use at home, and offering suggestions for boosting the child's self esteem. Teachers found that pupils at the secondary stage were less willing to work on homework together with their parents; there was a balance to be struck between allowing them to increase in independence and maintaining effective coverage of homework.

One parent's view of the work of this reading centre was given to the research by means of a covering letter sent with the questionnaire form reported in chapter 6:

> My son is severely dyslexic and I feel he has not been offered adequate help for his difficulties. . . . I have to say that I am happy with the quality of the teaching at the reading centre and the dedication of the staff. With hindsight, I now wish that I had put my son to a school where he would have had access to a reading centre on a daily basis.

One hour per week is not enough for a child with such severe reading problems. The secondary school he attends is not very sympathetic to his problems and there is a lack of co-ordinated help for him. He has very little chance of achieving pass marks in English and Maths at Standard Grade; at the moment the future looks very bleak for my son.

This parent's account highlighted the problems of providing for children with specific learning difficulties: even relatively lavish provision may still be too little. In this instance, however, if the reading centre objective of close collaboration with the school could be achieved, the parent's apprehensions for the future would be much diminished.

The main **voluntary body** discussed by the reading centre staff was the Dyslexia Institute (providing assessment and teaching on a fee-paying basis) rather than the Scottish Dyslexia Association and its branch associations. One psychologist expressed the view that children receiving teaching at the Institute 'may miss out as tutors do not have access to school. It might be a good thing if access could be made available'. This was dismissed by a teacher, who considered that the Institute programme was too inflexible to adapt to information from schools. Another teacher, however, suggested that greater flexibility was developing in the more recent versions of the programme. A degree of hostility to the Institute in schools was mentioned as a limitation on the benefits that voluntary organisations could deliver:

Secondary schools are very hierarchical . . Parents have children assessed and come up waving bits of paper and saying: 'Now do something'. There is a lot to be done on communications. We [reading centre staff] are far more accessible to schools and even we have a struggle at times.

Several teachers commented critically that the Institute would diagnose a case as dyslexia when only a very mild problem was involved. A psychologist explained:

The psychologists there describe what a child's difficulties are, not usually using the word 'dyslexia'. Parents get the report, listing difficulties and ways of alleviating them; they naturally go and ask for action. There is a sliding scale with specific learning difficulties; you could assess any child in these terms. Those who get to the reading centre will have at least a two year gap between reading age and chronological age, but that is an arbitrary cut off point.

This perception, from a standpoint accepting the *bona fides* of the Institute, gave a different gloss on the situation described scathingly by certain psychologists elsewhere, as 'false positives' (see chapter 7). The reading centre staff in general seemed to accept the voluntary bodies' roles of promoting public awareness, information and parental support, but reservations were expressed about their provision of tuition and assessment.

Recommendations for provision

The staff supported input to initial teacher education as an important way of improving provision for children with specific learning difficulties. They believed that the importance of direct teaching for such children should be stressed, in the light of recent developments in learning support which had been weighted towards other roles for the teacher such as co-operative teaching and specialist consultation. More work was seen to be needed on the management of the move from primary to secondary school; experience had suggested that the children with whom the centre worked could fall back at transfer. The main staff recommendation, however, was for the provision of more centres like their own; they felt that while points of detail might be improved, the pattern of work was the right one. Reorganisation plans, decided elsewhere, could result in altering the service to equalise provision throughout the local authority; staff considered that such a change might result in a damaging dilution. In 1994 these plans were still under consideration and were enmeshed with the process of devolving resources to schools. The further impact of lcoal government changes in 1996 leaves future development uncertain.

3.   A dyslexia unit in an independent school

The independent school dyslexia unit was situated in the learning support department of a large private day school with both primary and secondary sections. The same highly qualified and experienced teacher, a specialist in learning difficulties with a particular interest in dyslexia, was in charge of learning support and the dyslexia unit. The learning support department was situated in an attractive and comfortably furnished suite of rooms with plenty of computers and other equipment. No particular part of this accommodation was set aside for the dyslexia unit, which was just one of the aspects of the department. The teacher was visited and interviewed at length. No observation of teaching and learning was undertaken, as the teacher, who received many outside enquiries and visitors, preferred to keep the pupils protected from becoming objects of observation. We did not press the point.

The research addressed the following:

- the work of the dyslexia unit in the context of learning support in the school as a whole
- the teacher's views about the nature of dyslexia or specific learning difficulties, and the terminology in use
- teaching methods and materials in the dyslexia unit
- contacts with outside bodies, including the Scottish Examination Board and the Scottish Dyslexia Association.

The work of the unit

Children in P1 were observed by the senior learning support teacher, looking not for learning difficulties at that stage, but for physical/motor signs in the way they handled materials, held pencils, or put on their coats and moved about the classroom. Certain children might be noted and the class teacher alerted to look out for any points of interest. In P2, if the same or other children were showing any sign of learning difficulty they might have some short sessions of work with learning support, withdrawn as far as an alcove of the classroom. All children were given a group reading test in P3 as part of general screening. All those with low scores were tested individually. This ruled out those whose low scores were due to chance factors and identified a small number who required learning support, which might be given in the classroom or on an extraction basis throughout their schooling or as long as it was required. All kinds of learning difficulties were dealt with in this way, including slight emotional problems. Dyslexic pupils in primary classes could receive extra help in the unit once a day.

In addition to support for children already in the school, six children per year were admitted to the dyslexia unit from outwith the school. They had all been tested and assessed individually as dyslexic. The children then took the school's S1 general entrance examination with the support of scribes and readers arranged by the learning support teacher. This policy was being reconsidered.

The dyslexic children were placed in two S1 mixed ability classes which were timetabled for English and mathematics at the same time; this enabled the pupils to attend the unit as a group. This pattern continued as long as it was appropriate for the individual. The aim was to achieve a standard of literacy by the start of S3, at which point consideration was given to whether the dyslexic pupils could join the common course. However, even those who did join the general English class came into the unit each week, or were supported in class. Bright dyslexic pupils might be hard to place, as they could not cope with the amount of work required in a group aimed at their intellectual ability, but might lack stimulation in a lower group. In such cases the dyslexic group continued to attend the unit for Standard Grade work, with the scribe/reader that they would in due course require in the examination. The great majority of the dyslexic pupils were boys. Very few girls came into the unit; there were, at the time, only three girls out of the 36 attending the unit.

All the dyslexic children had reading and writing problems. Some had mathematical problems and attended the unit for mathematics. One learning support teacher had French in her degree, and took the dyslexic group together with some less able children for French. In other subjects the unit pupils followed their usual classes. Another pupil in each class was organised to supply the unit with copies of class notes in every subject. There were some unit pupils in the small boarding house of the school; volunteer helpers were organised to assist them with homework.

Applications for the dyslexia unit always exceeded the places available and the teacher worried about rejecting anyone. A total of sixteen applications were received for six places for the session 1991-92; some after-school voluntary classes were run as a service for some of the children who could not be offered places. The teacher also ran a teachers' course, the RSA one year Diploma in specific learning difficulties; thirty-eight teachers were taking this in 1991-92; some were from as far away as Aberdeen and Newcastle, attending weekly in their own time. Trust funds had been obtained to support the course.

The learning support staff consisted of three secondary staff including the head of department, and 1.5 primary. The head of department taught most of the dyslexic children, as continuity was seen as important. She also took mathematics groups, of dyslexic pupils and also within general learning support.

Terminology; the nature of the problem

This teacher preferred to use the term 'dyslexia'; in her view, it denoted a distinct phenomenon, however variously it may be manifested, and she was generally against using three words where one would do. However, she was quite willing to use 'specific learning difficulty' with teachers and psychologists outside her own institution in the light of the widespread professional opinion about the term.

The children in the dyslexia unit had been diagnosed as dyslexic from various sources. They were all tested individually when they were admitted, so that the teacher could identify the particular pattern of difficulties each individual had, whether they were auditory or visual dyslexics, and whether the difficulty was mild or severe. The commonly held view that any bright child with reading or spelling problems is dyslexic was rejected by this teacher, who pointed out that this combination can result from a number of different external causes. She rejected the frequent estimate that 10% of children were dyslexic, and suggested that the proportion was about 2%.

Her description of dyslexia was that of an uncommon but recognisable condition with a physiological or neurological basis. It could be indicated by a combination of characteristic signs, which might include cross-laterality, motor co-ordination problems, weak muscle control, possible involuntary eye movements, weak auditory discrimination or tone deafness. She believed there were certainly hereditary factors, and that dyslexic children were more likely to have been born by forceps delivery. Occasionally they had had meningitis, although any damage would have been minimal and not shown on a brain scan.

Teaching methods

Individual programmes of work were planned within a framework for the dyslexic pupils in each year group. They had to have an input of literature, as far as possible related to the work of the peer group, so that they did not feel isolated. Taped books were made in school by some teachers. The pupils followed the book while listening in order to identify the words heard with the print and to develop their concentration span. The teacher reported that children spontaneously described this work as 'reading'; they said they had 'listened' to a book if they had heard it without the book.

All were seen as needing help with spelling. The teacher believed that it was important to give attention to new ways to help with spelling; going back to spelling rules was undesirable because the children had been exposed to these for years. They all told her what they would like to be able to spell; she had found this provided a moving and revealing insight into the personal perceptions of the dyslexic pupils. Computers were used, and these sustained the pupil's interest, but they could never replace one to one teaching; even a child who was writing on the computer needed observation and guidance in order to make a sentence or paragraph, or use the spell check accurately.

It was suggested that reading came through listening; there was also a perceived need for plenty of short plays, and the children were given opportunities to read as a group. Following a sequence in order to read a play was regarded as good for them as sequencing was an area of difficulty which had prevented them learning their tables, knowing their date of birth or the days of the week. The teacher was wary, however, of over-emphasising phonic work:

> Phonic work is important but you have to be sensitive to the age; if an older child needs it, it must be introduced in a very adult way. I am very

168

keen not to offend their dignity. We must be careful as many have had an overdose of it. Some children need to clear their minds of sounding out every word. Their sight vocabulary is the one I have to work with.

Teaching materials: a wide variety of published materials were looked at, but use was eclectic and the teacher preferred to put together her own materials for the mechanics of reading and writing. She recommended reading series, for example *Starpol*, especially for pupils' free reading; even S4 pupils liked to choose large print readers for relaxation, although they might be far below the pupils' actual attainment. Schemes such as *Alpha to Omega* did not suit the teacher's personal style. Some software was in use, such as the Bangor spelling programme, but the computers were mainly used for word processing. Pupils made up their own spelling lists; and the school's information technology department had adapted computer games as an eye co-ordination pack to the requirements of the unit.

SEB special arrangements

A few pupils with mild dyslexia did not require any special arrangements by the time they reached S4, but for most of the unit's pupils a variety of special examination conditions were applied for. The pupils were used to working with scribes from S1 (S6 pupils provided a voluntary service). They preferred scribes to taping their work for examination purposes, although they were good at taping; the scribe provided a little personal touch.

The existence of the unit ensured that the school had six to eight dyslexic pupils per year, a total of over thirty-six at any one time. At examination times there could be up to sixty scribes coming in to cover the S4-S6 pupils, all on a voluntary basis.

Outside contacts

The teacher had been a member of the dyslexia association for many years, but while approving the teaching undertaken by the association she felt that a series of lessons isolated from the child's school experience was inevitably limited in the help it could give. Local authority reading units too involve taking the child away from the school, although parents with whom she had contact felt that reading units gave a very good service.

I am a great believer in success in your own school. In a unit like this within school, we are alerted to what is going on and the children are rubbing shoulders with each other. The children have got to take their place in society, and they must take part in the life of the school. With all their disabilities they do, very cheerfully.

4.   A paired reading scheme

On our fourth example we have rather less information than on the other three. Nevertheless, we felt we should report on it because it exemplifies a kind of support which can more readily be implemented in schools. The paired reading scheme was located in a largely rural region where there was a strong policy of mainstream integration for special educational needs. Extraction of pupils from their ordinary classes was officially frowned upon at the S1-S2 stages. A very small number of severely affected pupils were placed in special primary units. Within the mainstream, and especially at secondary school, learning support teachers were encouraged to rely upon co-operative teaching and consultation with subject teachers. These policy positions combined with scarcity of resources for dealing with referrals made it difficult to obtain outside assessment of any child's difficulties.

The learning support department in one school had decided to set up the paired reading scheme on a pilot basis. They were influenced by accounts of the benefits of paired reading from other parts of Scotland and used as a model a scheme and video from Perth Grammar School English Department. Pupils in S1 or S2 who had severe reading difficulties were identified, and paired with volunteers from S6 who had undertaken to contribute, generally one hour per week as a community service activity. Some of the volunteers were considering teaching as a career. The learning support teachers, one principal teacher and one assistant, chose the pairings sympathetically, on the basis of their knowledge of the individuals concerned. The younger pupils were asked if they had a preference for working with a boy or a girl. A few volunteers took two partners, but most had one; the organisers were concerned with establishing rapport between the partners and felt that it would be easier to develop a fruitful working partnership if the senior pupils had only one reading partner each.

The main problem of organisation was the negotiation of withdrawal time for each individual taking part, as there was no extraction allowed for on the timetable. Having obtained the agreement of the head teacher and other senior management staff, subject teachers were approached for each pupil and a timetable agreed. Once the initial pilot group were working satisfactorily, numbers were increased to between 20 -30, the majority being in S1. None of these pupils had been diagnosed as having specific learning difficulties by any outside agency; the principal teacher considered that 'quite a few of them had that type of difficulty to some extent' but was not concerned to identify these difficulties explicitly.

Evaluation of the scheme at the end of the year was positive. The learning support teachers and subject or guidance teachers concerned with the pupils who participated felt that it was worth pursuing and expanding during the next school session. All of the existing pupils entering S2 would be continuing, and possibly twenty of the new S1 would start, provided that enough suitable senior volunteer tutors could be recruited. The logistics of negotiating the withdrawal from one lesson per week presented some difficulty, but the principal teacher expected to be able to achieve this. Accommodation for an expanded scheme, however, might be difficult to arrange.

A group of five of the S6 tutors supplied 'unabridged and unexpurgated' evaluations of the scheme. Many of their fellow volunteers had already left the school when the opportunity arose. Extracts from the views expressed are given below:

A: Paired Reading served as a challenge to me at first and I think my first year reader saw it as more of a way to miss Maths. However, despite an initial shyness we both got to know one another reasonably well; eventually I was being told many different things in great detail. My reader did not have problems reading but was hindered by a lack of confidence which led to stammering and embarrassment on his part. After the first few reading sessions his confidence was growing and he began to ask to read alone. By the end of the time we worked together he was sitting, holding his own book and reading to me with only a few difficulties over words. To begin with, he told me he hated reading, his interests only stretching to comics. Recently he has been telling me 'what happened last week' in the story and pushing to get reading again ... I know that I enjoyed the time we spent reading. It was easy to sit and encourage him and it made everything worthwhile when he began to improve. I saw him recently and he actually stopped and asked if we would be reading again.

B: I thought the scheme was very educational for my paired reader. By reading together she built up her confidence, speaking quickly and more clearly. I found that one period a week was not enough; maybe two or three periods a week would increase the paired readers' skills more ... As 5th years graduate to 6th year I strongly recommend helping with the paired reading scheme.

C: I decided to join ... as I had a few free periods and thought that

171

some of this time could be spent helping someone else. I was paired up with a young girl in 2nd year whom I met at a special 'party' held for all those participating ... For 40 minutes, once a week, my partner and I met in a room where we were free from all noise and distractions. For the first few weeks we read together, but as we progressed she felt confident enough to read herself for long periods until she was soon reading totally independently. But I was still there to help her if she was unsure about a word, and I found the more praise and encouragement I gave her the better she read. I think my reader's biggest problem was that she lacked self-confidence and this made her feel awkward and clumsy in class; but it really made the time worthwhile to see her opening up and reading ... She told me she would quite like to do it next year if she felt she needed it, but she did say some people were inclined to tease those who needed the paired reading. ... it is extremely rewarding and satisfying to see someone progressing so much from just 40 minutes a week.

D: Since knowing S, my reading partner, I have found her to become more and more confident in herself and more perceptive in what she is reading. S is a very sensitive person and needs a lot of time and support; through this I am confident she will become a bright young student ... I think she is also more confident because she knows a sixth year [pupil] and is able to talk to me and get a laugh with me, whereas she wouldn't have been able to talk to me if the Scheme had not taken place.

E: When I met my reading partner we were both extremely nervous ... but after a couple of weeks things became easier and we had more to talk about. My reading partner, G, had no confidence in his reading whatsoever, but within a month his reading was more fluent. Personally I feel that the way in which the 'helpers' were told to work ... was not helpful. For example, my partner found it easier to split a long word up into 'bits' rather than being told the word and having to repeat it two or three times. G himself is not particularly interested in school but once I had found out from him what he liked doing, he became animated and a very lively talker. I hope the Scheme becomes a successful venture and that G tries to relax and enjoy school.

All the contributors focused upon confidence and personal relationships as key factors. (These descriptions were strikingly similar to some from the voluntary organisations, reported in chapter 7.) Only one mentioned a pupil's strategy in tackling words. Their evaluations of the pupils' progress were positive, and there was a clear impression that the experience also contributed to the personal development of the S6 pupils. The collaborative aspects of the scheme, involving negotiation with many different subject teachers, appeared to have had the potential to raise awareness across the school staff. It would be interesting to know if any gains in attainment across the curriculum were made by the pupils who took part. Unlike the marked preponderance of boys in the reading centres and dyslexia unit the paired reading scheme catered for a balance of boys and girls.

Summary and discussion

This chapter has provided illustrations of practice. The examples were by no means typical nor were they intended to be taken as exemplars; the first three were accounts of our attempts to observe some of the strategies used (and possible outcomes of those strategies) when children with specific learning difficulties are perceived as a discrete, identifiable group. The fourth example was a brief glimpse of a scheme which might benefit other children with reading problems as well as those who are the focus of this research. None of these accounts constituted a 'case study' because our data came entirely from providers' statements and our own (brief) observations. We did have some evidence from parents and voluntary organisations about provision of this type, but not about these particular examples; we had no information about other views (eg from mainstream schools) about this provision.

We summarise this chapter by comparing key features across the four examples. In the two reading centres and the dyslexia unit, all with a varying degree of emphasis on a discrete type of learning difficulty, **boys** predominated markedly. The paired reading scheme, based on the notion of continuum of difficulties which were not categorised, included a balance of boys and girls. **Identification** of specific learning difficulty might take place at any time from P1 in examples two and three, the larger reading centre and the dyslexia unit; it generally took place in P4 or P5 in example one, the smaller reading unit. **Provision** here was for late primary pupils only (P6 and P7); in example two, flexible patterns of support were arranged for children ranging from P3 to the middle years of secondary. In the independent school, example three, support could be given throughout a pupil's school life, from age 5-18; however, pupils specifically admitted to the dyslexia unit entered at S1. Example four, the paired reading scheme, was located wholly in the early secondary years, with identification of children with severe reading problems in S1, and support

173

offered in S1 and S2.

The **resources** of the four examples varied widely. Number four had minimal cost implications, and number one was established on an economical basis. The reading centre example two was more lavishly provided, especially in terms of staff, but also for teachers' and pupils' travelling costs, materials and accommodation. The facilities of example three accorded with those of the private sector in accommodation and materials; however, the level of support given depended largely on the extent to which the teacher in charge had obtained and organised volunteer assistance.

Turning to **teaching approaches**, example one stressed traditional phonic-based methods, and used taped materials and computers for word processing. Individual targets were negotiated with each child. Phonics were also important in reading centre two, with the Letterland system as a 'house style' and a wide variety of additional materials to build in individual programmes. Multisensory approaches were advocated. Decoding skills were emphasised in the primary years, with a developing shift to a semantic emphasis for older pupils. The dyslexia unit, example three, also adopted a largely semantic approach at the secondary stage; while phonic work was regarded as important, pupils in the unit might have had 'an overdose' of it. Specific difficulties such as sequencing could be tackled by, for example, reading a play. Taped materials were frequently made up within the school. The accepted paired reading approach, of one to one companion reading, with little or no instruction, was adopted in example four.

Our illustrative examples provided a range of linkage with the **mainstream curriculum**. Although number four was located within the mainstream school and negotiations to set up the programme for individual pupils may have raised teacher awareness, it was additional to curricular work. In example one, communication with the primary school was regular, at a low level of at least once a term. Written reports and liaison meetings took place during preparations for transfer of pupils to secondary school, but follow up contacts were minimal. In example two, the reading centre teachers maintained regular contact with primary class teachers, who consolidated the language programmes being undertaken. At the secondary stage, a team effort between the centre and the mainstream school continued to be an objective, but contacts were generally mediated by school learning support staff. Direct access to subject teachers was difficult for reading centre staff to arrange.

The third example, the dyslexia unit in the independent school, had the advantage that one teacher and her staff had the combined responsibility for general learning support and provision for children perceived as dyslexic. The experiences of this unit (example three) bore out the opinions of the staff in reading centre two, that close linkage of support programmes with the school

174

curriculum and mainstream teachers were required if children with a dyslexic type of difficulty were to have optimum access to the curriculum. In the case of this school-based special unit, the opportunity for continuing communication with subject teachers was clearly greater than it could have been for a regional or divisional centre.

This was the first instance of support for pupils with specific learning difficulties where we encountered the involvement of fellow **pupil volunteers**. They contributed to daily support by supplying copies of class notes in different subjects, and more senior pupils assisted with paired reading or acted as scribes. Other teachers played a part by making audio tapes of appropriate material from the curriculum.

Links with **parents** were not mentioned in our information from examples three and four. In the case of the two reading centres, both one and two held individual discussions when the child was admitted, an annual parents' night, and encouraged parents to telephone at any time. Reading centre two also involved parents in on-going homework support and feedback. Parents of the pupils at this centre ran a Dyslexia Support Group to their own agenda; staff reported that the group tended to encourage resistance to recommendations that a child's involvement with the reading centre be discontinued. The question of the **social class** of children supported in these examples was considered but not investigated. Again, no explicit information was obtained from examples three and four; in example three it was assumed that the socio-economic circumstances of families was similar to that of the private sector generally. Nothing in example four suggested any disproportionate involvement of children from middle class families.

Staff at both reading centres reported that placements were very unevenly spread between primary schools. In the case of example two, this was claimed to be unrelated to the social circumstances of the catchment. In example one, while there was no intention of directing reading centre support towards middle class pupils, it was acknowledged that the primary schools in the poorer parts of the district were the least represented. Home support was also given as a criterion for selecting a child for admission from among those nominated.

These accounts of practice have been largely descriptive. While they have provided ideas to think about, the absence in all of the examples of systematic evaluation of the effectiveness of the different programmes makes their value for policy decisions rather limited. There is enough informal or intuitive evidence to sustain interest in all these alternatives, but the crucial questions of whether they promote improvements in children's learning (and associated factors like parents' peace of mind), if so how much and how much does it all cost, have yet to be addressed in detail.

9 Provision for specific learning difficulties within the health service

The main thrust of this investigation of provision for children with specific learning difficulties has focused on the **education** services. Within the resources of the research project it has not been possible to explore in anything like a comprehensive way aspects of provision by the **health** services. However, as an illustration of this provision a brief consideration of three of its aspects is provided here. This comprises accounts of:

1   the role of three medical consultants
2   a unit in one major hospital's occupational therapy department
3   a view of the potential involvement of speech therapists.

The role of medical officers

Throughout the work with other groups involved in provision for children with specific learning difficulties, attempts were made to identify medical officers who might have helpful information and views to offer the research. Three consultants were identified in this way as having a particular interest in this area, coming from different large Scottish cities and with different kinds of appointment: a community paediatrician, an assessment unit medical officer and a paediatric neurologist. A semi-structured interview was used which sought to explore the part played by the medical officers in identifying the childrens' problems and meeting their needs, the kinds of diagnostic techniques used, the recommendations they would make to other professionals, their criteria for success and their involvement with others (voluntary organisations, parents' groups, other professionals.)

176

Medical officer involvement in diagnosis

All the medical officers reported that every week children with specific learning difficulties were referred to them. Mostly these referrals came from educational psychologists, but sometimes from other paediatricians or general practitioners (who may have been alerted to problems by parents either because they were dissatisfied with the provision made by the education authority or because the class teacher suggested they consult the doctor). Almost all the children seen were of primary school age with only a small number of adolescents; the vast majority were at the severe end of the spectrum of specific learning difficulties.

The typical involvement of the medical officers with the children was just one meeting. Follow-up provision and monitoring appeared to be the responsibility of other professionals: educational psychologists, occupational therapists, school doctors. The main role of the medical officers, therefore, was one of assessment and this often in the sense of 'ruling out' serious neurological disorders. This involved various neuropsychological tests, checks for chromosome abnormalities or other abnormal neurological signs (head size, co-ordination, reflexes), examination for visual or perceptual problems and assessment of language disorders, spatial relationships and gross motor abilities. The medical officers did not see themselves as being involved in what they termed the 'educational area' and only the community paediatrician took part (frequently) in the procedures for opening Records of Needs.

The concept of specific learning difficulties

None of the consultants was happy with the term 'dyslexia', but two found 'specific learning difficulties' acceptable. The community paediatrician applied this term to children with both average and lower 'intellect', who showed difficulties in aspects of their learning (eg motor control) which were out of keeping with their progress in other areas and could not be explained by specific adverse circumstances. The medical officer from the assessment unit saw specific learning difficulties as often manifest in a constellation of problems with reading, spelling, number, spoken language and clumsiness. Whether the problems were single or multiple, however, the children tended to have **some** areas of ability within the normal range. This interpretation introduced the idea of minimal brain damage as a causal factor, a point taken up by the paediatric neurologist. The view put forward by this doctor was that it was not appropriate to consider these children as a distinct group; they were, it was suggested, 'at the mild end of the spectrum of some more easily identifiable problems' such as cerebral palsy. This perspective suggested that the difficulties of the children were 'not all that specific'. On the one hand, they could be thought of as performing in particular areas at a lower level than that predicted from a 'normal IQ'; on the other hand, it was often the case that a whole range of 'other areas of everyday living' were affected by perceptual, motor, sequencing and dominance difficulties.

Meeting the children's needs

When it came to meeting the needs of children with specific learning difficulties, the medical officers themselves played very little part. They saw their role as passing the children on to occupational therapists, speech therapists, educational psychologists and learning support or class teachers. The community paediatrician suggested that provision for these children should be different from that for others with literacy problems. The distinctiveness arose from the typical intractability of specific learning difficulties and so the need to provide **alternative** routes to learning. An implication of this is that the emphasis is on **managing** rather than **resolving** the problems, with the aim of helping the children to participate in the curriculum rather than setting out to 'cure' them. It was interesting that this view was underlined by the criteria which all three medical officers used to judge the effectiveness of the provision: they stressed affective factors such as the satisfaction of the parents and the happiness of the child, but did not commit themselves in any way to improvement in the area of the specific difficulty.

Collaboration of the medical officers with other professionals was patchy and appeared most effective in the case of the community paediatrician. Indeed, the other doctors lamented the absence of such a post in their areas. Where this post did exist, there were good links with educational psychologists, school doctors and institutions educating teachers and others about specific learning difficulties. Apart from 'some skirmishing over terminology' there seemed to be little in the way of significant disagreement among the professionals on the type of provision best suited to these childrens' needs. What was of concern, however, was the dearth of resources available to support the collaborative, multi-disciplinary approach which was deemed appropriate.

The role of voluntary organisations and parents' groups was seen by the medical consultants as providing support for families, providing information about the needs of children with specific learning difficulties, educating parents and acting as pressure groups aiming to change attitudes towards provision. In particular, the organisations' emphasis was seen to be on helping professionals to gain access to information from each other, identifying ways in which the children could be helped in the early stages of their education, drawing attention to post-school provision and sponsoring courses, lectures and materials for the general promotion of the cause. All of the doctors had been involved in organisations' programmes at some time, mostly through giving lectures or talks, but in one case by being on the committee and having responsibility for organising meetings and conferences. There was a recognition of the danger that voluntary organisations' campaigns could 'put people's backs up', but a general view was that their approaches had become more sophisticated over the years and their avoidance of directly adverse criticisms of education service provision had led to good relationships with local authorities.

Overall, the medical officers expressed considerable sympathy for the education service. There was a consciousness of the belief perceived as being held among a minority of teachers, that if a child was not progressing it was the teacher's fault. The intractability of specific learning difficulties, the heterogeneity of children so impaired and the lack of material resources to help them manage their problems were seen as putting a 'massive imposition' on schools and teachers. One particular 'pioneering' example of a special unit, within the health service and with a capability to address some of these problems, was identified for us and it is to a discussion of this that we now turn.

1.   A special out-patient unit

It is important to remember that this example of provision is in no sense typical, it caters for children at what might be seen as the extremes of (and, indeed, beyond) specific learning difficulties, and because the features of the provision are likely to be starker than the more general picture, great caution has to be taken in generalising to other mainstream contexts. There may be, nevertheless, some lessons to be learned and there are certainly some very interesting features to be discussed. The children for whom this provision is made are those with 'motor/learning difficulties' who are referred through the Health Service and are almost without exception of primary school age.

Children with motor/learning difficulties

An Occupational Therapy Department (OTD) at a major Children's Hospital is involved with the diagnosis and treatment of children with **motor/learning difficulties** (or so-called 'clumsy children'). It is especially concerned to encourage collaboration with, and provide support for, parents and teachers (of both academic subjects and physical education). As well as face-to-face activities, this support has included the provision of written material (eg *The Child with Motor/Learning Difficulties: a guide for parents and teachers,* OTD, 1986).

Children with motor/learning difficulties are identified as those 'who despite normal intellect, stimulating environment, adequate teaching and no obvious physical handicap ... have difficulty with movement and with specific aspects of learning' (Stephenson, 1986, p.1). These may be manifest as gross motor, fine motor, eye movement, reading, writing, spelling, reversals, number, speech or language difficulties. Such children may also display behaviour and emotional problems, but are likely to have 'good days' and 'bad days'. Among the phrases used to describe sub-sets of these problems are 'specific learning difficulties' and 'dyslexia'. They are, therefore, of interest to this research but they are likely to be at the extreme of the continuum of problems in which we are interested; at the other extreme we would expect to find so-called 'normal children' who may well display mild forms of the difficulties.

The OTD unit endeavours to help parents and teachers to understand the underlying causes of the problems. It suggests that these arise from 'failure of the Central Nervous System to adequately interpret, integrate and process the information required to produce an appropriate response' (Stephenson, 1986, p.6). The method of helping children with these difficulties is described as eclectic and offers a 'total approach' which provides treatment for various motor problems in a safe environment, attention to emotional problems (in the individual, the family or the classroom context), physical or psychological therapy and remedial academic help. The programme for the individual child is specifically tailored to his or her needs and particular emphasis is placed on the improvement of the child's confidence and self esteem. The aim is to tackle the underlying cause of the child's problems rather than simply to provide opportunities for practice in reading, writing and spelling.

Support for parents

Parents who have been associated with the Learning Difficulties Support Group set up by OTD point to the frustration, guilt, anxiety, anger, disappointment, worry, embarrassment and, above all, feelings of isolation or rejection which they experienced when they first realised that their children had difficulties in performing simple tasks (OTD, 1986, pp.15-19). Their sense of relief when (i) the learning difficulty was identified, (ii) they became aware of their legal right to assessment of their child by the local authority and (iii) advice was made available about the best form of support for the child, is testament to the need the parents have for the support group. Without something of that kind the therapists found themselves spending an ever increasing amount of time coping with distressed parents to the detriment of the children (Stephenson and McKay, 1989, p.181). The parents' pressing individual needs were for information from, or workshops organised by, the therapists.

Eventually the therapists were able to relinquish the leadership role which had been thrust upon them; the parents gained knowledge and confidence and were able to think more constructively beyond the personal problems of their own families and to co-operate in providing support for each other. What is especially interesting is the length of time it took to establish the self-help group. It is a measure of the depth of their original feelings of desperation that it took three years for the group to become properly operational. Aspects of the OTD's research (see Chesson et al 1991) illuminated the impact that motor/learning difficulties of this kind can have on families. The stresses that were apparent on marriages, siblings, relationships with grandparents and general social activity were considerable. Little wonder that the parents' priority was to get whatever they could from the 'experts'. It is also interesting that the social class profile of the parents involved was broadly representative of the population of the area; the concentration in social classes I and II, which has been observed in some studies of children with specific learning difficulties and is reflected in our survey of parents, was not apparent.

The general run of parents with children with specific learning difficulties may, of course, have less acute levels of anxiety as their children's problems may be less extreme and of a more limited range. Furthermore, they may be less ready to 'bare their souls' in public than are parents who are at their wits' end from the disruption to the lives of their children and themselves which the severity of their child's difficulties is causing. There is, however, fairly strong evidence of a general need on the part of all parents of children suspected of having some measure of specific learning difficulty to have someone who is predisposed to recognise that something is wrong and to discuss the matter in a serious way.

Provision with a research base

A distinctive difference between the support provided by this OTD and that offered, for example, by local authorities to the wider population of children with specific learning difficulties, is the **research** base which is sought for the work. The interaction between research and practice is seen as important by the OTD in order both to gain more information about these kinds of disorders and the impact on families, and to provide a comprehensive history of each case as part of the assessment procedure (Chesson et al 1990, p.1). In particular, research is seen as crucial in the identification of characteristics of young children which may signal motor/learning difficulties and facilitate early diagnosis. A further advantage of taking essentially a research stance is that it offers opportunities for continuous evaluation of the treatment/remediation offered.

In one study it was argued that early recognition is more likely to facilitate remediation. Not only may younger children be more receptive to therapy but, also, families may be able to be more responsive to the demands of their offspring and develop appropriate 'coping and caring' strategies. (Stephenson et al, 1990, p.4)

The findings of this study of 31 children, all referred to the OTD by a hospital consultant paediatrician or child psychiatrist (though the referrals had often been initiated by educational psychologists or general practitioners), suggested that most had a history of earlier problems many of which had warranted medical or therapeutic intervention. The histories particularly highlighted placements in neonatal intensive care units soon after birth, referrals for assessment to the regional child development unit, early speech difficulties, absence of crawling before walking and problems with toilet training. They also demonstrated, however, the difficulties of diagnosis, the variety of routes through which children come to be referred to specialist units and 'the fact that frequently there were lengthy gaps between parental (and sometimes professional) suspicions and final confirmation' (Stephenson et al, 1991, p.91). The role of the educational psychologist was a crucial one, but few children had the opportunity for referral to the psychological service before entry to primary school.

Provision for meeting the needs of these children included weekly sessions of about one hour on a one-to-one basis at the OTD over a period of five to fifteen months, remedial work in school (reading, writing, spelling and number) and, for some, child and family psychiatry. The effectiveness of this treatment was assessed primarily through parental judgements of improvement. The majority of parents saw improvement in the children's self-esteem, school performance and general behaviour, in family and marital relationships (with a reduction in tension and fewer arguments over management of the child's problems) and in links with teachers. There were also, of course, some disappointments and fears for the future, but these were tempered with appreciation that the programme was attempting to meet the needs of the parents as well as the children. While it would be helpful to have other independent evidence of the outcomes of the provision, the evidence from the parents is extremely important. It confirms the notion that if they are given the opportunity to understand the nature of the disorders and have a realistic idea of the extent of improvement that can be expected, then they seem to be much more able to cope with the problems of both child and family generally. The frustration and panic that ignorance invokes gives way to constructive approaches for at least some improvements.

Implications for more general provision

There are four aspects of this work which appear to have implications for provision for the general run of children with specific learning difficulties; all of these follow from the **research** stance taken by OTD. The systematic evidence which this had provided offers a much more precise basis on which to review alternative courses of action and take decisions.

First, the documentation of the diagnostic histories of individual children (albeit fairly extreme cases) has helped to pinpoint areas in need of development (eg new and more specific assessment procedures), cues for the early identification of children likely to be at risk as they mature, critical ages for diagnosis and networks of professionals who need to co-operate in identification and diagnosis.

Secondly, the evaluation of the treatment of individual children through a variety of means suggests ways in which the less severely affected might have their needs met more effectively. It is possible that these children may need more than educational remediation; therapy to increase self-confidence and reduce tensions within the family may be an important ingredient. It may be that 'to regard the problem as solely educational is to take a restricted and partial view of the disorder, and is to ignore associated social and behavioural problems' (Stephenson et al, 1991, p.110).

Thirdly, the importance of providing for the whole family has been established. Although the occupational therapists carried out specific therapeutic work, it seemed that they were valued particularly for the information they offered (about the disorders, treatments available, educational services and facilities and appropriate follow-up activities to be undertaken at home), the support they provided for parents and the help they gave in liaising with teachers and schools. All of these functions could be carried out by people in other contexts where provision is made for children with specific learning difficulties. Prior to the referral, parents found that the advice offered to them often lacked cohesion, they had difficulty 'putting it all together', remediation seemed inadequate, children were often 'blamed' for bad behaviour and stress built up at home and in relations with the school.

Fourthly, a number of assumptions about specific learning difficulties have been challenged by the research. We have already noted that boys and middle class pupils are more likely than girls and working class pupils to be identified as experiencing specific learning difficulties. However, this particular group of pupils crossed the social class spectrum and there was a more even sex ratio. This might indicate that the usual process of identification is sex and class biased, or that the pupils who featured in the OTD research had significantly different characteristics from the majority of pupils identified as experiencing specific learning difficulties.

2. A special 'in-patient' unit

As well as the OTD unit, where children's and parents' needs were provided for on an occasional (but regular) 'outpatient' basis, there was provision in the same hospital of a second unit run more as an 'inpatient' facility by the Department of Child and Family Psychiatry (DCFP). The children in this unit had had considerable problems in school. Most had failed to cope with academic work, often because of emotional problems or gaps in their knowledge through work missed at an earlier stage of their learning. The head teacher in the unit suggested that many of the emotional problems may be associated with specific learning difficulties. Repeated failure with subsequent 'opting out' and lack of self-esteem or concentration on school work were characteristics frequently seen among this group, but they tended to be of average intelligence. Some individuals had additional perceptual or motor/learning difficulties. The direct implications for provision for children with specific learning difficulties were less obvious than was the case for the OTD unit, but it did offer an example where none of the remediation was carried out in the context of the mainstream school.

Children were in the hospital school on weekdays only and there are normally about 15 pupils, 10 on a residential basis and 5 with day places. There was a waiting list of referrals; those admitted were assessed over a 6 week period and might be offered further treatment after that. The geographical area served covered one mainland and two island authorities.

The philosophy of the school rested on the belief that children with these difficulties would benefit from a regular routine, some clear rules, individual programmes (which may include therapy) within class groupings, some group activities, project work and educational outings. As in the OTD there was emphasis on the development of higher self-esteem and special talents. Breadth of the curriculum was given some priority and it included physical education, swimming, art, music, baking and handworks as well as basic language and mathematics.

Considerable importance was placed on liaison among the members of the multidisciplinary team of nurses, occupational therapists, psychiatrists, psychologists, social workers and teachers. Meetings were frequent: of a daily 'hand-over' kind, for reports on children's progress or assessment (also attended by parents and sometimes mainstream teachers), of the staff support group to discuss any difficulties associated with different disciplines working together, and general ward meetings.

The ratio of teachers to pupils was good; for the fifteen pupils there were one head teacher (also acted as relief/supply teacher), two full-time teachers and two part-time teachers. In addition to teaching, the teachers had major responsibilities for liaison with the parents and maintaining links with the mainstream schools which the children attended prior to entry. When children returned to those schools the Unit's teachers took the primary role in the planning of that return. Unlike the OTD there was no specific initiative to provide support for families, but there were strong links between the two units. Many of the children in the DCFP unit, whose general problems were seen as arising from specific learning difficulties, spent some time in the OTD unit and were seen as receiving substantial benefit from the help they received there.

A possible contribution from speech therapists

The reports from the medical officers suggested that some of the children assessed for specific learning difficulties were subsequently referred to speech therapists. Robinson (1991), herself a speech therapist, has also reported that she and her colleagues have

> been receiving an increasing number of referrals from educational psychologists and from teachers of children of eight years and over who were showing impairment in literacy skills as well as in verbal language (p.2).

The research cited earlier (Stephenson et al, 1991) into the histories of children with such difficulties suggested that early difficulties in speech were common. However, because speech therapists have not traditionally provided a service designed **especially** for this group of children Robinson set out to explore whether (i) speech is indeed an important foundation for written language (and so whether a disorder in one might co-exist with or affect the other) (ii) particular kinds of early spoken language difficulty might predict later literacy failure and (iii) the involvement of a medically trained speech therapist in the management of learning disordered children whose main problems are identified in reading and writing rather than in speech would be advantageous.

From a review of the literature she concluded that:

1   literacy is a secondary skill learnt once a child has learnt to talk, to understand what is said, to recognise words as separate units of meaning, to hear sounds correctly and blend them in his or her own speech. (p.6)

2   the likelihood of reading impairment depends on the type and severity of any language disorder; in particular, problems of phonological processing (ie the division of words heard into their constituent sounds) appear to interfere with childrens' progression in reading and spelling (pp.8-9).

3   children with dyslexia may have very subtle high level language problems (in semantics, syntax, pragmatics and phonology) which may easily be missed; these have an adverse effect on their vocabulary and word labelling development and so act to the detriment of reading and spelling (pp.10-11).

4   there are no 'classic' dyslexics; an individual and descriptive approach has to be adopted in each case (p.14).

This analysis by Robinson led her to conclude that speech therapists were in a position to help to identify children at risk through an assessment, at the pre-school stage, of attributes such as phonological awareness and pre-reading skills. Furthermore, they were well placed to offer advice on suitable pre-literacy activities and management of the childrens' problems, given their training in phonetics as well as linguistics.

While this analysis was convincing in the sense of confirming that some children with specific learning difficulties might have a language disorder which affected spoken as well as written communication, and that speech therapists might have a role in identifying some of these high level language problems, the case for how the needs of these children could be met is still at the stage of hypothesis. In particular, the intractability of the difficulties may be a major problem, and the proposed support seems to depend on pre-school identification. We saw from the parents' survey, however, that such identification was most likely to occur after children in primary school had been seen not to be mastering basic reading and writing. Short of testing **all** children it is difficult to see how the speech therapists would move beyond the group to which they already have access through referrals. In addition, Robinson herself cautioned that the initiative would depend on speech therapists having 'special skills based on theoretical knowledge . . . a degree of specialist knowledge not normally covered in our basic training' (p.23).

Educationists' perceptions of links with health professionals

For the most part (the exception being in the geographical area of the hospital units described in an earlier section), teachers did not have much direct contact with medical officers. Their link was much more likely to be with educational psychologists and 73% of the sample of learning support teachers reported such links. A much smaller proportion (30%) reported collaboration with speech therapists and this was more frequently the case for primary than secondary teachers (see Table 9.1).

Table 9.1 **Learning support teachers reporting collaboration on specific learning difficulties with speech therapist by sector (Result of chi-square test)**

	Yes	No	Total
Primary	47 (44.8)	58 (55.2)	105 (55.6)
Secondary	13 (15.5)	71 (84.5)	84 (44.4)
Total	60 (31.7)	129 (68.3)	189 (100.0)

$p < .0001$
Missing values = 17

In about half of the regions, regional officers identified links with Health Board professionals. These tended to arise in the procedures for setting up Records of Needs or, in the case of occupational therapists, where specific learning difficulties were associated with motor disorders.

There was, however, a certain wariness among these interviewees in discussing this topic. They saw specific learning difficulties largely as an educational matter and the involvement of, say, paediatricians by parents produced some irritation. A philosophical divide between educational and medical perspectives was described, with educationalists emphasising 'the context and the curriculum' and medics the 'constitutional elements'. A referral to the psychological services of a child medically diagnosed as having 'constitutional developmental dyslexia' was considered to be 'unhelpful'.

A clinical diagnosis of dyslexia can aggravate the situation; it makes anxious parents more anxious. It is inappropriate; the implication is that it can be 'cured' and we can't cure these difficulties, just work at them and find strategies. [The medical officers] are never involved in the next stage [provision]. They don't say how difficult it will be and how slow progress will be. Also, they say it obviously means increased resources. Well it's not obvious to us and this causes tension. (Adviser)

Summary

It appeared that children, mostly from the primary sector, with more severe forms of specific learning difficulties were regularly referred to medical officers. These officers' main role was one of assessment and they played little part in meeting the needs of such children. They reported good relationships with educational professionals and agreement on how the needs should be met, though they were concerned about the lack of resources available for this purpose. The educational professionals were more cautious about these links. Indeed, there was some resentment expressed that those responsible for diagnosis then handed on to others the responsibility for meeting the needs of those with specific learning difficulties.

It is possible that some of this tension might be relaxed if there were more community paediatricians. Where such a post existed the medical officer played a part in the opening of Records of Needs and had the opportunity to communicate more effectively with education professionals. This could improve the chances of avoiding misunderstandings. For example, there was evidence that the regional education officers believed the medical officers encouraged parents' expectations of 'cures' for specific learning difficulties. Our information suggests this was not the case and the medical opinion emphasised 'managing' rather than 'curing' the problems. Unfortunately, appointments of community paediatricians were rare and this was regretted by all those we interviewed; a hospital consultant is not nearly so well placed for communication with those in education and is inevitably most concerned with those cases which are clinically most severe.

The medical personnel had good relationships with voluntary organisations and appreciated both the strengths and weaknesses of their work. There was, however, some disparity in the way the two groups have seen the nature of specific learning difficulties. Voluntary organisations welcomed the idea that specific learning difficulties resulted from minimal cerebral dysfunction which was genetic in origin. However, they were less comfortable with the idea that minimal brain damage was a causal factor of specific learning difficulties, or that such difficulties were mild versions of more easily identifiable problems such as cerebral palsy.

In addition to the part played by medical officers, this chapter has reported on another kind of contribution from health professionals: a special unit run by an occupational therapy department. This unit has dealt with some of the severest cases of specific learning difficulties and extended its work to parents and teachers. It has provided individually tailored programmes and aimed to tackle the underlying causes of the child's problems.

What was distinctive about this unit's success was the help it provided for families and the advances which it made in knowledge of the area by taking a distinctively research-oriented approach. The findings of its research and development with severe cases also had implications for improving the support for the general population of those with specific learning difficulties. This unit did not represent, however, the kind of provision more generally available across health boards. It was innovative and clearly expensive in its use of both human and material resources.

Finally the contribution from speech therapists was considered because so many people had referred to the part they should play in provision for specific learning difficulties. It appeared that the role of speech therapists in this area had been modest but might be increasing. We have described how one speech therapist put the case for more of such professional involvement in the future. This case rested on a view of the likelihood that literacy was a secondary skill which had to be based on oral, aural and recognition skills; that reading impairment depended on language disorder; and that children with dyslexia had high level language problems. Exactly what the role of the speech therapist should be, and how the children to whom such therapy is given are to be identified, are still at the level of hypothesis.

10 Specific learning difficulties: A focus for debate

A focus on perceptions

The purpose of this research has been to look at policies, provision and practice (in relation to children b 'ieved to have specific learning difficulties) through the eyes of a number of different groups of people. The emphasis has been on **perceptions** of whether such children are recognised as having a particular problem, the ways in which they are identified and how their needs are met. It has **not** attempted to extend knowledge by exploring either the 'objective reality' of what happens in classrooms (apart from a few snapshots of atypical provision) or the fundamental nature and causes of specific learning difficulties (if, indeed, such a phenomenon exists).

Policy and provision in this area have been the subjects of controversy. A study of this kind is intended to provide information which helps policy makers and providers to understand better the nature of that controversy and so help them decide what action should be taken. There are two arguments, one substantive and the other practical, for focusing on **perceptions** of the way things are. First, any human controversy rests not on what is **actually** happening but on what is **seen** to be happening (e.g. 'justice has to be seen to be done'). Secondly, children with specific learning difficulties are a small proportion of the population and are provided for largely in mainstream classes; the resources of this research project could not have achieved anything like a representative sample of provision, and a collection of appropriate case studies would have been virtually impossible to identify without first carrying out the study we report here. We have, of course, made brief forays into the land of 'how things really are' (e.g. in chapters 2, 3, 8 and 9 on policy documents, examination arrangements and illustrations of interesting practice).

In this final chapter we draw together the key ideas which have emerged from our diverse sources of evidence. The place of specific learning difficulties within the whole range of special needs is outlined, followed by discussion of the conceptual baseline for recognition of specific learning difficulties. While we do not attempt to resolve the debate on the nature of these difficulties, we use the three way model developed from our policy interviews (chapter 2): the discrete group view, the continuum view, and the anti-categorisation view. This model allows us to summarise the implications of each view for provision and practice. Findings with regard to identification and assessment are discussed, followed by a comparison of the views expressed by different groups with regard to current provision. In conclusion, six areas of conflict or tension central to decision making with regard to specific learning difficulties are drawn to the attention of providers.

The place of specific learning difficulties within the range of special needs

In any consideration of policy and provision there are questions about where specific learning difficulties might stand in relation to other special needs. The research was not designed explicitly to address this matter, but it is an important issue on which we offer a brief comment.

It was quite understandable that the parents who believed their children had specific learning difficulties expected the education system to make some sort of special provision for them. Several contrasted their own child's position unfavourably with that of others with, say, visual or hearing impairments and where, in their view, support was much more evident. Such comparisons, however, could not resolve the present question. In the cases of visual or hearing impairments there are high levels of agreement about whether such problems exist, the nature of the difficulties faced by children with such impairments, how they may be identified, whether they should receive special educational provision, how their educational needs could be met and the circumstances in which the emphasis should be on managing the problem rather than curing it. No such consensus exists in the area of specific learning difficulties.

These differences reflect a well known distinction between two kinds of special educational need. Barton and Tomlinson (1984) summarise this:

The notion of 'children with special needs' conflates what we have
here termed 'normative' conditions with 'non-normative'. That is,

there can be some normative agreement about certain categories of handicap or need - such as blind, deaf, epileptic, severe mental handicap, etc. The conditions affect children in families from all social classes and occupational groupings. On the other hand, categories such as educationally subnormal, maladjusted, disruptive are not normative. There are no adequate measuring instruments or agreed criteria to decide on these particular categories. (pp.71-72)

Looking at the last sentence of this quotation, it appears that specific learning difficulties, given the lack of general agreement about their existence and nature, should be categorised as non-normative. Certainly some would claim that, as in the case of the non-normative examples given above, specific learning difficulties would be included in Kennedy's (1980) general statement that 'the normal state against which we measure [these] abnormalities is a product of social and cultural values' (see also Clough and Barton, 1995). However, there are differences in two respects between the examples of non-normative conditions above and specific learning difficulties: the former are recognised predominantly among children with working class origins and the latter among those from the middle classes, and the latter have the support of determined campaigns which aim to get the difficulties recognised as a **normative** rather than non-normative condition.

Recognition of specific learning difficulties

There were substantial problems for this research which sought to explore the views of a range of different groups about something (in this case, specific learning difficulties) on which there was no agreed definition or, indeed, even a consensus recognition that it existed. We had to identify, however, some conceptual baseline for our discussion in this final chapter, and the 'discrepancy in the cognitive profile' concept of specific learning difficulties seemed the most suitable. We found that most people accepted that there were some children who had **specific difficulties in one or more areas of learning which showed discrepancies with their learning in other areas or their general ability;** such children might come from the whole ability range, but the problems were more easily identified in the average or more able child. There was no such consensus about the causes, nature or appropriate treatment of such difficulties.

The estimates of the proportion of children so affected among the general population were, however, fairly consistent: less than 5% (and probably closer to 1%) were seen as having problems of a discrepancy kind where the severity merited, in some people's view, special provision. 10% of the population would encompass not only those with milder forms but also others with literacy problems. Such figures have to be treated with caution, however, since everyone was reluctant to make guesses and we suspect that they were influenced by figures published for the incidence of specific learning difficulties in other contexts.

These published figures often estimate that about one in 25 of the population is affected. With reference to dyslexia Walker (1992 in Crombie's *Specific Learning Difficulties: a teacher's guide*) has pointed out:

> This means that in most classes there is at least one puzzling child who seems erratic in his learning, and who is struggling with the reading and spelling skills which the teacher expects of him. This makes survival in the classroom very difficult for that child. But we know from experience that there are children who do survive and go on to fulfil their potential in learning. They are usually the children who at some point have met with a teacher who was sympathetic and informed about dyslexic difficulties.

The use of the **male** pronoun in the extract is probably not accidental. The research has had contact with a number of examples of particular support for children identified as having difficulties of this kind; in all cases there were majorities (often large majorities) of boys over girls. Traditionally it has been assumed that more boys have this problem than girls. The resources of our project were not such that we could test whether this was the case or, alternatively, that society's pressure for boys to perform, parents' greater concerns for sons' achievements over those of daughters and teachers' gender-different responses to behaviour in classrooms have united to put the spotlight on the boys.

In at least some places where we looked at special provision within the education sector, more of it was being taken up by children from more affluent homes. Our findings did **not** support the hypothesis that specific learning difficulties (or dyslexia) exist only in the minds of middle class parents with dim or emotionally disturbed children (adaptation of a newspaper parody on the 'enemies' of the dyslexia lobby); but they did indicate that it was the children of middle class families which currently benefited most from any special provision that was made.

In addition to making use of the discrepancy model, we have concentrated on **problems of literacy**. The overwhelming majority of all those we talked to or surveyed by postal questionnaire focused on reading, writing and spelling, almost to the exclusion of other kinds of specific difficulties. Of the others, problems of numeracy were most frequently mentioned but the data available was at a much lower level of detail than those concerned with literacy. A separate study, in parallel with that reported here but using a different approach, was carried out to investigate problems in mathematics and this was reported in Weedon (1992).

The nature of specific learning difficulties

The research had as its first aim an investigation of the extent to which pupils with specific learning difficulties were recognised as a distinctive group with particular needs and how the nature of their difficulties was perceived. We have found it convenient to distinguish between three ways of looking at specific learning difficulties, all of which arose from the data: the **discrete group** view, the **part of the continuum of learning difficulties** view, and the **anti-categorisation** view. Because these views had implications for the assessment of children, provision for their needs and training of teachers, the 3-way classification enabled us more readily to discuss the differences among groups. It should be treated, however, as a useful tool, not as a fundamental and tested statement about psychologically different ways of conceptualising learning difficulties. Indeed, within the education system there were clear overlaps among the three perspectives and it was often difficult in the case of individuals, and was never the case for a regional authority, to say that one view was consistently adhered to in its entirety.

The discrete group view

This view identified (implicitly or explicitly) the origin of the specific learning difficulty as within the child. The problem was seen as constitutional, enduring, qualitatively different from more global learning difficulties although not amenable to precise specification. The difficulties were seen as variable and extending along a continuum from mild to severe. Assessment was regarded as a specialised procedure, usually to be carried out by a psychologist or other 'expert' using psychometric or medical techniques. The emphasis was on categorisation of the child and the provision of specialist one-to-one tuition to remedy the difficulties. This carried implications for special training for teachers on how to make preliminary identifications of such pupils and, once these were confirmed, to meet their needs. It also implied policies for provision which focused upon the particular group and were distinguished from those which provided more generally for children with learning difficulties.

194

Major resources and criteria for Records of Needs might be seen as central to any such policies.

Evidence for the existence of the 'discrete group' of children was equivocal. That it was not open to 'precise specification' weakened its case, and there was no medical evidence for either unambiguous diagnosis of specific conditions or particular symptoms displayed in, say, eye movements or sensitivity to light. There was, however, clear acceptance on the part of many people that specific learning difficulties were on a different dimension from the other kinds of learning difficulties which might manifest themselves in similar ways, particularly as problems of literacy.

This view was held by the voluntary organisations, the Scottish Examination Board and most of the parents surveyed by the research. Indeed, the majority of parents wished that instead of the term 'specific learning difficulties' the more distinctive and (in their view) precise word 'dyslexia' could be used. This word suggested the existence of a disability with underlying physiological causes; it was generally not used by educational psychologists and educators, who preferred the more inclusive term 'specific learning difficulties' carrying with it no connotations of causality. In explaining their preference for the term dyslexia, parents made clear that they wished a distinction to be drawn between their children and others experiencing more global difficulties. This was partly to avoid the stigma attached to low ability but was also to enhance their argument for the provision of intensive individual tuition. Clearly the voluntary organisations (all of which had the word 'dyslexia' in their titles) were in agreement with the parents.

The notion of a discrete group (and certainly the term dyslexia) did not reflect the ways in which most local authorities perceived specific learning difficulties, although about 30% of the individual officers interviewed did subscribe to that view. For the most part, the authorities (as policy entities) adopted the view of a continuum of learning difficulties from the specific to the global. Superimposed upon this there was also something of an ideological challenge which was presented as questions asking why children with specific learning difficulties, even it they **did** constitute a discrete group, should have special provision? Why should not others, whose literacy problems might indeed be more easily resolved, not have just as much if not more attention? In particular, why should special arrangements like those offered by the Scottish Examination Board not be available to **any** child whose performance would benefit from such support? It seems to have been in response to such arguments that the new Spoken English and Alternative Communication Standard Grade courses have been developed, (Chapter 3) thus moving the Scottish Examination Board towards the 'continuum position'.

The survey of learning support teachers suggested that a rather higher proportion (60%) than the education authority officers went along with the

195

'discrete group concept' and for some specific learning difficulties had a precise meaning synonymous with dyslexia. For others, however, it referred to **any** learning difficulty. The term 'dyslexia' was used by over two thirds of these teachers on at least some occasions and was defined more tightly than specific learning difficulties. The majority used it to refer to problems with decoding written symbols.

An important finding of the parents' survey was their dissatisfaction with the varying use of terminology which they encountered within different parts of the education system. They became anxious and confused when different professionals used a range of terms to describe the same phenomenon and interpreted the reluctance to use the term 'dyslexia' as a ploy to escape an obligation to provide support. Voluntary organisations, whilst willing to use the term 'specific learning difficulties' in negotiation with education authorities, preferred the term dyslexia and used it with parents. These discrepancies in the use of language were not merely semantic but derived from an underlying uncertainty over the manifestation and origin of the problem.

Among the pre-service teacher educators none subscribed to the 'discrete group' concept. Those involved with in-service, however, were divided. While one college seemed wedded to the continuum model (see next section), staff in the other college saw specific learning difficulties as one dimension in the multi-dimensional complexity of learning difficulties more generally: a discrete group but with shades of grey.

The perceptions of the medical officers tended to be based on the most severe cases of specific learning difficulties. While the BMA in 1980 designated this area as **not** a medical problem, health professionals clearly have had a rôle in differentiating children with such difficulties from others with more profound neurological disorders. Perhaps as a result of the kinds of cases they see, the medical officers' views were within the 'discrete group' model although they rejected the term 'dyslexia'. They described a continuum of severity of difficulties within this group, with some problems so intractable that they had to be accepted (as does a severe physical impairment) and to have ways round them sought. The underlying causes were seen as minor brain damage (and, indeed, a continuum of brain damage was introduced with specific learning difficulties located at the mild end). This way of conceptualising the problem was criticised by the voluntary organisations (who challenged the notion of 'damage', but might well accept an explanation of anatomical anomalies in the brain structure) and rejected by parents (who saw it as yet another aspect of stigmatisation of their children). It was perhaps in the health service provision, however, that we first had a clear sense that the 'problem' was one of the whole family and should be treated as such.

This view was held by almost half of the individuals interviewed in the local authorities. They saw specific learning difficulties not as a distinctive dimension within a multi-dimensional complex of learning problems, but rather conceptualised specific difficulties as a loose grouping of pupils on a continuum on which more global learning difficulties were to be found at the other end. This concept was not tightly defined and individuals overlapped with the 'discrete group' view in admitting that at the extreme end of the continuum there were a small number of children who had 'discrete features'. They were not prepared to define a cut-off point to distinguish this group, however, and further lack of clarity was introduced by overlap with ideas about mild and moderate learning difficulties.

There appeared to be a number of reasons for this cautious approach to conceptualising specific learning difficulties and the preference for the continuum model. First, there had been disagreement in the literature about whether the problems which children with such difficulties have are qualitatively different from other literacy problems. Secondly, there was a general reluctance to categorise and label children, in the light of the damage which some other labelling had been shown to inflict on some of its recipients. Thirdly, the implications that recognition of particular groups had for specialist provision within already overstretched budgets could have a profound effect on how authorities looked at particular educational problems. Fourthly, many of the world's experts on reading (e.g. Marie Clay, Margaret Meek and Frank Smith) have expressed scepticism about whether the remedies for children believed to have specific learning difficulties should be any different from those for other children. And fifthly, perceptions of the promotion of the case for dyslexia as a middle class pressure group activity, and the likelihood that it could deflect resources from other areas seen as more deserving of priority treatment, made education authorities reluctant to give recognition to a discrete group - a fear of the 'floodgates opening'.

There was dissatisfaction expressed among a few individuals, however, that despite this concept of a continuum of difficulties, some authorities were reluctant to commit themselves to policies which would cater for its full spectrum of problems, including specific learning difficulties. The principal educational psychologists in one region produced a document on dyslexia in 1988 which stated:

> A continuum of difficulties . . . should be matched by a continuum
> of provision, ranging from help and advice from a coordinator for
> learning difficulties working within the school and providing the

class teacher with materials and programmes to intensive help in a specialist centre.

Within the continuum view a range of assessment techniques was used, including normative/standardised tests, criterion-referenced assessment and observation methods. However, in contrast to the discrete view, normative assessments were not necessarily carried out; assessments were done by learning support teachers in the first instance and a psychologist was not always involved.

Authorities where the continuum view was dominant did not go out of their way to raise teachers' awareness of specific learning difficulties. The emphasis was on training learning support teachers to cope with the range of learning difficulties they might encounter and specific learning difficulties was included as part of that range. They reported that learning support teachers were reluctant to resume the old (i.e. before the HMI report on learning difficulties in 1978) remedial rôle, preferring to offer support to all children through a differentiated curriculum. Much emphasis had been placed in recent years on training learning support teachers to adopt the role of consultant; their reported preferences might well reflect a response to perceived policy developments. The underlying assumption that learning difficulties were essentially problems of the curriculum and should not be regarded as deficits within pupils was evident. Perhaps in line with that, there was a sense that giving one-to-one tuition was neither a desirable nor central part of the learning support and that was another reason for not accepting the discrete group model. Children with specific learning difficulties were regarded as an integral part of the whole population of those with literacy problems and should be catered for within the **general** policy framework for special educational needs.

In the learning support teachers' survey (chapter 5, discussed further in Duffield, Brown and Riddell, 1995) and in the illustrations of practice (chapter 8), it appeared that a rather larger proportion of these classroom practitioners than regional officers were prepared to accept the 'discrete group' concept. We do not have data from the other important group of classroom practitioners, mainstream teachers, but we suspect they would tend towards the continuum view. That judgement is based partly on informal conversations, but also on the large majority of pre-service teacher educators who regarded specific learning difficulties as part of a broad range of learning difficulties and might be expected, over the years, to have had a substantial influence on the profession. Certainly they appeared to have ensured that a large majority of student teachers were familiar with the **term** specific learning difficulties, although a rather smaller proportion than expected recognised the 'discrepancy in the cognitive profile' definition favoured by the teacher educators (and most other people). The primary student teachers were likely to accept a definition of visual or auditory handicap; in other words, many interpreted it as 'a difficulty which can be specified' rather than 'a difficulty specific to learning'.

The 'anti-categorisation' view

This view was essentially unstructured in the sense of making no assumptions about the existence of either a discrete group or a continuum of difficulties. Just under a quarter of the education authority officers rejected any kind of categorisation of pupils, regarded all learning difficulties as matters concerning the **individual** child and stressed the importance of the whole child and the whole context. The emphasis was on the children's strengths rather than their weaknesses; withdrawal for one-to-one tuition was disapproved of because it was seen as bringing about impoverishment of the child's curriculum. Those holding the 'discrete' view were criticised for, so it was said, regarding the child as the recipient of the 'magic formula' which would bring about a 'cure'. The proposed approach was to eschew formal identification and assessment and concentrate on diagnostic teaching strategies to see what the child could or could not do in relation to the curriculum and then find ways to enable him or her to learn.

> There are no special approaches for the different categories of reading failure, no different methodologies for different groups. So what's the point in separate categorisations? If the diagnosis doesn't differentiate the management, is the diagnosis worthwhile? (Psychologist)

> There is no unified theory and therefore no unified prescription about what you should do. Don't think the notion of dyslexia is helpful: the cure model is not appropriate. (Psychologist)

The Scottish Examination Board regulations sat ill with the anti-categorisation viewpoint as did any approaches which set out to identify and classify children according to their disabilities.

> If you take the point of view that some people's failure to learn is difficult to explain, then you can identify these children, but if you take the view that the problem is about the difficulty in getting people to realise their potential you end up with a different model. (Psychologist)

Here, as with the continuum model, the goal was not to produce specialist teachers, but (in line with the 1978 HMI report) to equip all staff (mainstream and learning support) with the skills necessary to teach the range of abilities they encounter, including children with specific learning difficulties. However, INSET for mainstream teachers in the area of learning difficulties was only mentioned in two regions and considerable variation in the skills of learning support staff was reported as a result of different approaches to training. Most authorities were tackling the latter problem, however, through a development programme for learning support teachers aimed at training them to Diploma level.

Those authorities which espoused an anti-categorisation perspective had essentially rejected a dichotomy between specific and global difficulties. In doing so, they had the laudable aims of combatting the stigma which others attached to the difficulties under **both** headings ('non-problems all in the mind of pushy middle class parents with dim children' and 'mental handicap' respectively) and of attempting to organise a response to children's needs on an individual basis. The analogies of bespoke tailoring and à la carte menus, however, suggest that more lavish provision is required to achieve individually adapted programmes. Within realistic resources, it may be necessary to have a measure of categorisation and to apply it as flexibly as possible. That would imply that parental demands for a rigorous definition of specific learning difficulties and unambiguous allocation of children to a discrete group would continue to be resisted, but a systematic strategy of provision based on a philosophy which consciously blurred the edges of categories would be visible.

The identification and assessment of children with specific learning difficulties

Parents' disquiet about what they saw as deficiencies and delays in the proper identification of their child's difficulties was a feature of the research findings. Because our sample was made up entirely of parents whose children had been identified as having specific learning difficulties, it may well be that there were others which escaped such identification altogether. From the schools' perspective, nearly 70% of learning support teachers in primary schools and 50% in secondary schools reported that their school had systematic procedures for identifying such difficulties; in most cases responsibility for this was shared between learning support and mainstream teachers, though in secondary schools there was a higher chance that this fell on the former.

One of the problems seems to have been different perceptions of levels of communication. Almost all learning support staff met parents at the schools' parents' evenings and a large majority (85%) reported discussions with individual parents about their child's progress. This was not reflected in the findings from the parents' survey where a view emerged that communication was poor and the Warnock ideal of partnership between parents and school had by no means been achieved. Many parents still saw themselves as having had to make strenuous efforts to persuade the schools and local authorities of the nature and urgency of their child's problem. As a reward for this, they perceived teachers as tending to stereotype them as neurotic or inadequate and not taking seriously the valuable information they had to offer about their own children.

The usual stage at which identification occurred was P3 or P4: secondary school was regarded by most people as too late. By this time the school had had the opportunity to observe the puzzling discrepancies apparent in some children's cognitive profiles. The routine screening carried out by some education authorities was unlikely to reveal such discrepancies. A majority of regions used the Warnock five-stage procedure for identification and assessment (1 and 2 school-based, 3 by educational psychologists, 4 and 5 by multi-disciplinary teams). There was variation in how this was used: some seldom went beyond the second stage while others routinely went to the third. Only the more severe cases tended to proceed to medical consultants for assessment, and the intention here was to eliminate some of the possible serious neurological disorders.

The Warnock Report had placed great importance on inter-professional collaboration in this area. Such collaboration seemed to focus almost entirely on the rôle of the educational psychologists. Nearly three-quarters of the learning support teachers reported such links as did all of the medical consultants; direct contract between teachers and health service professionals, however, was relatively rare.

The identification/assessment process was seen by no one as a simple matter. Although a repertoire of different kinds of tests was in use, there were important limitations (and in some cases dangers) associated with all of them and concerns at inconsistencies in the level of training of learning support staff to carry them out. Classroom observation was clearly important but not well defined; in most cases it was the necessary first step and played the major part in detecting uneven performance/ability across different areas. A crucial element in the process seemed to be the opportunity teachers had to gain extended experience with the various assessment approaches so that, with practice, tests and other measures would be used to **demonstrate** rather than **discover** the specific learning difficulties; the discoveries would be made directly by the teachers as their professional craft knowledge in this area improved (see also Reid, 1993, 1994). Another aspect where the teachers were in need of support, was in dealing with parents who are understandably distraught, but often also apparently unreasonable, in their concern for their own child in an area of education which is still ill-understood and without clear policy guidelines.

Voluntary organisations, parents, psychologists and teachers all put considerable priority on the **early** recognition that certain pupils had learning problems that were unrelated to their general ability. Not only was this seen as offering the best chance to resolve or manage the problems, it was also expected to help to prevent the disruptive behaviour to which specific learning difficulties, in some cases, could lead.

Before moving on to matters of provision we should comment on the 'other side of the coin' of parents' dissatisfaction with the identification procedures in the public sector of education. Learning support teachers and regional officers were uneasy about assessment of children in the voluntary or private sector. The risks of false positive identification were seen as very real. These were regarded as unfortunate in the sense that they could well engender inappropriate expectations among parents and delay the children concerned receiving a suitable form of support for their difficulties.

Meeting the needs of children with specific learning difficulties

The kind of **special** provision for children with specific learning difficulties, which was suggested by those whose views we collected, tended to emphasise

- regular withdrawal from class
- one-to-one tuition
- highly structured teaching approaches including repetition and over-learning
- an eclectic programme of instruction tailored to individual needs
- practice in phonics (especially at the primary stage)
- concern with the whole family
- a readiness to stress how to **cope** with the problems if they could not be **resolved**
- specialised units or centres (e.g. occupational therapy units or reading centres)

There appeared to be no evidence to suggest that measures like drug therapy, diet or vitamin supplements would be of any help.

In many instances, the provision recommended for these children was also seen as appropriate for others with literacy problems. Those who drew a distinction tended to focus on organisation, withdrawal and one to one tuition, rather than differences in materials and pedagogy, where there was considerable overlap. The only explicit distinction put forward was that for generally low achievers, the conceptual content of learning materials would have to reflect an earlier stage, while for children with specific learning difficulties, the conceptual complexity could be consistent with the child's chronological age.

In two thirds of the regions, provision was entirely in mainstream classrooms supported by learning support teachers. Three, however, had specialist units or centres of some kind with pupils attending full-time or part-time and outreach work for teachers. The trend appeared to be towards in-class rather than in-centre support in the hope that this might prove to be of more long term benefit for the children and maintain a more stable pattern of integration with the rest of the population in the spirit of the national policy documents of 1978 (Warnock and HMI Reports). From an economic point of view, such a move was demanding of resources; outreach provision was expensive in terms of teachers' time and the peripatetic life could be unsatisfactory for professionals.

The policies of the late seventies, viewed as enlightened and liberal at the time, saw it as important that the withdrawal of pupils from mainstream classes be kept to a minimum; indeed, it appeared that many people interpreted those polices as taking an even harder line against withdrawal. Most educational psychologists and some teachers, however, believed that many children with literacy problems would benefit from intensive one-to-one tuition. The arguments against such provision were that it was against the spirit of the move away from the old remedial education, the children would lose touch with the mainstream curriculum, schools were inadequately staffed to undertake such work and any individual provision for children with special needs would necessarily be at the expense of the other children. If more emphasis were placed on individual tuition the learning support teacher would have less time to work as a consultant or co-teacher with the mainstream teacher (see SCOSDE, guidelines 1990; SOED 1993), advising on teaching methods to allow all children access to the curriculum and developing differentiated materials. Less than 20% of learning support teachers placed such tuition as the most important aspect of their work.

The views of parents and voluntary organisations were firmly in favour of intensive one to one tuition. Particular examples of practice, such as reading centres, were given very positive ratings and most parents in our survey reported that their child was being withdrawn from class for some individual tuition. Despite this, more than a third of the parents were dissatisfied with the provision. It is worth noting that the parents surveyed were by no means a homogeneous group. They varied in the particular nature of their child's difficulties, their view of appropriate learning support and their level of satisfaction with services provided. They did, however, share a number of concerns and one of these related to levels of resourcing. Pumfrey and Reason (1991) argued that parents' expectations have been raised by measures such as the 1981 Act, which emphasised the responsibility of the education authority to meet the needs of children with learning difficulties. Parents' comments indicated that they had a sense of entitlement to adequate provision and were prepared to stake their claim against those of other disabled groups. We examined this clash of expectation further in Riddell et al, 1994a. In the light of such competing claims, education authorities were being thrust into public debate on the establishment of priorities.

At one level this could be seen as disaffection caused by poor communication and some improvement could be effected, no doubt, by encouraging more active links between parents and professionals and among different professionals. It could be argued that this might help alleviate parental concerns about the appropriateness of the provision for their child or, indeed, offer a means to get the provision changed. In our view, however, the dissonance goes deeper than that.

Policy on special educational needs has been pulling in two directions. The 'liberal' Warnock and HMI reports of 1978 eschewed the categorisation of children into groups labelled by their disability. Whether the general public changed their thinking to embrace the new approach, which shunned the notion of the deficit residing in the pupil and shifted the 'blame' to the curriculum, is a moot point. It was clearly the case, however, that parents who believed their children had specific learning difficulties continued to see them as constituting a category (discrete group) and wished them to be so defined and provided for. Other 'market forces' policy pronouncements, especially the 1981 Act, the 1992 Parents' Charter and the document *A Parents' Guide to Special Educational Needs* (SOED, 1993a), have given them more power to 'fight back'. They are now demanding, with the support of the voluntary organisations, that the Warnock ideal of partnership becomes a reality rather than a pious hope and they have more say in the decision-making. They have resented education professionals (who are obliged to ration scarce resources) using negative stereotypes to dismiss the claims of parents and have perceived themselves as victims of that process. The new policies have put them in a more powerful position to resist this, but those same policies have not provided the extra resources needed to fulfil parental ambitions for the education of their children.

Learning support teachers may find themselves at the centre of a conflict which hinges on differing conceptualisations of learning difficulties and differing views on how such difficulties should be met. They are aware of the needs of individual children in their class and the demands of parents for individual tuition. At the same time, they have heeded the advice of HM Inspectorate to focus their energy on co-operative teaching and consultancy. Clearly, it may not be possible to fulfil both sets of expectations simultaneously. Learning support teachers' comments revealed the tensions created as they struggled to reconcile these conflicting demands.

The 5-14 *Support for Learning* document (SOED 1993b) goes some way towards making the place of specific learning difficulties more explicit; indeed, the new document refers plainly to 'pupils with dyslexia' (p.22) rather than the circumlocution 'specific learning difficulties including those of a dyslexic kind' of SCOSDE (SOED 1990 p.22). The new list of roles (SOED 1993b p.21) is closer to the roles as perceived by the teachers in our survey, still prioritising consultancy but giving more weight to teaching. Under 'teaching and tuition' the document includes withdrawal of individuals or groups from class 'as circumstances dictate' (p.22); the exercise of learning support teachers' judgement in this area, which we found in nearly all primary and most secondary schools, is here officially acknowledged. One example of tuition is 'providing special programmes in reading and writing for pupils with dyslexia' (SOED 1993b p.22). There is still no explicit reference to identifying children's difficulties; but since these pupils are now officially deemed to exist, and learning support teachers are to provide for them, by inference identification forms part of the task. The complete absence of such guidance in the 1990 version expressed opposition to categorising difficulties; the new policy takes a cautious step towards recognising the kind of expertise revealed in our survey data.

In our brief illustrations of provision in reading centres, we saw something of the variety of approaches that can be taken under this head, and were aware of parental satisfaction with this kind of provision. We were struck, however, by the lack of any evaluation of the effectiveness of the outcomes of these initiatives in terms of resolving or managing the children's difficulties. Even the criteria on which evidence might be sought about such effectiveness were unclear. This also applied (but perhaps less so) to the occupational therapy unit within the health service.

Provision for children with special educational needs has an obvious link with the opening of Records of Needs. In the case of those with specific learning difficulties, local authority practice varied from it being a routine (almost automatic) procedure to a relatively rare event. There was also variation among parents in how it was viewed. It was probably some parents' increasing awareness of the extra support that a Record should ensure for their child that led to increasing use of the recording process. There are other parents, however, who were sensitive to the perceived stigma of having a child labelled as 'recorded' or who felt that provision for children with specific learning difficulties should be included in the normal classroom repertoire. Our research was unable to unearth any significant differences in provision between those who were and were not recorded.

In conclusion

The controversial nature of this area of education and the plethora of different perceptions of specific learning difficulties ensure that the research cannot offer a set of clear recommendations to those who provide for young people with special educational needs. However, we believe the information we have collected will be of value in alerting providers to the factors they have to take into account in making decisions. There is, of course, no solution to the 'problem' that will be satisfactory to everyone involved or, indeed, completely satisfactory for anyone.

There is a sense in which many people believe that the problems might be resolved if more funds were available to provide individual support for children with learning difficulties. We suspect that such resources might well bring some improvements. However, we think it significant that one question which we formulated in our research proposal we have been unable to address; this concerned the reliability and comparability of statistics held by health boards and education authorities about their expenditure on specific learning difficulties. We found no such statistics. In our view, it would be virtually impossible for authorities to calculate costs in this area, given the absence of shared understandings and priorities.

At one level there are improvements that could be made in communications between the education system and parents and among different professionals. No doubt people could be made to feel better informed and, as a result of that, more comfortable. Setting up the mechanics of communication, however, is unlikely to make the major improvements in this area for which many would hope. There are six major areas of conflict or tension which are not open to easy resolution.

First, there is friction between competing **policies** in the public sector which reflect different ideological stances about learning difficulties. On the one hand, national and regional policies over the last decade have increasingly focused on concern for the learning difficulties of all children ('every child is special') and the promotion of integration into mainstream education rather than segregation into special schools or classes; along with this has gone a much greater propensity to see the difficulties as located within the curriculum rather than as a deficit in the child. On the other hand, within the move towards policies which stress market forces and the primacy of the customer, there is increasing empowerment of parents; in this case, such empowerment takes the form of demands that their children have special provision in the form of one to one tuition. The implication is some kind of withdrawal from the mainstream class and a recognition that the problem lies within the child.

The differences embodied in the two aspects of policy above are reflected in the second focus of dissent which is **economic.** Education authorities have responsibilities and concerns for all pupils but parents' priorities are for their own child. Learning support teachers are pulled, on the one hand, by the emphasis on providing co-operative support to mainstream staff for all pupils in classrooms and regarding problems as essentially curriculum problems and, on the other hand, by the belief that there are circumstances in which children's needs are not met by these strategies and withdrawal for individual tuition to deal with a difficulty located within the child is needed. Parents often see local authorities (perhaps rightly) as dragging their feet because of the resource implications of providing for pupils with specific learning difficulties. However, resources are scarce and the authorities, even if they return to the old ways of thinking about learning difficulties as groups of pupils characterised by particular kinds of disabilities, have to balance provision for all groups with varying kinds and levels of disability, whether or not the parents are applying pressure. With greater devolved management of resources to schools, individual schools might choose to accord greater priority to pupils with specific learning difficulties but inevitably that will be at the expense of something else. If we go even further along the self-governing line, and schools acquire greater freedom to select their pupils, the problem may become one of whether such pupils are able to find places in the schools of their choice. That will depend on the extent of the incentives or otherwise to schools to accept children with special needs.

The third area of tension concerns the fundamental differences about the **nature of these difficulties** between many professionals and parents, within professional groups and between different aspects of government policies. The main area of disagreement focuses on whether children with specific learning difficulties form a discrete group, are part of the continuum of all children with problems of reading and writing, or are individuals whose difficulties are not amenable to any kind of categorisation. There are also differences in whether the problems are seen as necessarily enduring. Certainly some professionals and the voluntary organisations would argue that such difficulties are not open to cure, but only to management (usually by circumvention). In cases where children do, in fact, get over their problems of, say, literacy, should we conclude that they did not have specific learning difficulties in the first place? There are calls for more training of teachers on the assumption that this could resolve some of these conceptual tensions. Such calls seem also to assume that there is a body of knowledge and acquirable skills available to plug into the gaps in teachers' expertise. Unfortunately, there is no such resource of shared understanding, and academics are as much in debate about the issue as everyone else.

A fourth controversial focus is the **recognition** of specific learning difficulties. We have documented in this report the differences among the various groups involved in our study. There is some evidence that small numbers of professionals (though much smaller than parts of the media and some parents would have us believe) regard such recognition as directing attention to children (mainly sons) of middle class parents who want to distinguish their offspring from those pupils (usually working class) who are generally less able. To some extent this view is reinforced by the fact that the major part of the provision which we observed did go to support middle class families. In its most convincing form, however, recognition of specific learning difficulties sees no social class differences in occurrence nor is it expected to appear only in children of average or above average ability. It is more difficult, of course, to observe discrepancies in the cognitive profiles of low ability children and there is a tendency to explain poor performance of children from the less affluent areas on other factors such as culturally deprived home backgrounds or some idea of inherent general low potential for learning. The question of gender is more problematic; there is an argument that the predominance of boys could be a social artefact of the importance given to their achievements rather than a basic gender difference in occurrence.

The fifth area of uncertainty is concerned with **what constitutes effective provision.** Without measures of effectiveness of different kinds of provision, policy decisions are difficult to make. It is unlikely, for example, that parents' satisfaction with reading centres will prevent such centres from being vulnerable to spending cuts in education. We have described a variety of approaches illustrating the considerable demands of a task which tries to explore the possibilities of providing the individual tuition, seen by many as essential for these children, within the current economic stringencies and, at the same time, avoiding the pitfalls of loss of contact with the general school curriculum and social interaction with peers.

Finally there are conflicts of **emotions.** At one level, there are the irritations felt by educationists who feel constrained by their limited resources and under pressure from what they see as pushy parents supported by voluntary organisations; the latter are seen as having the great advantage of being able to act as a pressure group for one small section of the school population without carrying any of the responsibility for the vast majority of pupils (Riddell et al 1994a, 1994b). Parents, on the other hand, are frustrated by what they see as the education system resisting valuable information which they have to offer, treating them as if they had little to contribute to the education of their own children and failing to communicate with them about matters of crucial importance to the family. At a deeper level, however, there is in parents' minds a fear of the stigma attached to any notion that their children are identified with generally low achieving pupils (fears of 'mental handicap' labelling), or as 'recorded', or as 'brain damaged'. This concern, perhaps as much as the difficulties themselves, ensures that the whole family becomes enmeshed in the problem. In the Scottish education system there has not been a tradition of supporting the whole family, and schools' perceptions of parents (especially the articulate middle class) as pushy have exacerbated the situation.

An account of six areas of tension and uncertainty may seem a sombre note on which to end this study of policy, practice and provision for children with specific learning difficulties. However, the common aim, which we share with the many teachers and education professionals, campaigners and parents who have contributed to the study, is to enable children to overcome obstacles standing in the way of their learning. By setting out the various strands of the problem in the changing context of education in the 1990s, we hope that we have established firmer ground from which the next steps can be taken.

References

Allan, J, Brown, S and Munn, P (1991), *Off the Record: Mainstream Provision for Pupils with Non-Recorded Learning Difficulties in Primary and Secondary Schools*, The Scottish Council for Research in Education, Edinburgh.

Barton, L and Tomlinson, S (1984), 'The politics of integration in England' in Barton, L and Tomlinson, S (eds), *Special Education and Social Interests*, pp.65-80, Croom Helm, Beckenham.

Bowe, R and Ball, S J (1992), *Reforming Education and Changing Schools*, Routledge, London.

Bradley, L (1990), 'Rhyming connections in learning to read and spell', in Pumfrey, P D and Elliott, C D (eds), *Children's Difficulties in Reading, Spelling and Writing*, Falmer Press, London.

Brown, E N (1978), 'Attentional style, linguistic complexity and the treatment of reading difficulty' in Knights, D and Bakker, D J (eds), *Rehabilitation and Management of Learning Disorders*, proceedings of the 1978 Nato International Conference.

Bryant, P E (1985), 'The question of prevention' in Snowling, M (ed), *Children's Written Language Difficulties*, NFER Nelson, Windsor.

Bryant, P E (1990), 'Phonological development and reading' in Pumfrey, P D and Elliott, C D (eds), *Children's Difficulties in Reading, Spelling and Writing*, Falmer Press, London.

Bryant, P E and Bradley, L (1985), *Children's Reading Problems*, Blackwell Scientific Publications, Oxford.

Bryant, P E and Impey, L (1986), 'The similarities between normal readers and developmental and acquired dyslexics', *Cognition*, 24, pp.121-137.

Carroll, H C M (1972), 'The remedial teaching of reading: an evaluation', *Remedial Education*, 7, 1, pp.10-15.

Chesson, R, McKay, C and Stephenson, E (1990), *The Child with Motor/Learning Difficulties: a study report for parents*, Royal Aberdeen Childrens Hospital, Aberdeen.

Chesson, R, McKay, C and Stephenson, E (1991), 'Motor/Learning difficulties and the family', *Childcare, health and development*, 16 (2), pp.123-138.

Closs, A (1994) 'All change but has training lost its way?' *Times Educational Supplement Scotland* 16/12/94 p.4

Clough, P and Barton, L (eds) (1995) Making Difficulties: *Research and the Construction of Special Educational Needs*, Paul Chapman Publishing, London.

Critchley, M (1981), 'Dyslexia: a overview' in Pavlidis, G and Miles, T R (eds), *Dyslexia Research and Its Applications to Education*, Chichester, Wiley.

Crombie, M (1992), *Specific Learning Difficulties: A Teacher's Guide*, Jordanhill Publications, Glasgow.

Dane, G (1995) 'Pass the keyboard please' *Times Educational Supplement Scotland*   6/1/95 p.16.

Department of Education and Science (1972), *Children with Specific Reading Difficulties*, Report of the Advisory Committee on Handicapped Children (The Tizard Report), HMSO, London.

Department of Education and Science (1975), *A Language for life*, (The Bullock Report), HMSO, London.

Department of Education and Science (1978), *Special Educational Needs*, (The Warnock Report), HMSO, London.

Department of Education and Science (1979), *Developments in Provision for Children with Specific Learning Difficulties*, (The Fish Report), HMSO, London.

Division of Educational and Child Psychology of the British Psychological Society (1983), *Specific Learning Difficulties: The 'Specific Reading Difficulties' versus 'Dyslexia' Controversy Resolved?*, DECP.

Duffield, J, Brown, S and Riddell, S. (1995) The post-Warnock learning support teacher: where do specific learning difficulties fit in? *Support for Learning* Vol 10, No 1 1995 pp.22-28.

Grampian Regional Council Education Department (1987), *Guide to Educational Services for Children with Special Needs*, Grampian Regional Council, Aberdeen.

Grampian Regional Psychological Service (1987), *Reeling and Writhing: Children with Specific Learning Difficulties*, Grampian Regional Council, Aberdeen.

Kennedy (1980), 'Unmasking medicine' in *The Listener*, 6/11/80.

Lawson, J (1994) 'English-Spoken must not be allowed to fail' *Times Educational Supplement Scotland* 28/10/94

MacLeod, D (ed) (1988), *Ten Years On: a review of developments since the publication of the HMI report on pupils with learning difficulties*, JCCES/Moray House, Edinburgh.

Moses D, Hegarty S and Jowett S (1987) 'Meeting special educational needs: support for the ordinary school' *Educational Research* 29(2) pp.108-115

Newton, M, Thompson, M E, Richards, I L (1979), *Readings in Dyslexia: A Study to Accompany the Aston Index*, Bemrose UK, London.

Pumfrey, P D (1990), 'Testing and teaching pupils with reading difficulties' in Pumfrey, P D and Elliott C D (eds), *Children's Difficulties in Reading, Spelling and Writing*, Falmer Press, London.

Pumfrey, P and Reason, R (1991), *Specific Learning Difficulties (Dyslexia) Challenges and Responses*, NFER Nelson, Windsor.

Reid, G (ed), (1993) *Specific Learning Difficulties (Dyslexia) Perspectives on Practice* Moray House Institute of Education, Edinburgh

Reid, G (1994) *Specific Learning Difficulties (Dyslexia) a handbook* Moray House Institute of Education, Edinburgh

Riddell, S, Thomson, G O B and Dyer, S (1992), 'A key informant approach to the study of local policy-making in the field of special educational needs', *European Journal of Special Needs Education*, 7, 1, 47-63.

Riddell, S, Brown, S and Duffield, J. (1993) 'Specific Learning Difficulties, learning support teachers and the impact of changing policy' Chapter 29 pp 409-429, *Specific Learning Difficulties (Dyslexia) Perspectives on Practice* ed. Gavin Reid, Moray House Institute of Education, Edinburgh

Riddell, S, Brown, S and Duffield, J.(1994a) 'Parental power and special educationial needs: the case of specific learning difficulties'*British Educational Research Journal*, Vol 20 No 3, 1994

Riddell, S and Brown, S (eds) (1994b) *Special educational needs policy in the 1990s: Warnock in the Market Place*, Routledge, London

Riddell, S, Brown, S and Duffield, J. (1995) 'The ethics of policy-focused research in special eductional needs: researching specific learning difficulties for the Scottish Office (Education Department), in Clough, P and Barton, L (eds) *Making difficulties: research and the construction of SEN*, Paul Chapman Publishing, London

Robinson, N (1991), *Should Learning Support Teams Include a Speech Therapist?*, unpublished paper presented to Edinburgh and South East Scotland Dyslexia Association conference 21st September 1991.

Rutter, M, Tizard, J and Whitmore, K (1976), *Education, Health and Behaviour*, Longman, London.

Scottish Committee for Staff Development in Education (1990), *Award Bearing Courses Within the 3 Tier Structure: Guidelines for Diplomas in Special Educational Needs*, SCOSDE, Edinburgh.

Scottish Education Department (1978), *The Education of Pupils with Learning Difficulties in Primary and Secondary Schools in Scotland: A Progress Report by HM Inspectors of Schools*, HMSO, Edinburgh.

Scottish Education Department (1981), *Education (Scotland) Act 1981 - Implementation*, Circular 1087, HMSO, Edinburgh.

Scottish Examination Board (1990) *Guidance on examination arrangements for candidates with special educational needs*, SEB, Edinburgh

Scottish Office Education Department (1992), *The Parents' Charter in Scotland*, HMSO, Edinburgh.

Scottish Office Education Department (1993a), *A Parents' Guide to Special Educational Needs*, SOED, Edinburgh.

Scottish Office Education Department (1993b), *Support for learning: special educational needs within the 5-14 curriculum*, Scottish Office, Edinburgh.

Scottish Office Education Department (1994), *Higher Still*, Scottish Office, Edinburgh.

Smith, F (1990), *Reading*, Cambridge: Cambridge University Press.

Snowling, M J (ed) (1985), *Children's Written Language Difficulties: Assessment and Management*, NFER Nelson, Windsor.

Snowling, M J (1990), 'Dyslexia in childhood: a cognitive-developmental perspective' in Pumfrey, P D and Elliott, C D (eds), *Children's Difficulties in Reading, Spelling and Writing*, Falmer Press, London.

Stephenson, E (1986), *The Child with Motor/Learning Difficulties: A Guide for Parents and Teachers*, Occupational Therapy Department, Royal Aberdeen Children's Hospital, Aberdeen.

Stephenson, E and McKay, C (1989), 'A support group for parents of children with motor-learning difficulties', *British Journal of Occupational Therapy*, 52

(5), 181-183.

Stephenson, E, McKay, C and Chesson, R (1990), 'An investigative study of early developmental factors in children with motor/learning difficulties', *British Journal of Occupational Therapy*, 53 (1), 4-6.

Stephenson, E, McKay, C and Chesson, R (1991), The identification and treatment of motor/learning difficulties: parents' perceptions and the role of the therapist, *Childcare, Health and Development*, 17, 19-113.

Strathclyde Regional Council (1992), *Every Child is Special: A Policy for All*, Strathclyde Regional Council Education Department, Glasgow.

Tansley, P and Panckhurst, J (1981), *Children with Specific Learning Difficulties*, NFER Nelson, Windsor.

Tobin, D and Pumfrey, P (1976), 'Some long term effects of the remedial teaching of reading', *Educational Review*, 29, pp.1-12.

Tomlinson, S (1982), *A Sociology of Special Education*, Routledge, London.

Weedon, C (1992), *Specific Learning Difficulties in Mathematics*, Stirling University Department of Education & Tayside Region.

Weedon, C (1995) 'English for all' *Times Educational Supplement Scotland* 3/2/95

Young, P and Tyre, C (1983), *Dyslexia or Illiteracy? Realizing the Right to Read*, Open University Press, Milton Keynes.

Yule, W (1976), 'Issues and problems in remedial education', *Developmental Medicine and Child Neurology*, 18, pp.674-682.

Appendix A
Definitions of specific learning difficulties

Literature survey: definitions of specific learning difficulties

The area of specific learning difficulties is typified by disagreement over terminology. In the literature a wide variety of different labels has been used, for instance specific developmental dyslexia, specific reading retardation, word-blindness and, most recently, specific learning difficulties. The definition used varies from profession to profession and has considerable implications both for the estimated incidence and for the type of assesment and provision deemed appropriate. The problem is that the concept (specific learning difficulties/ dyslexia) does not appear to indicate a syndrome which is distinct in terms of aetiology, intra-individual abilities, prognosis and response to treatment. The central issues of the debate revolve around:

a)   the identification of children with specific learning difficulties: Are children with specific learning difficulties psychologically different from other poor readers, or are they part of a continuum of reading ability?

b)   the origin of specific learning difficulties: Is the deficit in the child or in the curriculum?

Since 1970 the pressure on education authorities to make special provision for children with specific learning difficulties has increased due to the demands of various bodies representing dyslexic children and the recommendations made in DES and SED reports and Acts of Parliament. These recommendations are summarised below. The focus in section A is on the issue of terminology and the definition of the concept, while section B concentrates on policies and provision.

1968 - World Federation of Neurology defined both 'dyslexia' and 'specific learning difficulties'. Dyslexia is defined as '... a disorder in children who, despite conventional classroom experience, fail to attain the language skills of reading, writing and spelling commensurate with their intellectual abilities'. Specific developmental dyslexia is defined as '... a disorder manifested in learning to read despite conventional instruction, adequate intelligence and socio-cultural opportunity. It is dependent upon fundamental cognitive disabilities which are frequently of constitutional origin'.

1970 - Chronically Sick and Disabled Persons Act. LEAs were required to provide 'special educational treatment' in maintained schools for children suffering from 'acute dyslexia'. The ambiguity of the term 'acute dyslexia' led the Secretary of State to refer the matter to the Advisory Committee on Handicapped Children, which led to the following report:

1972 - DES, Tizard report, *Children with Specific Reading Difficulties*

The term 'acute dyslexia' was rejected and the evidence for a 'specific syndrome of developmental dyslexia' was similarly discounted. The preferred term was 'specific reading difficulties', used to describe 'the small group of children whose reading (and perhaps writing, spelling and number) abilities are significantly below the standards which their abilities in other spheres would lead one to expect' (Tizard, 1972, p.3). The educational needs of these children was considered as part of 'the wider problem of reading backwardness of all kinds' (the continuum view) and it was recommended that children who are backward in reading, including those with specific reading retardation, should normally be given skilled remedial teaching in their ordinary schools (p.8).

1975 - DES, Bullock Report, *Language for Life.* The use of the term dyslexia to describe the small group of children whose difficulties in learning to read are not attributable to 'limited ability or... emotional or extraneous factors' (Bullock, 1975, p.268) was criticised and the term 'specific reading retardation' was suggested instead. 'Specific reading retardation' is operationally defined as a 'syndrome characterised by severe reading difficulties which are not accountable for in terms of low intelligence and which are not explicable merely in terms of the lower end of a normal distribution of reading skills' (Rutter & Yule, 1973). Bullock recommended that these children be given intensive treatment in a remedial centre or reading clinic, with the support of an adviser with special responsibility for children with learning difficulties. However, the borderline between children included in this category and children excluded has been controversial (DECP, 1983). The criticism has also been made that the term 'specific reading retardation' is not broad enough to describe the complexity of dyslexia (Critchley, 1981).

1978 - DES, Warnock report, *Special Educational Needs* recommended that the term 'children with learning difficulties' be used to describe both children then classified as ESN and children receiving remedial education. It was suggested that children with particular learning difficulties, such as specific reading difficulties might be described as having 'specific learning difficulties'. Warnock recognised that there were problems in distinguishing these children fom other poor readers but considered that 'distinctive arrangements' should be provided for 'children whose disabilities are marked but whose general ability is at least average' (Warnock, 1978, para.11.48). Warnock also lists specific learning difficulties as one of the potential difficulties experienced by pupils with moderate learning difficulties, which shows that the term is not confined to children of average or greater than average intelligence. This report changed the conceptual framework for special educational provision from one based on discrete categories of handicap to one based on a continuum of special educational needs and led to the 1981 Education Act and to an important survey of the field by Tansley & Panckhurst (1981).

1978 - SED (HMI progress report), *The Education of Pupils with Learning Difficulties in Primary & Secondary Schools in Scotland*
No reference to specific learning difficulties as such is made in this report. The phrase 'pupils with particular learning difficulties' is used at one point in connection with 'certificate courses' (para.2.22) but the meaning of this term is not defined.

1979 - DES, Fish report, *Developments in provision for children with SLD*
This report concluded that specific learning difficulties in reading, writing and spelling indubitably exist and that the problems and needs of these children should be more widely known to schools and advisory services. The difficulty in identifying these children was acknowledged , one of the problems being that present procedures for screening and assessment are not sufficiently discriminating. In particular, the report referred to the problem of distinguishing children with SLD from children whose backwardness in reading, writing and spelling 'may have been caused by social, cultural and less obvious emotional factors'.

1980 - In the **BMA News Review** the British Medical Association advised its members that dyslexia was an educational rather than a medical problem, hence diagnosis was the responsibility of educational psychologists rather than medics.

1981 - Tansley & Panckhurst, *Children with Specific Learning Difficulties.* Tansley and Panckhurst offer the following definition: 'Children with specific learning difficulties are those who, in the absence of sensory defect or overt organic damage, have an intractable learning problem in one or more of reading, writing, spelling and mathematics, and who do not respond to normal teaching. For these children, early identification, sensitive encouragement and specific remedial arrangements are necessary' (Tansley & Panckhurst, 1981, p.259). The term specific learning difficulties was chosen because it has breadth of meaning, subsumes a wide range of difficulties and does not confine the concept to children of average or greater than average intelligence. While it was recognised that retarded readers (children underachieving according to their general intelligence level) could be differentiated from the mass of backward readers (children whose reading is less than average for their age), such a division was not considered helpful since both groups of children may have the same type of learning difficulty and benefit from the same type of remedial treatment. It was recommended that any special provision for reading difficulties within schools should be across the board: 'The evidence is clear that there are, as the Warnock Report says, "children whose disabilities are marked but whose general ability is at least average", but it is difficult to accept the conclusion that there should be "distinctive arrangements" made for these children without such arrangements being made for all children with specific learning difficulties - including those of below average intelligence' (p 259).

1981 - Hansard (4.3.81) reports debates in both Houses of Parliament in which 'dyslexia' was named and recognised as a handicapping condition During the Fifth Sitting of the Special Standing Committee on the Education Bill, 1981, the Under Secretary of State for Education said that 'dyslexia' would be covered by the Act (DECEP,1983).

1981 - Education (Scotland) Act. The Act states that a child has 'special educational needs' if he has a 'learning difficulty' which requires special educational provision to be made to meet those needs. A child has a learning difficulty if 'he has significantly greater difficulty in learning than the majority of children' (Section 3,1d). (Children whose difficulties are solely attributable to their first language not being English are not included in this category). The onus is placed on the education authorities to establish which children have

219

'pronounced, specific or complex special educational needs which are such as require continuing review and to open and keep a Record of Needs of each such child or young person' (Section 4, 2b). The Act was seen by the British Dyslexia Association as a gesture of 'good faith' by the government, making it the duty of LEAs to provide appropriate remedial resources for dyslexic children (TES, 27.11.81).

1981 - SED Circular 1087: Education (Scotland) Act 1981 - Implementation
This circular was issued to education authorities to provide guidance on the Act and the regulations made under it. It expands on the distinction between 'special educational needs which can be met within the normal resources of primary and secondary schools and those which are pronounced, specific or complex, cannot be so met and are of a continuing nature' (para 1, Rec 2). For the latter recording procedures should be implemented. Pronounced, specific and complex needs are not defined. The description of specific educational needs includes 'needs dictating a particular curricular approach e.g. arising from dyslexia' (Appendix, Rec 2).

1983 - Report of a Working Party of the Division of Educational and Child Psychology of the British Psychological Society, *Specific Learning Difficulties: The 'Specific Reading Difficulties' Versus 'Dyslexia' Controversy Resolved?* (DECP report).
Although the term used in the enquiry was 'specific reading difficulties', specific learning difficulties was the term finally recommended. This umbrella term was generally accepted within the maintained sector, but the various establishments within the private sector did not agree on terminology and many of the issues stemming from it . The adoption of a generic term - SpLD - was seen as counter to the interests of parents and voluntary organisations who have campaigned to get dyslexia acknowledged as a handicapping condition, requiring a specific kind of remedial treatment. The report made the point that the new Act helps make the debate on terminology irrelevant by emphasising individual problems and needs rather than nomenclature. Where a child presents significant specific learning difficulties, the detailed assessment and monitoring procedures specified in the Act should be implemented.

1983 - Young & Tyre, *Dyslexia or Illiteracy*
Young and Tyre reject all terminology as unhelpful:
'Their spurious use of 'specific' neither determines a species nor is it precise. Suggesting that a disparity between "intelligence" and reading ability is a "specific retardation" is as fatuous as talking about "specific singing retardation" or "specific swimming retardation". If you have difficulty in

220

singing or swimming that's it. "Specific learning difficulties in reading" begs the question whether the specificity is in the learning, in the difficulties or in the reading. All it means is that a child has difficulties in learning to read and there is no need to be any more specific than that (p19).

B *Provision for children with specific learning difficulties*

1979 - DES, Fish Report, *Developments in provision for children with Specific Learning Difficulties*
In February 1977 the DES conducted a survey of the facilities provided by local education authorities for children with reading difficulties. 79 of the 104 responding local education authorities provided reading centres, clinics or remedial centres. The remainder based their provision either on peripatetic teaching services or on special classes. A notable difference was whether individual policies concentrated on within-school or external provision. The survey suggested that local education authorities were aware of the needs of children with reading difficulties but showed that there is considerable variability in both policies and provision for these children. Later on in the year the HMI visited clinics run by Dyslexia Associations, hospital clinics and the local education authority establishments identified in the survey. They found that the children attending independent clinics differed in a number of ways from those attending local authority establishments: children attending local education authority clinics were younger, from a wider range of social backgrounds and more often perceived to have emotional/behavioural problems in addition to reading difficulties. Although it was generally considered that the children required long-term support, most help was discontinued after about 2 years and there appeared to be no agreed criteria for this step. There was little evidence overall of any systematic follow-up of the children's progress, although the local education authorities were slightly more likely to continue monitoring the children's progress than the independent establishments. The conclusions of the report included the recommendation that more guidelines should be developed for dealing with SLD within ordinary schools, with specific reference to the long-term help these children may require.

1978 - SED (HMI Progress Report) The Education of Pupils with Learning Difficulties in Primary & Secondary Schools in Scotland
This report assesses the remedial provision made for pupils with learning difficulties *in the lower half of the ability range.*[1]

---

[1] It is not clear whether children with specific learning difficulties are included. Identification was subjective: 'based almost entirely on the failure of pupils to make

1978 - DES, Warnock report, *Special Educational Needs*
Five increasingly more complex stages in assessing (and meeting) special educational needs were outlined. The first three stages are school-based, starting with class and head teachers and progressively involving specialist help in the identifying and meeting of needs. The multi-disciplinary assessment at stages 4 and 5 (leading to recording) was recommended only for children whose needs could not be met within the ordinary school. The development of special facilities and teaching was advocated to enable as many pupils as possible to receive special educational provision in ordinary schools. The setting up of school-based resource centres, such as reading clinics, was recommended for the use of non-recorded pupils in ordinary schools. The children would be withdrawn to these centres, which would be specially equipped and staffed by teachers with special qualifications. With reference to children with specific learning difficulties,   Warnock notes that there has been an increase in the number of clinics and centres both inside and outside the education service to meet these children's needs (cf. Fish,1979) and recommends further work to

---

progress in reading their class reader' (para 3.2,p16). A more precise identification of learning difficulties was left to remedial teachers, who sometimes used standardised reading tests when deciding whether to accept pupils for special tuition. The report states that it 'was not normal practice for schools patiently to diagnose the sources of difficulty and match remedial action to need' (Ibid).   Children with learning difficulties were withdrawn from their class individually or in small groups and taken by the remedial teacher where available or by a promoted member of staff. Withdrawal normally began at P3 and continued to P5. In secondary schools there was considerable variability regarding the proportion of pupils withdrawn for remedial tuition.   While the main criterion for selecting a pupil was the difference between his reading and chronological age, different standards were applied and ultimately the final number tended to depend upon the availability of staff.   Remedial provision was only made at the S1 and S2 level.   Few schools had a clear policy for keeping pupil records and discussion of children's problems tended to be informal.   Child guidance services were much more involved in the primary than the secondary school: their main concern being with children whose reading difficulties were severe.   The lack of communication with parents, who were frequently not informed that their children were receiving special tuition, was lamented.   The curriculum was identified as a major source of learning difficulties;   in particular, the withdrawal of children for remedial classes often resulted in an impoverished curriculum. 'Appropriate' rather than 'remedial' education was recommended and the responsibility for providing this was placed firmly in the hands of the schools.   In conclusion, the lack of progress made in developing efficient systems of support for pupils with learning difficulties was lamented.   There was no standard means of identifying pupils with learning difficulties in primary or secondary schools; whether or not a pupil received remedial tuition depended on the subjective judgments of staff and school resources.   Even it if it was available, the type of support provided was not necessarily appropriate.

evaluate the effectiveness of the different approaches being followed. In the meantime the committee advocates that 'a more discriminating approach to children with reading, writing and spelling difficulties' be adopted (para 11.48).

1981 - SED Circular 1087: Education (Scotland) Act 1981 - Implementation
Both HMI (1978) and Warnock (1978) advocated a school-based approach to the assessment, identification and (where possible) resolution of pupils' learning difficulties with the help, if necessary, of specialist teachers. The circular recommends that arrangements for school-based asessment should include the following:

i) 'prompt action by the class teacher along defined lines when learning difficulties first become apparent;
ii) explicit provision for referral by class teachers for further advice;
iii) maximum involvement of parents; and
iv) regular monitoring at agreed intervals of the effect of specific interventions on the pupil's progress in accordance with an express policy formulated by the education authority on the assessment of and provision for special educational needs'.

1981 - Tansley & Panckhurst, *Children with Specific Learning Difficulties*.
The evidence suggests that those identified as having specific learning difficulties do not all receive appropriate help and that the remedial treatment provided is not always effective.

1983 - DECP Report (op cit)
Over half of the responding local education authorities agreed that specific learning difficulties/specific reading difficulties existed in some form or another and they had been sufficiently concerned about it to formulate a policy. Provision for children with specific reading difficulties was seen by all responding chief education officers as 'essentially part of the wider approach to the provision for children with special needs' (p.20). Specific reading difficulties were viewed within the context of reading difficulty at large. The dominant concern was to help teachers to identify and educate children with reading problems in ordinary schools. Children with specific reading difficulties were most frequently identified through referral to school psychological services. The type of provision most frequently named was remedial teaching in ordinary schools (89% of responding local education authorities) with additional help from peripatetic services also well favoured (78% of responding local education authorities). The conclusions were that local education authorities in England and Wales recognise the existence of

specific learning difficulties/specific reading difficulties and are doing 'as much as they consider necessary to meet these needs' (p.25).

The pattern of responses from principal educational psychologists concerning policy and practice was generally similar to that of the education officers. Opinion was however divided between those who viewed specific learning difficulties within the general context of special needs and felt provision was adequate and those who saw specific learning difficulties as a special category of need, requiring extra provision. (The term 'dyslexia' was not favoured either by education officers or psychologists, because it has medical rather than educational connotations.)

Appendix B
Definition of social class

Definition of social class used in the study

Because both fathers and mothers contribute to the economic and cultural status
of families, we felt it was important to use a definition of class which took
account of both parents' attributes. Class was therefore assigned to a particular
family according to the broad definitions used in the Registrar General's
Classification of Occupations. Parents' occupations were grouped thus: (1)
professional and managerial; (2) intermediate (semi-professional); (3a) white
collar; (3b) skilled manual; (4) semi-skilled manual; (5) unskilled manual.
Families were considered middle class if either the father's occupation was 1,
2 or 3a or if the mother's occupation was 1 or 2. The families of women in
group 3a were not considered middle class because their pay and status is more
comparable with that of manual workers. Critics of the Registrar General's
Classification of Occupations have argued that it is inadequately theorised, but
it is difficult to find any definition of class thta pays equal attention to the status
of women and men, and so despite its inadequacies it seemed to provide a
useful working definition.

Appendix C
Summary of education authority policy documents

Summary of education authority policy documents

Policy documents from ten Regions were made available to the team and are discussed below, along with other documents which were provided.

Region 1

1.1   A Teacher's Resource Centre housed a Special Needs Library containing an identified section of books and materials on dyslexia. Lists of these materials were presented; under the heading 'Dyslexia: pamphlets and books for Parents and Teachers.'

Region 2

2.1   The Regional *Guide to Educational Services for Children with Special Needs* comprised a 30 page booklet, addressed to parents or members of the public (1988).   It outlined regional policy for special educational needs, detailing lines of responsibility. Parents were encouraged to consult authority staff in named posts and the psychological services if difficulties arose. Various sections outlined the ways in which children with special needs were identified, covering a wide range of particular needs and areas of provision. The development of services was presented as part of a ten year plan. Five pages of useful addresses at the end reinforced the message that members of the public were intended to use the services to the full.

Specific learning difficulties were not dealt with in an identified section of this guide.   They were subsumed under the learning difficulties section and provision was described within a section on learning support services in primary and secondary schools.

The confusions arising from the word 'specific' were exemplified in the section introducing special schools and units for 'some one and a half percent of the school population'. The Guide suggested: 'They range from children whose difficulties are pronounced, specific and complex on the one hand to some whose intellectual abilities are not strikingly low but who . . . persistently fail to cope with the demands of their local school.' The facilities described were generally designed for children with mild, severe or profound mental handicap.

The reports on which the policy was based were identified, and the provision was described as: based on P2 screening with follow up diagnostic testing; primary school learning support with individual, group and co-operative teaching; arrangements to support the transition of children with learning difficulties to secondary school; and secondary learning support noting direct tuition, team teaching and learning support input into courses and materials. It was stressed that support was given as needed, 'whatever the child's level of ability'.

The only direct reference to specific learning difficulties was in four lines at the end of this section. It described a small primary age unit for children with severe specific learning difficulties, with places for only six pupils.

2.2   The region's psychological services conducted a survey into the incidence and provision for children with specific learning difficulties in 1985-86, following meetings between officials of the Education Department and representatives of the local Dyslexia Association. All referrals to the psychological service during the survey year which fulfilled set criteria indicating possible specific learning difficulties were included.   Initially 32 returns from three divisions were analysed in the main report; 12 returns from the fourth (city) division were analysed separately owing to a delay. In the event, clear differences emerged, with the main sample conceived in terms of a relatively discrete group of difficulties, and the latter group perceived in broader terms, with the difficulties partly attributed to environmental factors. Findings pointed to the need to raise awareness in schools, so that earlier referral could be made. The survey was considered to confirm the existence of specific learning difficulties; while help was always available, it was 'not always sufficiently intensive to be of maximum benefit.'

2.3   Internal documents were supplied, of more recent dates than the survey and the guide to services. They confirmed that the region had followed up its previous stance of progressive development of appropriate education. An internal summary on specific learning difficulties dated 1990 noted increased awareness and demand for provision. Incidence was discussed with reference to the 44 pupils out of a school population of over 80,000 identified in the 1986 survey. This 0.05% of pupils was compared with the estimated 20% having special needs of any kind. A small proportion of the pupils considered to have specific learning difficulties required individual intensive tuition of the kind provided in the small special unit; two later documents detailed the plans to open two further units. These provided full time teaching for pupils mainly at the P4-P6 stages. A period of 18-24 months was recommended as the probable duration of placements. The units were situated at primary schools so that a measure of integration could be achieved. Significant gains in reading age and general educational competence were reported for the unit's pupils.

The region had also undertaken a planned programme of staff development in relation to specific learning difficulties. The psychological service had been associated with the development of a one year Diploma course at a college of education and ten experienced learning support teachers per year had been seconded to take this additional qualification since it began in 1990. The aim was that every Area Special Educational Needs Team (i.e. the learning support teachers for a secondary school and its associated primaries) should have at least one member holding the specific learning difficulties Diploma. However, the documents noted recent (July 1990) budget restrictions on learning support staffing levels.

Region 3

3.1 Policy statement (1990): *Regional provision for Children with Severe Specific Learning Difficulties.* The difficulties were defined as including dyslexia, dysgraphia and dyscalculia; no position was taken on incidence, with the range of quoted estimates given as 2% to in excess of 20%. While recognising the existence of children with severe specific learning difficulties, the authority concluded that only a 'very small' proportion of children would require a Record of Needs to be opened. Intervention would range from sympathetic handing of child and parents by the class teacher, through school learning support, support by the five regional learning support specialists, to speech therapy, occupational therapy or alternative means of decoding or encoding information.

At this level, access to various aspects of technology, including tape-recorders, word-processors and communications aids is often a

228

feature of provision; in this Region a child with this degree of difficulty would possibly be considered to require a Record of Needs; . . . . The emphasis would be on making the necessary provision to address his special needs while maintaining his contact with the curriculum and his status as a mainstream pupil.

Intervention in the secondary school was outlined; scribing and the preparation of tapes might be required together with modified Standard Grade Courses and exceptional examination conditions. The whole approach was described as pragmatic rather than theoretical.

Region 4

4.1 A proposed *Policy Statement on Dyslexia* (1991) perceived dyslexia as part of a continuum of specific learning difficulties and located educational provision within overall provision for pupils with learning difficulties. Relevant experience and organisational structures already existed in the region and could be built upon at levels involving the school, parents, flexible deployment of learning support, the psychological service, provision of appropriate technological aids, and attention to current research. A range of in-service training on specific learning difficulties had already been offered, and it was recommended that this programme be further developed in order to raise the awareness of all staff with regard to specific learning difficulties. A 30-hour module had been developed with a college of education for use within Learning Support teacher training, and consideration was being given to seconding teachers to attend courses offered by the Scottish Dyslexia Association.

The rights of parents in relation to voluntary associations were emphasised. While any support including tutoring from voluntary sources was external to and outwith the normal school day, 'the Authority is desirous of establishing and maintaining good relations with all such voluntary organisations.'

Region 5

5.1 Documents forming relevant parts of the total policy on learning difficulties were supplied: *The Multiple Roles of the Remedial Specialists within the Context of a Whole-School Policy* and *Pupils with Severe and Specific Learning Difficulties*. These items were evidently dated 1988, but the series of policy documents originally dated from 1980, following the HMI Report on learning difficulties of 1978, and different sections had been periodically updated. The underlying principles of the policy were the provision of appropriate education through the whole curriculum. The responsibilities of class and subject teachers for the education of children with learning difficulties were stressed. 'More of the energies of promoted and remedial staff should be used ... [in] getting the initial teaching right rather than picking up the pieces afterwards.' Direct tuition, was accepted as the third aspect of the role of learning support teachers, seen not as an isolated function but as interacting with the consultative and co-operative roles. Extra help provided through direct tuition was not intended to be a substitute for the pupil's class lessons in English or mathematics and withdrawal for this purpose should not normally take place. However, 'such help offered outside the ordinary classroom can often deal with the really severe cases without embarrassing them in front of their peers.'

The starter paper on specific learning difficulties offered guidance on a small minority of pupils; the main emphasis of their work should remain within the classroom but a planned programme including individual withdrawal might also be helpful. An operational definition and guidance on the recognition of pupils with specific learning difficulties was given. Key principles were: early identification, the involvement of parents, the provision of opportunities to participate widely in the curriculum and a clear programme of tuition in the area of difficulty. Decisions would have to be taken on an individual basis and reviewed regularly. Points of management and organisation of support were described for primary and secondary schools and for the stages of transfer to and from the secondary school. The paper was designed to supplement aspects of regional policy and should be seen in the context of appropriate curricula and whole school policies. It was intended to be amplified through in-service training.

Region 6

6.1 *Guidelines on Specific Learning Difficulties*, an updated leaflet, was prepared by a regional Psychological Service. It suggested that individual patterns of strengths and weaknesses should be sought rather than the 'tempting' diagnostic label. The purpose of assessment was to decide how to help the pupil, and followed the same basic principles that were used in assessing any student. Consultation with parents and between the class and learning support teacher, observation and experimental teaching to find out what works should all be used. Assessment might proceed to specialised testing and referral to the educational psychologist and other agencies.

Intervention also relied on educational principles that were unchanged by the fact that a child experiences specific learning difficulties. Clear aims, individual programmes, working to strengths, raising expectations of success, consultation and clear communication with all others involved were among the points described. Teachers were recommended to avoid talking and thinking of the student as one of a category.

Region 8

8.1 Copies of internal memoranda (1991) between a Director of Education , Principal Psychologist and Adviser in Special Educational Needs were made available to the research. The Director consulted the other staff about rising demand for provision in relation to specific learning difficulties, raising the question whether these could 'throw into further turmoil the new progressive role of our learning support staff.' Both the psychologist and the adviser took a positive view of the upsurge. The psychologist regarded it as 'a predictable outcome of the on-going movement of encouraging parents to become involved,' and fully supported parents in demanding appropriate education for their children. The adviser suggested that growing demand in this area arose from good assessment by class and learning support teachers; this is 'the direct result of good training.' Staff training developments were planned to continue. The region's psychological and learning support services were working well together, unusually so, in the adviser's view. The adviser suggested the possibility of a parents' self support group in relation to specific learning difficulties.

Region 9

9.1 Within the draft guidelines on recording for Special Educational Needs, 1990, the notes on grounds for recording included a brief paragraph on specific learning difficulties. The definition was based on marked discrepancy between school work in the area of difficulty and 'general ability', and lack of access to other areas of the curriculum. While all pupils placed in special schools or units should be recorded, Records of Needs for pupils remaining in mainstream schools should be opened only if extra staff input was required, over and above normal learning support provision. Schools had the responsibility for identifying and referring pupils with learning difficulties. However, it was noted that there was usually a waiting list for assessment by the psychological service.

Region 11

11.1 An updated regional draft entitled *Learning Support Policy* was addressed to teaching staff. This document was strongly based on the HMI Report on learning difficulties of 1978, with the theme of moving from remedial to appropriate education and stressing the curriculum as a major source of learning difficulty. Sections on the roles of staff, to which teachers were invited to respond, were included for learning support teachers, head teachers, class and subject teachers, principal teachers and guidance staff. The description of the learning support teacher's role gave detailed guidance on the consultative and co-operative elements; its outline of the direct tuition role was slight. There was no explicit reference to specific learning difficulties.

Region 18

18.1 The document entitled *Regional Policy for Special Educational Needs (1992)* encompassed a new comprehensive policy which was the outcome of a consultation exercise involving 621 responses. It stressed the inclusive nature of policy in this area. Key principles were positive discrimination in favour of the disadvantaged, acknowledgement that every child had individual learning needs and the non-segregation of children with special needs. It was acknowledged that certain highly specialised facilities would continue to be required. The discussion of financial implications stated that the bulk of the finance needed for developing mainstream support for special educational needs would have to come from special school closures, emphasising that if this was not done, and all receipts reallocated to mainstream provision, the policy could not be implemented during the early 1990s.

None of the sections on particular categories of need related to specific learning difficulty. The section on recording cited specific learning difficulty as one of the grounds for the recording of school age children. The continuum of learning support available for all pupils experiencing learning difficulties was described, moving through escalating levels of input from the school's own resources, through peripatetic specialist support, referral to the psychological service, recording of needs with additional specialist support and finally special placement.

18.2 An internal report on dyslexia to the Director from the principal psychologists had been under consideration in 1988, in response to proposals raised by a divisional officer. The matter was brought forward in relation to the extension of parents' rights to appeal against an education authority's decision not to open a Record of Needs. The psychologists fully supported the recommendations for provision made in the earlier paper within, they emphasised, the context of regional provision for learning difficulties in general. They preferred the term 'specific learning difficulties' as it avoided the notion of a discrete group of children all requiring specialised help. 'We would recognise that within the group who have specific difficulties there are some for whom the label "dyslexia" would be appropriate, but we would not view their educational needs in isolation from the wider group'. Their estimate of incidence was 5% to 10% of the school population, contained within a larger group experiencing a continuum of difficulties, and a continuum of provision was outlined. This largely corresponded to that in the 1992 regional policy, but the 1988 paper did not mention Records of Needs as marking the boundary of additional provision. For children who needed support beyond that given by school and peripatetic learning support, the paper recommended that part-time attendance at a specialist centre dealing with specific learning difficulties should be available. 'Most divisions already have centres which could be further developed to meet these proposals.' Summaries of this local provision were given.

Relations with the Dyslexia Institute were discussed under a separate heading. It was acknowledged that parents' genuine anxiety about the scarcity of appropriate provision might lead them to seek help from the Institute or Dyslexia Association. 'While accepting that this may fulfil an unmet need, there is a danger that the approach taken by such bodies is divorced from the overall curriculum of the school and utilises narrowly-based diagnostic and remedial procedures.' It was suggested that

> The region, while remaining sympathetic, should not view these bodies as viable alternatives to the region's own services. The region already possesses a base of knowledge and expertise in the area of specific learning difficulties. Given regional support and appropriate resources this can be extended to develop a comprehensive provision including direct help for children together with training and role development for staff.

18.3 A Divisional Working Group Report, 1990, *The Concepts of Learning and Learning Needs* focused on the concept of a continuum of need; however, specific learning difficulties were discussed fully as an important sub-set of difficulties. Early identification, preferably before the child left the infant department, close co-operation with parents, and constant encouragement of the child to foster awareness of his capabilities as well as his difficulties were recommended. Detailed sections on Management of Learning Experiences and on Support Systems did not treat specific learning difficulties separately. An Appendix on Paired Reading was included.

18.4 Another Division supplied five documents:
   i) *Learning Difficulties* 1988 Primary Study Group Report

A working group of a senior psychologist and four primary head teachers had made a survey of 20 primary schools in order to identify examples of effective whole school policies for pupils with learning difficulties and establish practical strategies to meet the needs of such pupils. Appendices included information on one such strategy of recording the progress of 'slow learners', known as Teacher Initiated Monitoring and Evaluation or T.I.M.E.; and also guidelines for paired reading .

   ii) *Specific Learning Difficulties (Dyslexia): a Guide to Provision* Divisional Psychological Service, no date.

This brief paper outlined the nature of specific learning difficulties and the help available in the division. It covered the role of class and subject teachers, school and area learning support, the work of the divisional psychological service, and the reading centres in the division. Staff development and the involvement of parents were highlighted.

   iii) *Dyslexia* 1985 Paper by psychologist

This earlier paper summarized the debate on a discrete syndrome or a continuum of learning difficulties, and offered guidance to the class teacher in identifying and assisting children displaying difficulties of this type.

   iv) *Learning Support Pupil Profile forms*, 1991, for use by schools in the Division.

A letter from an education officer reminded primary head teachers that profile forms should be in use in all schools to record aspects of support, appropriate methodology and monitoring of action taken for pupils with learning difficulties.

v) *Monitoring and Evaluation*, information to schools 1990.

Another letter to primary schools from the principal psychologist also referred to the Teacher Initiated Monitoring and Evaluation (TIME) strategy, as an approach to learning difficulties particularly for slow learning children. The progress of the initiative was outlined.

Index

ability grouping, streaming 63, 91, 113, 115
advisers, learning support, special needs 16-34, 35, 134-135. 86-87
Allan 5
Alpha-Omega 28, 80, 169
anti-categorisation 6-8, 17-20, 40, 68, 93, 127, 190-191, 194, 199, 200
aphasia 131
area learning support 26, 135, 156, 163, 234
assessment of SPLD 24-25, 61-62, 78, 123-124, 182-183, 187, 196, 200
Association of Scottish Principal Educational Psychologists (ASPEP) 35, 39, 41
Aston Index 24, 32, 61, 77,

Bangor Dyslexia Test 24, 32, 77
Barton 191, 192
B.Ed. primary 48-56

Blackwell's Spelling Workshop 147
Bowe 9
Bradley 10, 11, 158
brain damage 177, 189, 196
British Ability Scales 149
British Medical Association 12, 196, 219
Brown 11
Bryant 10, 11, 158

Carroll 4
Chesson 181
classroom support 25, 33, 43, 46, 77-81, 105-108, 112, 128, 138, 203-205
Clay 197
Closs 61
Clough 192
cognitive abilities 15, 38, 51, 71-73, 98-99, 146, 149-152, 177-178, 192
college of education 47-66, 124, 228, 229
continuum 3, 6, 7, 18-21, 31, 59, 60, 64, 66, 69, 142, 174, 180, 191, 194, 195, 196-200, 207, 216-218, 229, 232-234

co-operative teaching 5-7, 54, 55, 65, 83, 106, 112, 165, 170, 205, 227
Critchley 12, 218

Dane 45
defict approach 49, 58, 66, 135, 139, 206
Department of Child and Family Psychiatry (DFCP) 184
devolved school management 8, 33, 165, 207
diagnosis 12, 24, 32, 43, 51, 76, 103, 113, 177, 179, 181-183, 188, 195, 199, 219
differentiated learning 49, 54
(DipSEN) Diploma in Special Educational Needs 57, 69, 88, 90-91, 162
direct tuition 26, 27, 54, 55, 63, 66, 203, 227, 230, 232
directorate see education officers
discrete group 18-20, 31, 50, 72, 127, 140, 195-197
Division of Educational and Child Psychologists of the British Psychological Society (DECP) 2, 24
Duffield 198
dyslexia 1-3, 7, 9, 12, 14, 19, 24, 32, 35, 36, 40-44, 51, 58, 60, 63, 67, 69, 70, 71, 73, 74, 77, 80, 85, 89, 91, 93-95, 101, 102, 105, 113, 116-119, 121-131, 134-144, 147, 154, 156-158, 161, 163-170, 173-175, 177, 180, 186, 188, 189, 193, 195, 196, 197, 199, 205, 216-224, 226-229, 232, 233, 234
Dyslexia Association, British 123-

125, 134, 156, 220
Dyslexia Association, Scottish 14, 35, 41, 58, 93, 94, 105, 121, 123-130, 134, 135, 154, 156, 164, 166, 170, 220, 227, 229, 233
dyslexia associations 12, 94, 118, 121, 129, 131, 134-136, 221
see also voluntary associations
Dyslexia Institute 12, 69, 105, 121, 123, 131, 134-136, 158, 164, 233

Education Act 1981 (Education Scotland Act 1980 as amended) 6, 116, 126, 203, 220, 223
education authorities 8, 16, 44, 89, 124, 130, 133, 196, 197, 201, 204, 206, 207, 216, 219-221, 223
education officers 14-17, 20, 21, 31, 35, 38, 42, 188, 223, 224
educational psychologists 2, 12, 14, 15, 24-26, 31, 33, 35, 38, 52, 70, 86, 94, 95, 117, 127, 129, 134-137, 177, 178, 182, 185, 187, 195, 197, 201, 203, 219, 224
emotional and behavioural difficulties 61, 100, 147, 151, 160, 184-185
England and Wales 8, 9, 12, 114, 223

Fish Report 218, 221-222
five to fourteen (5-14 curriculum) 9, 33, 205

gender 96, 193, 208
General Teaching Council for

Scotland (GTC) 124

handwriting 113
head teacher 35, 38, 40, 41, 43,
    116, 161, 162, 171, 184, 185
Hickey 28, 125, 158
Higher Still 9
HMI, Scottish (Report 1978) 3-5, 77,
    198-199, 203-204, 218, 221-
    222
home support 78, 145, 160, 176
homework 85, 125, 161-164, 167,
    175
hospital school 184

in-service training (INSET) 30, 43,
    162, 200, 229, 230
incidence of spld 22-23, 31-32, 73-
    74, 123, 134, 168, 192-193
independent schools 25, 41, 97,
    106, 114, 131, 138, 143, 145,
    165-170, 173-175
Inspectorate 6, 205
integration 25, 161, 170, 203, 206,
    228
intelligence 18, 64, 71, 122, 129,
    149, 158, 184, 217-220
Irlen H, (coloured filter methods)
    13, 27

Kingston Manual 125

language disorder 160, 186, 189
Lawson 45
learning support 5-9, 14-16, 19,
    21-30, 33, 35, 38, 39, 43,
    45-47, 49-55, 57, 58-65,
    67-91, 94, 95, 100, 103, 104,
    106, 110, 112-121, 125,
    127-129, 135, 137-139,
    141-145, 153-156, 159,

161-163, 165, 166, 167, 170,
    171, 175, 178, 187, 195, 198,
    200, 201-205, 207, 227-234
learning support teacher 6, 7, 21,
    49, 52-55, 59, 62-65, 67-91,
    103, 104, 106, 112, 118, 119,
    128, 135, 143, 144, 153, 156,
    161, 163, 166, 167, 203, 229,
    230, 232
Letterland 142, 158, 162, 174
literacy 2, 8, 10-14, 17, 18, 27, 31,
    33, 50, 64, 69, 72, 73, 80, 90,
    94, 99, 119, 125, 147, 167,
    178, 185, 186, 189, 193-195,
    197, 198, 203, 207
local government, reorganisation 9,
    33, 165
local management of schools 8

Macleod 59
mainstream 4-6, 8, 23, 25, 26, 30,
    32, 33, 47, 59, 63, 66, 67, 73,
    75, 77-79, 84, 88, 90, 111-
    112, 119, 127-130, 138, 141,
    142, 147, 155, 161, 170, 174-
    175, 179, 184-185, 190, 198,
    200, 203, 206, 207, 229, 231,
    232
mathematics difficulty see numeracy
medical role in spld 12-13, 86-87,
    104, 176-189, 196
Meek 197
memory 99-100, 122, 152
middle class 42, 43, 46, 51, 96, 97,
    99, 101, 106, 108-111, 119,
    131, 134, 138, 139, 140, 145,
    157, 176, 183, 193, 197, 200,
    208, 209, 225
Moses 77
motor difficulties 99-100, 122, 166
multisensory approach 11, 33, 66,

129, 135, 138, 174

Neale Analysis 77
Newton 24
numeracy 2, 17, 69, 90, 100, 157, 167, 194

occupational therapy 106, 115, 176, 179, 189, 202, 205, 228
Occupational Therapy Department (OTD) 176, 179, 189

paired reading 78, 85, 142, 143, 158, 163, 170-175, 234
PAL computer software 159
parents 3-8, 13-15, 17, 21, 23, 32, 36, 41, 46, 51, 61-63, 67, 70, 71, 82-120, 122, 124-127, 129-142, 147, 154, 155, 157, 161-165, 170, 174, 175, 176-189, 191, 193, 195, 196, 200-209, 220, 222, 223, 225, 226, 228-234
Parents' Charter 8, 204
PEP 16, 20, 23, 24, 26, 27, 144 see also educational psychologists
phonics 11, 30, 80, 111, 139, 144, 158, 168, 174, 202
physical disability, illness 37, 89, 100, 151, 160
postgraduate certificate of education (PGCE) 48-56
pre-service teachers see student teachers
primary stage 22, 32, 56, 62, 75-79, 89-90, 142-147, 156, 158-160, 166, 202
principal educational psychologists 2, 14, 15, 24, 31, 35, 94, 95, 197, 224
private tuition 106, 107, 115, 119,

133
progress of pupils 125, 149-153, 160, 171-172
psychological services 21, 26, 32, 35, 38, 39, 62, 63, 66, 94, 96, 97, 101, 104, 106-110, 119, 131, 135, 137, 139, 187, 223, 226, 227
Pumphrey, P 10
pupil volunteers 78, 167, 169, 170-173, 175

Quest screening 77

reading, teaching of 10-14, 22, 28, 33, 45, 50, 56, 62, 65, 72, 80, 88-89, 98, 103, 111, 113-115, 129, 138, 142-151, 153-175, 185, 186, 193, 197, 199, 202, 203, 207, 208, 216-224, 228, 234
reading centre 25, 28, 58, 89, 142, 155-165, 174-176
reading skills 10, 28, 89, 186, 217 see also literacy
reading unit 25, 26, 82, 94, 106, 107, 114, 115, 142-150, 153-155, 159, 160, 165, 166, 167-170, 173-177, 179, 180, 182, 184, 185, 189, 205, 227, 228
Record of Needs 6-8, 21-23, 26, 27, 32, 65, 79, 108, 109, 115, 117, 119, 129, 136, 156, 220, 228, 229, 232
Reid 13, 201
remedial teacher 4, 5, 222 see also learning support teacher
research questions 1, 14, 17, 47, 57, 67, 92, 121-122, 166
Riddell 7, 198, 204, 208

Robinson 185, 186
Rutter 123, 217

sampling 68, 93-96, 108, 133
SCOSDE guidelines 7, 8, 61, 63,
    77, 203
Scottish Dyslexia Association see
    Dyslexia Association, Scottish
Scottish Dyslexia Trust 51, 60
Scottish Examination Board (SEB)
    14-16, 35, 44, 51, 67, 95, 166,
    195, 199
Scottish Office Education
Department (SOED) 1, 2, 8, 9, 33,
    60, 68, 116, 203-205
screening 22, 77, 130, 166
scribe 37, 38, 42-45, 167, 169
secondary school 9, 22, 25, 28, 58,
    75, 78, 85, 90, 95, 101, 108,
    113, 116, 127, 142-144, 153,
    154, 157, 159, 162, 164, 165,
    170, 175, 201, 222, 227-230
secondary stage 29, 90, 142, 156,
    163, 174, 175
self-confidence, self-esteem 72, 113,
    115, 125, 139, 147, 172, 182,
    183, 184
slow learners 28, 33, 73, 80, 88, 89,
    234
Smith 10, 197
Snowling 10, 11
socio-economic status see middle
    class, working class
special educational needs advisers
    see advisers
special school 4, 8, 37, 41, 106,
    107, 206, 227, 231-232
speech therapists 13, 58, 86, 155,
    176, 178, 185-187, 189
spelling 10, 17, 50, 55, 80, 99, 111,
    113, 114, 122, 144, 146, 147,

149, 151, 158-162, 168, 169,
    177, 180, 182, 186, 193,
    217-219, 223
staff development 5, 29, 63, 89,
    126, 154, 162, 228, 234
Standard Grade examinations 36,
    41, 43, 45
Stephenson 180, 182, 183, 185
student teachers 14-15, 47, 48, 50,
    52-57, 64, 65, 83, 141, 198,
    199

Tansley 24, 218, 219, 223
teacher, mainstream class or subject
    2, 4-7, 14, 15, 21, 25, 26, 30,
    35, 38, 40, 41, 43, 48-55, 57,
    59-68, 70, 73, 75, 77, 80, 84,
    86-91, 103, 104, 106, 107,
    111, 112, 114-116, 118, 119,
    126, 128-130, 135, 136,
    141-150, 153-171, 174, 175,
    177, 179, 184, 185, 193, 196,
    198, 203, 222, 223, 226,
    228-230, 232, 234, 235
teacher education 2, 14, 15, 47-66,
    141, 165, 195-196, 198
teaching materials 25, 67, 80, 90,
    169
teaching methods 11, 27, 28, 49, 67,
    79, 90, 111, 113, 131, 132,
    136, 137, 148, 166, 168-169,
    203
technological aids (computers, tape-
    recorders) 28, 45, 62, 112,
    125, 138, 143-145, 155, 159,
    229
terminology 1, 2, 9, 10, 37, 39, 41,
    42, 44, 87, 90, 117, 121, 122,
    157, 166, 168, 178, 196, 216,
    220
Tizard Report 217

Tobin 4
Tomlinson 2, 10, 191
transition primary-secondary 43, 114,
    153-154, 165
tutor service 124

voluntary organisations 15-17, 35,
    44, 55, 67, 80, 85, 92, 94, 96,
    97, 99, 101, 103, 104,
    106-110, 119, 121-141, 161,
    164, 173, 174, 176, 178, 179,
    188, 195, 196, 202-204, 207,
    208, 220, 229

Walker 193
Warnock Report 3, 4, 6, 8, 32, 36,
    201, 218, 219, 222
Weedon 2, 17, 45, 194
WISC test 149
withdrawal tuition 4, 7, 27, 33, 45,
    54, 55, 63, 77-79, 83, 90, 106,
    107, 129, 130, 138, 141, 171,
    199, 202, 203, 205, 207, 222,
    230
working class 96, 97, 101, 106,
    108-111, 119, 131, 133, 183,
    192, 208

Young and Tyre 220
Yule 4, 217